FOUNDATIONS

Foundations

HOW THE BUILT ENVIRONMENT MADE
TWENTIETH-CENTURY BRITAIN

SAM WETHERELL

PRINCETON UNIVERSITY PRESS
PRINCETON & OXFORD

Published by Princeton University Press
41 William Street, Princeton, New Jersey 08540
99 Banbury Road, Oxford OX2 6JX

press.princeton.edu

First Paperback Printing, 2023
Paperback ISBN 9780691241760

The Library of Congress has cataloged the cloth edition as follows:

Names: Wetherell, Sam, 1986– author.
Title: Foundations : how the built environment made twentieth-century
    Britain / Sam Wetherell.
Other titles: Pilot zones
Description: Princeton : Princeton University Press, [2020] | Revision of the
    author's thesis (doctoral)—University of California, Berkeley, 2016, under
    the title: Pilot zones : the new urban environment of twentieth century Britain. |
    Includes bibliographical references and index.
Identifiers: LCCN 2020009358 (print) | LCCN 2020009359 (ebook) |
    ISBN 9780691193755 (hardback) | ISBN 9780691208558 (ebook)
Subjects: LCSH: Architecture and society—Great Britain—History—20th century. |
    Cities and towns—Great Britain—History—20th century. | Sociology, Urban—
    Great Britain—History—20th century.
Classification: LCC NA2543.S6 W458 2020 (print) | LCC NA2543.S6 (ebook) |
    DDC 720.1/03—dc23
LC record available at https://lccn.loc.gov/2020009358
LC ebook record available at https://lccn.loc.gov/2020009359

British Library Cataloging-in-Publication Data is available

Editorial: Ben Tate and Josh Drake
Production Editorial: Natalie Baan
Jacket/Cover Design: Layla Mac Rory
Production: Danielle Amatucci
Publicity: Katie Lewis and Alyssa Sanford
Copyeditor: Cindy Milstein

This book has been composed in Arno

For my parents,
Margaret Wetherell and Jonathan Potter

CONTENTS

ACKNOWLEDGMENTS

SPENDING THE BEST part of a decade writing a book about the history of Britain's built environment seems like a strange thing to do, but here we are. My gratitude to those who have helped me do so is fathomless. This book was in the background as my life and the world changed in ways that were profound and unexpected. It has spanned more than eight years, taking me to three universities on two continents. It has followed me from London to Berkeley, from Berkeley to New York City, and from New York City to Old York, and it predates my marriage, the birth of my nephew and niece, and the passing of two grandparents.

Let's start at the beginning. The road to this book started with an email from James Vernon that arrived in my in-box on a rainy February morning in 2011 when I was working at a dismal office job in London. I will never begin to be able to repay the emotional, intellectual, and professional debts that I owe James. He persuaded me to think big and maintain a political investment in my work, and I am constantly amazed at his humanity and generosity. It is no exaggeration to say that I came to Berkeley and became a historian because of him. I am also grateful for the mysterious and magical wisdom of Thomas Laqueur, who has always pushed me to inject my work with a lyricism and cosmic significance that I fear it still lacks. At Berkeley, Robin Einhorn, Teresa Caldeira, and David Henkin pushed me to think beyond Britain and broadened my historical imagination.

Some of the most important relationships that I made during those magical years at Berkeley were friendships. The wise and kindhearted Chris Casey picked me up from the San Francisco airport when I arrived and dropped me off again six years later, waiting like a patient father for me to disappear out of sight through security. A few years later he would sit with me in the Library of Congress canteen, helping me turn the book's six chapters into a single Word document. Joey Kellner has been a perpetual source of humor and magical ideas, and opened my eyes to new ways of seeing the United States. I am especially indebted to the brilliance, humor, and companionship of Trevor Jackson, who has taught me so much over the years. Tehila Sasson has been a vital and caring mentor since the day we first met and I cooked her a disappointing stir-fry in London. I will miss eating terrible Chinese food and drinking cheap wine with Sophie Fitzmaurice and Liz Chadwick, then going on glorious, arduous runs the next morning with Sarah Stoller and Dave Hayden. Tim Wright and Edith Fox have both been wonderful housemates, great friends, and fellow foot soldiers in the perpetual war against rats in our Oakland apartment. During our many lunchtime discussions at the "circle," I learned what can only be described as a new way of thinking from Daniel Kelley. Camilo Lund and Robbie Nelson have each kept me sane in different ways and been there at times of crisis. Thanks along with a huge amount of love also go to Melissa Turoff, Ari Edmundson, Erica Lee, Brendan Shanahan, Julia Wambach, Aaron Hall, Sheer Ganor, Ivana Mirkovic, Katie Harper, Yana Skorobogatov, and Mircea Raianu. Many of those listed above were fellow members of the "People's 285" writing group, which laid the groundwork for chapters 1 and 6 of this book.

I want to thank Susan Pedersen for hiring me for a life-changing yearlong stint as a visiting professor at Columbia University. Her honesty, diligence, and sage advice have changed the way that I think about history and my own work. It is also impossible to understate the multitude of ways that Guy Ortolano has made this book possible. Guy has been there from the beginning as a wellspring of advice, consolation, and intellectual stimulation. I am immensely grateful for many of my colleagues at the University of York whose friendship and support helped me weather a difficult transition back to Britain. In particular, I want to thank Tom Johnson, Lucy Sackville, Lawrence Black, Chris Renwick, Harry Munt, Oleg Benesch, Shaul Mitelpunkt, Amanda Behm, and my many other fantastic colleagues on "A Block." I especially want to thank David Huyssen and Mary Reynolds for making me feel at home in York as well as providing hours of wonderful conversations. These relationships were strengthened on freezing picket lines and crowded teach-outs, and I am grateful for my colleagues' solidarity as well as friendship. In Britain and the United States, all my colleagues who began PhDs in the years after 2008 have had to piece together lives in the shattered remains of an academy that is hemorrhaging jobs and money. This experience has bought many of us together as we have sought to rethink our own lives and the future of our work. In that spirit, I also want to thank some of my brilliant and radical students for giving me hope for the future and meaning to the work of teaching—particularly Olivia Wyatt, Claire Burgess, Tom Ward, Adonis Li, and Luke Cregan.

This book is indebted to the work of fellow British urban historians, especially those who have rejuvenated the field over the last several years. Simon Gunn has been a wonderful advocate for British urban history and supported this project from an early stage. Otto Saumarez Smith has spent years forging a vibrant community of people working on the history of the modern British city, and always patiently and humorously answered many hastily emailed questions about architecture and design. I am also particularly grateful for the friendship and brilliant work of fellow urban historians Erika Hanna, Tom Hulme, Divya Subramanian, Christopher Lawson, Alistair Kefford, Sarah Mass, Claire Wrigley, James Greenhalgh, and Judith Walkowitz. David Ellis, with his brilliant eye for detail, helped me get over the finish line by reading drafts, answering questions, and challenging me on some of my ideas. I would also like to thank Frank Trentmann, Rebecca Wright, and Charlotte Johnson for sharing their ideas about the politics of domestic energy as well as helping organize the Domesticating Energy workshop in Cambridge in 2017. Thanks too to Sabine Clarke and David Clayton, who helped me think through some aspects of the first chapter. Over the years, different strands of the argument for this book have been presented at conferences and workshops across the world, and I am always grateful for the feedback and questions that I have received.

My thanks also go to the countless archivists and librarians whose work made this book, and history as a discipline, possible. In particular, I would like to thank the staff of the more than twenty local authority archives that I visited up and down the country, whose records made up the bulk of the source material for this book. They are precious spaces for historians, many of which are being gutted by some of the same historical processes that this book seeks to chart. Alice Coleman was kind enough to meet with me in person and allow me to look at some of her personal papers. She will no doubt disagree with some of the conclusions of this book, but I am immensely appreciative of her help. Images for the book were made possible by a grant from the Scouloudi Foundation in association with the Institute for Historical Research. A generous image grant from the Society of Architectural Historians of Great Britain was also crucial in funding the many images reproduced in this book. Thanks to Nick Hedges for allowing me to use some of his wonderful photographs of 1970s Glasgow and Kevin Atherton for allowing me to reproduce an image of his sculpture at Stockley Park. Thanks also to Thomas Williams at the *Oxford Mail* for letting me into the paper's archive.

At Princeton University Press, my editor, Ben Tate, took a punt on this book at an early stage and supported it all the way through. I am enormously grateful for his faith in my work as well as his competence and flexibly. Thanks also to Natalie Baan, who helped organize the production of the book, and Cindy Milstein, who copyedited the final manuscript. Many others have read some or all of the book and provided invaluable comments, suggestions, exclamations, and funny cartoons. Thanks so much to Trevor Jackson, Joey Kellner, Sarah Stoller, James Vernon, Margaret Wetherell, David Ellis, Chris Casey, and Guy Ortolano for their honesty, care, and attention. Thanks to Gena-mour Barrett for supplying a much-needed journalist's eye. Thanks also to Laura Gutiérrez, Daniel Eltringham, Koshka Duff, Barnaby Raine, Lotte Houwink ten Cate, and Amy Edwards for the many profound conversations that have shaped the politics and ideas that underpin this book.

Before turning to my family, I want to first thank three friends who are as close to being family as it's possible to be. I owe an indescribable debt to Harriet Williams, who has been such a brilliant friend, traveling companion, confident, and interlocutor over so many years. I also want to thank Harry Kennard for his constant humor, wild schemes, and thousands of endless, rambling conversations. It is no exaggeration to say that this book would not exist without Felicity Taylor. With my family living overseas, I have stayed in Felicity's beautiful London house on and off for the last seven years as a lodger, then as a guest, and then as a friend. It was her hospitality that allowed me to stay in Britain and London for long spells of research. "Brooky" has become the closest thing to my family home in Britain. Despite being in her eighties, Felicity has the youth of a millennial, and I look forward to many more evenings drinking white wine and bickering with her about politics in the kitchen.

Finally, I want to thank my eccentric and globally dispersed family, which spans Britain, New Jersey, California, and New Zealand, particularly Alexa Hepburn, Pete Williams, Marion Hepburn, Steven Weeks, Chris Jewell, Jane Jewell, Simeon Jewell, and Amy Jewell. Hopefully I never again need to answer the question, "How are the shopping malls going, Sam?" While writing this book I have lost two grandparents, Mary Potter and Percy Potter—a loss that was tempered by the birth of my indomitable nephew, Kaspar, and niece, Rosa. I met my wife, Hannah Jewell, by chance at a party in Oakland in 2012. That the decisions I have made put me in the same place as her means that I will never have any regrets. Her love and crazy humor mean everything. My debt to her is endless, and I look forward to paying it back over the rest of our lives. This book, however, is dedicated to my parents, Margaret Wetherell and Jonathan Potter. Their love and support has never wavered, and my decision to follow them into academia is, I hope, a testament to this love rather than a lack of imagination on my own behalf.

FOUNDATIONS

Introduction

IMAGINE YOU ARE sitting in the window seat of a plane beginning its descent into Heathrow Airport. As the plane comes in to land, it flies low over the entire length of London, from east to west.[1] If it is a clear day, it is possible you will be able to see many of the types of spaces whose history this book sets out to tell. First, on the eastern fringes of London, on a marshy, southern bank of the Thames, you may be able to make out a labyrinthine cluster of concrete walkways, imposing tower blocks, and square artificial lakes. This is Thamesmead, a vast public housing project initiated by the Greater London Council, and announced as a triumph of architectural and social engineering. Shortly after its first residents moved into their new homes at the end of the 1960s, the Greater London Council commissioned a documentary about their lives.[2] At one point the film shows a small group of young children gathered in the classroom of a brand-new school erected on the grounds of the development. The children were milling around a graying cube of papier-mâché about two feet high, being encouraged by a beaming teacher to design their own housing project similar to Thamesmead. To Britons alive today, this image of a group of children, happily ensconced within a newly minted utopia and encouraged by a teacher to play modernist planner for the afternoon, seems to belong as much to a lost *ancien régime* as a Napoleonic battlefield or witchcraft trial.

A few seconds later, as the plane continues its course, it will approach the East End of London, an area of former docks and factories that has been transformed by more than thirty years of intensive urban regeneration. The epicenter of this new landscape is the Olympic Stadium, built for the 2012 London Olympics and now, to the horror of many of its fans, the new home of West Ham Football Club. Just to its north, almost the same size as the stadium and built at the same time, is Westfield Stratford City, a monumental shopping mall, one of more than a hundred similar malls owned by the Westfield Corporation across Europe and North America. The mall is a glowing, angular cube, peppered with shards of decorative glass. Inside its cavernous, brightly lit atriums, more than 250 stores and 65 restaurants face off along miles of concourses. There is a cinema, bowling alley, twenty-four-hour casino, "biodiversity playground" for children, and concierge service tailored toward elite visitors. It is one of the biggest of its kind in Europe.

Seconds later, and just a mile farther west, the plane will pass over a development that looks from above like a large, red-brick, nineteenth-century factory that has been carefully scrubbed clean. This is the Bow Quarter, a colossal gated housing development that was retrofitted on the grounds of a former match factory and opened in 1988. The match factory, which closed in the late 1970s, was once the stage for the successful 1888 matchgirls' strike, a canonical event in the annals of British labor history. That year, hundreds of young women rebelled against the brutal working conditions imposed by Bryant and May, a rapacious match-manufacturing firm with factories across the country (and later the world). The women had been working fourteen-hour days, shrouded in toxic clouds of white phosphorous and suffering from disfiguring health conditions. Behind its high walls, the transformed factory has been broken up into more than seven hundred apartments as well as a swimming pool, gym, and restaurant. During the 2012 Olympics, the Bow Quarter became central to the controversial counterterrorism operation that accompanied the games after it was decided that an antiaircraft missile battery would be fitted onto the development's roof. The matchgirls strike is commemorated by a small blue plaque, which sits beside the development's tall security gates.

As the plane passes farther west, flying over central London, the curvature of the Thames now fully in view, these types of spaces repeat themselves with gathering intensity. High-density housing estates built in the mid-twentieth century still permeate the city, appearing in stripes through Wandsworth south of the river, gathering in spiked clusters in Fulham and Notting Hill west of the city center, and lining the arterial roads that fan out to the north. These estates persist, despite wave after wave of privatization and demolition. They are interspersed with private, comprehensively planned, high-end residential developments, a substantial number of which will be younger than the jet you are sitting in. Many of these new developments are empty and silent, owned as investments by distant millionaires who will never set foot in them. If you are landing at night, many will be eerily unlit. The flight path may take you directly over the now-defunct Battersea Power Station, a grand 1930s municipal building whose surplus energy was once preserved and used to heat hundreds of nearby homes. It is now is almost invisible, obscured beneath a choking tangle of apartments built for the rich. If you take a more northerly route, you may catch a glimpse of what was once the Enfield Royal Small Arms Factory, a government-managed armory built in 1816 that once churned out hundreds of thousands of guns for distribution across Britain's empire, and from 1989 on was repurposed as a private housing development. The flight path might also take you over Westfield London on the western fringes of the city center, a shopping mall almost identical to Westfield Stratford City, which is owned by the same international property developer. In 2014, Westfield London, a product of US suburbia, fell victim to an unsanctioned eruption of a different kind of globalization when it was stormed by hundreds of Black Lives Matter activists who staged a "die-in" in the wake of a murder by the police of a young black man in New York.

As the plane begins its final descent over the western fringes of the city, the last thing you might see before touching down is a sudden rush of green. This will be the grounds of Stockley Park, a gigantic landscaped business park developed throughout the 1980s, and so close to Heathrow that its buildings were designed to be seen from above. This business park, with its ambling curvilinear streets, ornamental lakes, and symmetrical coil of low-rise buildings available for businesses to rent, was designed to resemble a patch of Silicon Valley, nestled up against the busiest airport in Europe. Its architects sent delegations to the United States to scour the high-tech complexes of the San Francisco Bay Area, the Research Triangle in North Carolina, and the working landscapes of Atlanta, Denver, and New Jersey for inspiration. Beneath a rumbling chain of landing planes, Stockley Park was designed to map out the future of high-tech, flexible knowledge work in Britain. If you think that the grass looks a little too green and the trees a little too young, that's because the park is an entirely constructed space, its verdant fields and golf courses having been layered over what was once a gigantic garbage dump.

This book is a history of twentieth-century Britain told through the transformation of its built environment. It tells a story about the rise of a developmental social infrastructure, and its privatization, demolition, and rearticulation under a new neoliberal consensus. It reveals the types of subjects and visions of society that emerged alongside these transformations as well as the new relationships between Britain and the wider world that they entailed. It does so by charting the emergence and spread of six different types of urban space. The first is the industrial estate. These were planned developments that provided footloose industrialists with ready-made factory buildings and infrastructure networks. Initially conceived of by private developers, dozens of industrial estates were built across the country by the state to help solve regional unemployment problems in the 1930s, 1940s, and 1950s. The second is the shopping precinct. These were municipally planned shopping centers built in the first three decades after the Second World War to form the centerpieces of new towns or redevelop existing towns and cities. The third is the council estate, the British equivalent of the US public housing project. These were comprehensively planned, often high-density residential developments, built by the hundreds across Britain throughout the twentieth century but peaking in the 1950s, 1960s, and 1970s. The fourth is the private housing estate. These took the form either of an existing council estate whose residents had purchased their own homes from the state or one of the new high-density housing developments that were built by private developers in the late twentieth century. The fifth is the shopping mall. These were a new type of privately owned, fully enclosed retail environment that consciously followed similar developments in the United States. The sixth is the business park, also known as the science park or office park. These were privately built working landscapes designed to house high-tech manufacturing or elite knowledge work.

Taking a cue from US theorist of technology and cities Lewis Mumford, I call these types of spaces "urban forms." In his book *The City in History*, Mumford concludes a chapter on the history of Rome by indexing all the different types of space that could be found there: "six obelisks, eight bridges, eleven public baths . . . two circuses, two amphitheaters, three theatres, twenty-eight libraries, four gladiatorial schools . . . 290 storehouses and warehouses."[3] These were discrete, recognizable, and portable types of space. They comprised a familiar set of components that would have been identifiable to all Roman citizens. Although this book opens in the skies above London, we could draw up a similar index of almost every British town or city at the millennium using the six urban forms whose histories this book charts.

The first three forms—the industrial estate, shopping precinct, and council estate, which comprise the first three chapters of the book—helped usher into being a new kind of state between 1930 and 1970, one oriented toward full employment, urban redevelopment, managing consumer demand, modernizing domestic life, and fabricating community out of proximity. The second part of the book shows how these forms were each reinvented in the 1970s, 1980s, and 1990s as privatized and securitized spaces. Private housing estates, shopping malls, and business parks all thrived in the wake of the promarket urban policies introduced by Margaret Thatcher's government in the 1980s. Unlike Britain's mid-twentieth-century urban forms, planners and politicians did not expect that these three spaces would contribute to a national project of state-directed development. While Britain's midcentury urban forms were tailored toward subjects who were malleable and knowable, people whose consumer desires were predictable, or who under the right architectural circumstances could be molded into discrete communities of friends and neighbors, Britain's late twentieth-century urban forms were not called on to make such claims. Instead of making new subjects, the private housing estate, shopping mall, and business park were planned in order to minimize crime, marshal infinite reserves of consumer desire, and stimulate inspiration and well-being among elite knowledge workers.

These six forms do not comprise, of course, a comprehensive list. Other candidates could include prisons, schools, hospitals, research laboratories, motorways, football stadiums, and refugee camps.[4] I have chosen these six for two reasons. First, because besides being at home, shopping and working consume so much of our daily lives. It is possible, for instance, to imagine a Briton who lived in the 1960s, in the new town of Harlow, who commuted from a planned housing estate every day to work in the town's industrial estate, while shopping on weekends at Harlow's shopping precinct. Second, I have chosen these forms because they are each, in different ways, a fraught blend of public and private space. Shopping malls have their public concourses and private shops, council estates have their communal corridors and courtyards as well as individual flats, and both business parks and industrial estates wrap individual enterprises in a sheath of collectively managed amenities and landscaped space. Each of these urban forms posed a set of questions about how space itself should be theorized and parceled out, the answers to which changed as time passed. They show how space was the outcome of history rather than merely the terrain on which it unfolded.[5]

Encoded in these six urban forms were the prevailing political, social, technical, and economic assumptions of their age, and each was an agent in reproducing these assumptions. The built environment, however, is also made up of urban forms that have outlived the guiding political assumptions of those that designed them. The urban forms that accompanied Britain's midcentury moment of developmental politics awkwardly endure. The industrial estates have outlasted the regional industrial policies that fostered their growth as well as the forms of light industrial work that they were built to house. The shopping precincts built in new towns and redeveloped city centers after the Second World War are no longer called on to plan precisely for future consumer demand. The hundreds of council estates that still encircle British towns and cities reflect an optimism that new communities could be forged by architecture—an optimism that is no longer felt. I argue that Britain's neoliberal political formation has been characterized by this uneasy interplay between old and new. While the ideas, calculations, and practices of government are prone to rapid and often devastating upheavals, the buildings and plans, factories and infrastructural networks left behind by previous political moments stubbornly remain. In this sense, the built environment can be seen as a giant museum, exhibiting the decrepit and shabby remains of prior means of capital accumulation along with obsolete visions of society.[6] Just as John Maynard Keynes claimed that we are slaves to some defunct economist, our daily lives unfold in cities and among buildings that were designed and built during times that are radically different from our own.[7]

This book comes in the wake of a revival of interest in the history of Britain's twentieth-century built environment both inside and outside the academy. When it comes to studying the built environment in Britain, history is beginning to catch up to other disciplines, particularly geography but also sociology. Urban histories are shaped at their outset by questions of topic, theory, and scale, and although the subject area may feel superficially similar, the books and articles produced by recent urban historians have been diverse. In recent years there has been a revival of scholarly interest in the history of planning, architecture, and the lived experience of urban life in twentieth-century Britain.[8] Some have written histories of specific towns and cities as synecdoches for broader historical themes and narratives.[9] Others have examined Britain's modern built environment not for its own sake but instead as a source for understanding some of the significant metanarratives of modern British history, including the emergence of an affluent consumer economy, the uneven work of decolonization, or the reproduction or subversion of gendered and sexual identities.[10] There has also been a revival of interest in the history of Britain's twentieth-century built environment outside the academy. The demonstrative inequality of Britain's contemporary housing market along with the encroaching privatization and securitization of public space have led many writers and journalists to reevaluate as well as celebrate aspects of Britain's mid-twentieth-century urban landscape, while others have launched urgent and direct attacks on Britain's present-day failing urban infrastructure.[11]

Building on these important contributions, this book takes a different methodological approach, beginning with particular types of space and moving outward—watching as they develop, mutate, spread, and become implicated in different historiographical questions. This approach allows us to see how these urban forms developed their own autonomy and logic, often escaping the ability of any single actor to contain or shape them.[12] It is another way that we can understand twentieth-century historical change without deferring to the causal primacy of politicians and political parties. The urban forms that I describe were not totalizing machines that instantly brainwashed all who passed through them. Some shopping malls have been reclaimed as spaces for association, dates, protests, or even just killing time. Workers on industrial estates went on strike. Residents of council estates have formed different kinds of communities from those that their planners imagined. Indeed, space has always been used by people in ways that are unanticipated or unsanctioned.[13] Documenting, or better yet, participating in resistance to and reappropriation of these spaces is urgent and important work. While there are instances of resistance and reappropriation throughout this book, I focus more on the ways that urban space molded its subjects rather than the other way around.

Each chapter of this book tells the history of a different urban form and has a different configuration of structures and agents. One aim of this book is to reveal and chart the fascinating histories of each of these spaces—hopefully showing the historical fragility and downright weirdness of places that have come to feel mundane and familiar to so many of us. There are many subplots, including histories of consumerism, crime control, racial segregation, gendered forms of work, energy and heating, industrial policy, and community formation. Running through all the chapters, however, are also four strands of interrelated thought and argument, which the rest of this introduction will outline.

Development beyond the Market

The first three urban forms—the industrial estate, shopping precinct, and council estate—each contributed in different ways to the material, social, and economic development of mid-twentieth-century Britain. In this sense, they each did certain kinds of *work*, anticipating and becoming technically complicit in what I call "developmental social politics," a midcentury state of affairs bound up with welfare and warfare, macroeconomic management, and the nationalization of industry.[14] The decades between 1930 and 1970 saw massive, state-led revolutions in energy generation, transportation, domestic work, warfare, and agriculture. These three forms were a product of this historical moment and opened up new and more radical possibilities for state-directed development.

I shy away from using the common phrases "social democracy" or the "welfare state" to describe this political formation. I do so in order to avoid telling a story about the Labour Party or welfarism, and to escape, as much as it is possible to do so, the specificity of domestic British high politics and its periodizations. After all, similar attempts to manipulate the built environment in the name of public sector development could be found in a variety of radically different political regimes during this time. For example, comprehensively planned, high-density public housing complexes, the likes of which I discuss in chapter 3, were built between 1930 and 1970 by a startlingly diverse range of ideological formations across the world. They feature in Robert Moses's New York City, Juscelino Kubitschek's Brasilia, Nikita Khrushchev's Moscow, and Benito Mussolini's Milan as well as in 1930s Red Vienna and postwar imperial Hong Kong.[15] Meanwhile, industrial estates were built in Britain to help solve the problem of unemployment in deprived areas of the country, but they were also built in Britain's empire in West Africa and the United States' empire in Puerto Rico. In other words, there is nothing necessarily democratic about this built environment. The term "social democracy," with its attendant nostalgia, implicit periodization, and sheen of prelapsarian unity, is a problematic moniker when it comes to portraying Britain's mid-twentieth-century built environment.

Each of these first three urban forms mediated between the state and market, allowing the former to guide the latter in the service of development. Industrial estates were a key part of a broader mid-twentieth-century attempt to control the location of industry. By laying out a grid of factory buildings, canteens, training programs, and infrastructure networks, all owned by bodies founded and funded by the government, they helped the state to channel industry, and therefore jobs and capital, to places like the North East, South Wales, western Scotland, and underdeveloped parts of its empire. In other words, they were the outcome of a state-sanctioned historical geography of British capitalism. They were an admission that the massive economic imbalances between north and south created by the Depression, the collapse of shipbuilding and other industries, and the increasing concentration of new kinds of industrial jobs in the Home Counties and Midlands would not right itself without direct state intervention.

Shopping precincts, meanwhile, acted as instruments for urban development and redevelopment. At a time of increasing anxiety about the social and environmental consequences of unplanned, tentacle-like suburban sprawl, they were a means of re-centering British urban space and purging automobiles from town centers. Their commensurability meant that shopping precincts became go-to centerpieces for many of the more than thirty new towns built by state development corporations after the war. Shopping precincts also allowed planners and politicians to attempt to measure, and thus anticipate and plan precisely for, different types of consumer demand. Given a population of a hundred thousand people, for example, economists, geographers, and urban planners attempted to develop sophisticated models that they believed could predict exactly how many stores selling different products would be required, and make space for them.

Lastly, council housing had removed almost a third of households from the private housing market by 1980. Needless to say, this fact alone was a significant statement about how the lines of relation between the state, the market, and the individual citizen were drawn in the mid-twentieth century. But there were other, subtler ways in which mass council housing posed profound challenges to the market. Many planners and politicians believed that the density and portability of council estates allowed them to modernize domestic life en masse by centralizing and collectivizing various services, such as heating, plumbing, and waste disposal as well as health care and community development. This book will dwell particularly on the surprisingly fascinating, if unglamorous, world of indoor central heating—a novelty for almost all the first generation of council house occupants. The density of new housing estates along with their ownership by the municipal authorities meant that radical experiments in providing heat and hot water outside the domain of the market could be undertaken. "District heating," the heating of entire tower blocks, housing estates, neighborhoods, and even small towns with vast boilers, preferably heated with the runoff energy of nearby industry or power plants, was the boldest iteration of this idea.

These three urban forms, then, formed the technical basis for a directed program of modernization. Although architects of the industrial estate and shopping precinct were making spaces for manufacturers and stores—they were not, by any means, "anticapitalists"—many were proud of building frameworks in which individual enterprises could be planned for and closely managed by the state. Some realized, early on, the radical potential of the forms that they were trading in, and in doing so indulged openly in speculations about the different futures that they would enable. For example, Kenelm C. Appleyard, who oversaw the construction of Team Valley, Britain's first state-owned industrial estate in the 1930s, believed that industrial estates were experiments in practical state socialism. He called for the dismantling of Britain's entire industrial landscape—in his words, "a slum clearance of factories"—and the relocation of all light industry to government industrial estates. During the 1930s, he also praised the totalitarian governments of Soviet Russia and imperial Japan, and he toured Nazi Germany in 1938 to promote Team Valley. Meanwhile, Victor Gruen, the inventor of the shopping mall, was a socialist refugee who had worked as an architect for the municipal socialist regime in Vienna before fleeing to the United States after the Anschluss. Gruen believed that shopping malls could cure the evils of US suburbia, becoming art galleries, theaters, and community centers. Lastly, during the Second World War, the government's Building Research Station, a state agency created to research housing and urban planning issues, gathered information about the vast municipal heating systems, powered by industrial runoff, that were built in Soviet Russia during Joseph Stalin's five-year plans. Impressed by what it saw, the agency recommended that bomb-damaged cities and new towns should be planned around enormous municipal boilers, heated, if possible, by nearby industry. The new technical possibilities that these forms opened up therefore had an accelerating and contagious logic. In some instances, they represented the limit case of Britain's mid-twentieth-century developmental moment.

Neoliberalism and Thatcherism

During her eleven years in power, Thatcher unleashed an urban transformation that was arguably more profound than anything that has been seen before or since in Britain. While the 1945–51 Labour government scaled up ideas and practices that had accreted at the municipal level over the previous five decades, and comprehensive redevelopment in the 1960s altered the look and feel of a great number of British town centers, Thatcher's government introduced a series of policies that in the space of a few years changed the very idea of what cities were *for*.[16] This transformation lay not in a reduction of the overall size of the state, or in the rate at which the government intervened in the management and planning of the built environment.[17] Instead, what changed were the ends to which that money was spent and new legislation was passed. Where once local authorities had owned and maintained infrastructure as well as provided jobs and housing, now they were forced to compete against one another to attract private capital to do this work.[18] The second major argument of this book is that the last third of the twentieth century saw a reinvention of Britain's developmental urban forms—a transformation that illuminates the particularities of British neoliberalism.

While both Labour and Conservative governments in the 1960s and 1970s had attempted to manage the problems of urban and industrial decline by channeling state funds or restricting the location of new industries, the new Conservative government of the 1980s introduced a raft of measures to attract private capital to cities.[19] Enterprise zones (1981) were miniature tax havens created in poor neighborhoods to stimulate inward private investment. Urban development grants (1982) delivered small amounts of public money to local authorities *only* on the condition that it was spent on specific projects completed in partnership with the private sector. Derelict land grants (1983) and national garden festivals (1984) used small amounts of public money to clear away decaying industrial ruins and prepare land for private development. Many of these interventions were managed and implemented by urban development corporations (1981), planning authorities that had the power to overrule democratically elected local councils. Finally, the Housing Act (1980) incentivized millions of public housing residents to purchase their own homes at heavily subsidized rates. All these processes were lubricated by a wave of financialization and attempts to stimulate the popular ownership of capital.[20] They occurred during a time when the autonomy of local governments and their access to funding were heavily restricted by Westminster, and nationalized industries and local authorities were put under extreme pressure to sell their landholdings on the private property market.[21]

This political transformation is the canvas on which the second half of this book unfolds, but it is far from the full story. Many of these policies were formal rather than substantive. The state created the conditions for a new kind of private sector urbanism, but what did private capital build when it arrived? The answer, more often than not, was housing developments, shopping malls, and business parks, owned and managed by private developers.

Instead of dwelling on policies or politicians (although of course, these both feature), this book looks at the new spaces that emerged during this transformative period—spaces that, unlike their predecessors, did not have to bear the burden of state-directed development. Some of these forms started their lives as insurgents, battling against the grain of developmental urban planning. The Cambridge Science Park, Britain's first high-tech business park, which opened in 1973, was initially refused planning permission by the Board of Trade. The gigantic Brent Cross shopping mall, built in the northern suburbs of London, had been ensnared in more than fifteen years of protracted, bitter discussions by the time it opened in 1976. In other words, these forms were latent before Thatcher's election in 1979—regional curiosities lying in wait for the emergence of the political conditions under which they would thrive.

This book comes in the wake of decades of unresolved and intense debate about the meaning as well as use of the term "neoliberalism." For some scholars, neoliberalism is a class project imposed from above by elites that entailed a global reorientation of the way that capital has been accumulated since the 1970s.[22] Others have followed the framework set out by Michel Foucault's 1979 lectures at the Collège de France, arguing that neoliberalism is characterized by the new type of enterprising subject whom it calls into being: a *homo economicus* who has internalized the logic of market competition and elevated it into a reality principle.[23] Others have sought to historicize rather than theorize neoliberalism, with many historians having traced the emergence of a discrete set of ideas popularized among mid- to late twentieth-century economists, and implemented as policy in the 1970s, 1980s, and 1990s in different parts of the world.[24] Frustrated with the different scales and registers across which these discussions have played out, others have called for the term to be jettisoned entirely, contending that it is ethereal and immobilizing.[25]

I argue that the term still has some utility. It allows us to connect and name a set of processes that are common across the world, and in doing so, helps us to think through political alternatives that can begin to transcend the parochialism of national electoral politics. To invoke neoliberalism is to make an assertion about change rather than continuity in the last third of the twentieth century. For the purposes of this book, I take the essence of neoliberalism to be a form of free market fundamentalism—one that, to quote sociologist Will Davies, seeks to "anchor modernity in the market," making "economics the main measure of progress and reason."[26] To take this definition is to maintain that the important transformations in late twentieth-century politics and economics had little to do with the overall amount of public money spent by states, or extent to which they intervened in their economies. Instead, neoliberalism meant the abandonment of the developmental and social aims that guided mid-twentieth-century regimes, and their replacement with the market as the ultimate arbiter of political action.

The history of Britain's changing built environment, however, allows us to go one step further with this definition. In the second part of this book, I will argue that neoliberalism should be understood as being a type of market fundamentalism that is layered on top of the ruins of mid-twentieth-century developmental projects. As a well as the proliferation of new types of urban space, the 1980s and 1990s also saw the privatization and redevelopment of older urban forms. With parts of Britain's midcentury built environment proving architecturally unsuited for private ownership, this process frequently entailed a set of awkward and messy modifications. Council estates, for example, had to be reorganized to suit the new criminological common sense that crime was about opportunity rather than inequality—a problem inherent in the sharing of public space by strangers. When the shopping precincts commissioned and owned by local authorities or state development corporations were sold to property developers, doors to the street were installed or locked for the first time, and new legal questions emerged about how significant parts of town centers, once public and now private, were allowed to be used. Sometimes this process raised unsolvable problems. Thatcher's attempts to turn Britain into a property-owning democracy through the sale of millions of council homes, for instance, were limited by an urban fabric that resisted the logic of private ownership, as it turned out to be extremely difficult to uncouple council apartments in large estates from the collective infrastructure in which they were embedded. In housing projects where half the residents were tenants of the state and the other half had bought their apartments outright, exasperating disputes over the management and funding of collective resources ensued. While some urban forms were retrofitted in ways that made them compatible with new ideas about crime, public space, or landscapes of productive work, others were demolished, reimagined, and rebuilt.

The British neoliberal city was, therefore, made distinctive by the ways that a host of new urban forms were retrofitted to an older, increasingly shabby social infrastructure. Rather than being theoretical or abstract, Britain's modern built environment helps us understand how neoliberalism was a political formation characterized by its relationship to history—a developmental stage rather than a menu of policies or philosophical program.[27] Unlike the liberals of the nineteenth century, neoliberals in different parts of the world were forced to critique, dismantle, or reimagine a prior developmental infrastructure that had transformed the mid-twentieth-century world. The uneven ways in which Britain's developmental built environment was reorganized to suit the private property market in the late twentieth century are one way in which we can see this. Most important, viewing neoliberalism from the mezzanine of a shopping mall or the courtyard of a council estate where half the residents have purchased their own homes from the state allows us to see how political change was worked out in practice on the ground. Doing so takes away some of the causal autonomy that has been bestowed on elite politicians, intellectuals, or the movements of the global economy. It allows us to see the new kind of society and new kind of subject that the neoliberal built environment attempted to conjure into being, and it is to this that we now turn.

Making and Unmaking a New Society

Each of these different urban forms were manifestations, sometimes implicit and sometimes explicit, of different claims about the nature of the individual and the social world to which they belonged. This book's third argument is that the transition from a developmental to neoliberal political formation in Britain resulted in a loss of faith among planners and politicians that urban space could be used to make new kinds of people. The industrial estate, shopping precinct, and council estate each operated during a time when it was assumed that individuals and the social were raw materials waiting to be shaped by external forces.[28] Industrial estates, with their canteens, communal leisure centers, and generous training programs, existed to maximize the health, fitness, and productivity of workforces. Shopping precincts operated with the assumption that populations had a finite and calculable set of needs that could be provided for in advance. Council estates—often dense, inward looking, and set apart from their surrounding urban fabric—were intended to create thriving communities out of erstwhile strangers. They each assumed that the social was an aggregate of individuals who were knowable—people whose desires could be met, and whose relationships with each other could be altered in predictable ways. These claims were made in spite of the social body's evident diversity during this period. Many firms on early industrial estates were managed by German Jewish refugees (nonnative-speaking managers complained about being unable to understand the thick local accents of their employees), and many employed more women than men at different times in their history. The planners of council estates boasted that they were producing new communities of strangers at the same time as increasing numbers of Commonwealth migrants were de facto excluded from these spaces. The mid-twentieth-century urban forms described in the first half of this book were agents in reproducing the inequalities of gender and race that ordered the social world in which they emerged.

Britain's neoliberal urban forms—the private housing estate, suburban shopping mall, and business park—called into being a different type of individual and manifested a skepticism about the very idea of a manipulable social body. A new kind of criminology, emerging in the United States in the 1970s and moving to the heart of the Thatcher government by the 1980s, posited that the generous amounts of public space and shared resources characteristic of many council estates—the courtyards, corridors, and walkways where new communities were supposed to arise—went against the grain of human nature itself. In the 1980s and 1990s, council estates were redesigned in ways that maximized private over public space in the name of crime control. All of a sudden, the respectable raw material of community development had become, in the eyes of politicians, threatening, unpredictable, and in need of urgent policing. Meanwhile, although shopping malls were intensively regulated types of space—developments whose lighting, heating, and music were carefully calibrated to internationally agreed-on standards—they were tailored to more intangible forces of leisure and desire. Necessity was traded for pleasure, and shopping malls became otherworldly family destinations rather than functional and feminized sites for routinized daily shopping. Lastly, high-tech business parks were spatially ordered to maximize the productivity of a new kind of worker—"flexible" and "creative." With their pubs, verdant grounds, and public art, they set out to foster inspiration as well as cultivate a vague and cozy feeling of well-being, as opposed to developing their workforces in a rational and linear manner. Britain's neoliberal urban forms inherited the unequal social order of their predecessors. Council estates were securitized and reordered in the 1980s, at the same time that they were becoming home to substantial numbers of people of color for the first time. Shopping malls in the 1980s attempted to exclude unproductive subjects—for the most part unemployed men—via a strategy that resulted in protracted legal battles. The affluent knowledge work practiced in business parks in the 1970s and 1980s was coded as male and oriented toward elite workers rather than the cleaners, receptionists, gardeners, or security guards who also worked in these spaces.

The ideal users of these new types of spaces were individuals whose subjectivity existed beyond the frontiers of power; they were people whose desires and relationships had to be discovered rather than produced, enabled rather than prescribed, and policed rather than reformed. Together, they show that the ideal neoliberal urban subject is one who could *not* be planned for and was formed beyond the reach of any kind of political or architectural intervention. While much has been written on the neoliberal subject as an entrepreneurial *homo economicus*, this pessimism about the use of state power to reshape instead of enable individual subjects, borne out by the design of urban space, is less well understood.[29] Premonitions of this complex and unknowable urban subject, immune to being shaped by power, abound among critics of the high modern, developmental projects of the midcentury. This subject can be found among Michel de Certeau's elusive pedestrians or Henri

Lefebvre's lyrical descriptions of the citizens of Navarrenx, his medieval hometown in the Pyrenees. It can be found amid the "vernacular" forms of architecture celebrated in Las Vegas by Robert Venturi, Denise Scott Brown, and Steven Izenour, or, perhaps most famously, in Jane Jacobs's evocation of the "sidewalk ballet" that unfolded outside her Greenwich Village apartment each day.[30]

These thinkers were right to be critical of mid-twentieth-century attempts to remake society. In Britain, these experiments were coercive, patriarchal, and tied inexorably to the inequalities produced by empire both at home and abroad.[31] A return to midcentury social politics should not form the basis for a political program in the present. What remained after the tide of developmental social politics had receded, however, were a series of shattered, privatized, and depoliticized spaces. The neoliberal vision of society and the built forms that have enabled it have proved compatible with staggering levels of inequality, intensive policing of space, and ownership of infrastructure by distant and unaccountable private bodies.[32] It is also a landscape that is spatially hostile to the effective mobilization of political resistance. This is something that anyone who has tried to organize a protest in a shopping mall or canvass a private housing development secured by an entry phone already knows.

It was the starkness of these two different visions of the individual and the social that, when they clashed on privatized council estates or in renovated shopping precincts, accounts for the distinctiveness of the British neoliberal built environment. Any given historical moment always contains accumulated traces of what came before; Saint Paul's Cathedral still stands, as does York's medieval city walls. But perhaps never before have the guiding principles governing the organization of urban space in Britain been inverted as quickly they were during the last third of the twentieth century, when a vision of society as an aggregate whole, capable of being remade by planners, fragmented and gave way.

Aligning Britain with the World

Lastly, these six urban forms had lives that stretched far beyond Britain itself. The fourth and final argument of this book is that these spaces acted as mechanisms for aligning the look and feel of everyday British life with that of the wider world. Throughout the twentieth century, Britain exported urban plans and policies. The ideas of British new town planners and development corporations shaped the urban landscapes of Latin America, West Africa, the Indian subcontinent, and elsewhere.[33] Enterprise zones, a neoliberal urban planning strategy developed by the Thatcher government that created small, exceptional tax havens in impoverished inner-city areas, were exported to the United States, France, and Italy, among other places.[34] The first chapter of this book shows how the industrial estate, an urban form invented on the banks of the Manchester Ship Canal in the early twentieth century, spread through imperial networks to West and East Africa as well as to the Pacific Rim by the end of the 1950s.

Despite its empire, however, and its exemplary status within Cold War modernization theory as the first country to urbanize, Britain was a net importer of urban forms from the Second World War onward. Particularly in the last third of the twentieth century, Britain's built environment was shaped by the world rather than vice versa. Britain has, of course, always existed in global and imperial networks of trade and migration. But in the postwar period, and particularly since the 1970s, the look, feel, and purpose of the British built environment has been shaped by the wider world to an unprecedented degree.[35] When it came to mass council housing, many towns looked east. Cities such as Glasgow and Sheffield sent delegations of architects, councillors, and planners to western Europe to marvel at Le Corbusier's Unité d'Habitation in Marseille or traipse among the soaring towers of the Bellahøj housing development in Copenhagen. Reams of technical material about the planning of large-scale district heating systems were requested from Soviet technical journals and translated in the hope of emulation. Britain's new towns program imported as well as exported urban expertise, often employing former colonial officials at crucial stages in their planning and development.[36]

The most significant global alignment, though, was between Britain and the United States in the last third of the twentieth century. Both the shopping mall and the business park were direct imports from US suburbia. They were each born in the same decade—the 1950s—the former in the Midwest, where freezing winter temperatures demanded new forms of enclosure, and the latter in what has since become known as Silicon Valley in Northern California. Iterations of these forms in Britain were standardized by international networks of experts, frequently with the help of institutions such the International Council of Shopping Centers and the International Association of Science Parks. The repetitive, almost banal modularity of these urban forms across global space allowed many to be owned by distant, overseas property developers who bought and sold them without setting foot inside, safe in the knowledge of what they looked like. The last twenty years has seen the emergence in the United States of what has become known as the "New Suburban History," a historical turn that has looked to postwar suburbanization to answer important questions about race, gender, and the collapse of New Deal liberalism.[37] While these histories have tended to halt at the US border, the new urban forms generated in the US suburbs have spread across the world.[38] By showing how they migrated to and thrived in a new urban environment on the other side of the Atlantic, this book picks up where many US historians have left off. Likewise, while the British route to neoliberalism has often been explained as emanating from a transatlantic network of think tanks sharing ideas and policies, this book demonstrates how physical spaces as well as ideas washed up on Britain's shores during the period when neoliberalism was in ascendency.[39]

These urban forms, then, passed *through* Britain and beyond, crossing borders with the ease of passing clouds. Now imagine that the plane journey with which this book began had originated in the United States. During your flight, you may then also have seen the boreal forests of Newfoundland and frigid emptiness of Greenland, but the city you are about to land in may feel uncannily familiar to that which you departed from.

1

The Industrial Estate

WRITING IN THE early nineteenth century, Scottish physician Andrew Ure described factories as being analogous to the human body. The factory, he wrote, "involves the idea of a vast automaton, composed of various mechanical and intellectual organs . . . subordinated to a self-regulating force" with "mechanical fingers and arms" that are "regularly impelled with great velocity by some indefatigable physical power."[1] His account was based on his observations of the mechanized textile factories in Lancashire and Cheshire, many of which he visited during the course of the 1830s. The industrial estate, an urban form that emerged in early twentieth-century Britain, marked the antithesis of Ure's conception of the factory.[2] Industrial estates are spaces created in advance for industrial production, where multiple factories and workshops cluster together under the supervision and management of a single authority. This authority provides these factories with energy, infrastructure, access to labor markets, and sometimes even buildings and machinery. By the mid-twentieth century, many industrial estates resembled mini towns, with stores, railway networks, canteens, hotels, playing fields, and football teams. Here, business owners were reconceived of as tenants, fleeting consumers of systems of infrastructure that would long outlive their presence. If 1830s textile factories were like mechanized human beings—individuated and self-sufficient—then the factories on mid-twentieth-century industrial estates were like bees in a hive, existentially dependent on and existing in service to a bigger endeavor.[3]

This chapter is about the emergence and spread of the industrial estate as a new type of twentieth-century space. The history of this space begins on the outskirts of Manchester in the 1890s, when an ancient aristocratic family sold its land to a shady property speculator. The result was the creation of a monumental planned industrial complex called Trafford Park. As Trafford Park developed in the early twentieth century, hosting Henry Ford's first British-based car-making plant along with hundreds of other enterprises, it was joined by a handful of similar, smaller developments built in southern suburban towns such as Slough and Welwyn Garden City. It took the interwar economic crisis, however, to realize the potential of the industrial estate as a new urban form. As the restructuring of Britain's economy in the 1920s and Depression in the 1930s decimated the workforces of significant regions of the country, the British government built its own industrial estates, modeled on places such as Trafford Park and Slough, as a means of incentivizing factories to move into areas of high unemployment. In the late 1930s, three government-financed industrial estates in areas of high unemployment—Team Valley in Gateshead, Treforest in South Wales, and Hillington on the outskirts of Glasgow—were employing tens of thousands of people. Following the example of these spaces, this new urban form spread rapidly after the Second World War. By 1960, there were upward of eighty industrial estates in Britain, employing more than a quarter million, mostly in new towns or regions of the country that were deemed to be in economic distress.[4] The workers in these estates often included women as well as men, particularly in those factories specializing in electric assembly-line production. With government-financed industrial estates offering an easy place for the settlement of Jewish business owners fleeing central Europe in the 1930s, it was frequently the case that the tenants of early industrial estates were German-speaking émigrés. After the war, industrial estates became an international phenomenon, seized on by colonial administrators and economists as a means of catalyzing industrial development across the world. None of this was ever really supposed to happen. The setting aside of small amounts of money by the government to build and service industrial estates in 1936 was an emergency measure—a last resort that came about only after the government had failed to persuade private developers to shoulder the burden.

My aim here is twofold. First, I want to demonstrate how industrial estates came to be promoted by a new kind of developmental state in the twentieth century and offered the possibility of remaking both Britain's workers and its economy. The government-financed industrial estate was forged in the service of a state-sanctioned historical geography—an idea that Britain's economy could be spatially altered in ways that were conducive to full employment, national economic development, and the closure of regional disparities of wealth.[5] These spaces were organized around a particular type of industrial subject: a worker whose health and productivity could be maximized by elaborate fitness centers and canteens serving scientifically balanced meals.

Second, I want to show how industrial estates had a radical logic, one unforeseen by its creators and even many of its early promoters. The success and portability of this new type of space was infectious, and within a few years after the opening of the first government-financed estates, they were pulling politicians, planners, colonial administrators, and international development agencies behind them in their slipstream. In less than a generation, the state had become the landlord for hundreds of factory owners across the country, and, in many instances, was locked in heated disputes with capitalists who were banding together to contest the conditions of their leases, threatening, in some cases, to withhold their rent. What's more, they allowed some planners to indulge in more radical fantasies about the future relationship between the state and industry—fantasies that were ultimately unfulfilled. Some planners believed that these new urban forms would solve some of the problems that British capitalism faced after the Depression, imagining future worlds in which all industry of a certain type would be housed on nationalized industrial estates. Others believed that industrial estates would help rapidly industrialize parts of Britain's empire. In this sense, these spaces had a demonstrative significance that went beyond their contribution to midcentury industrial policy in both the metropole and the empire. They were showcases for an emergent future of town planning and a new type of capitalism tamed by the state, spaces that were visited by government ministers, monarchs, and international delegations.

Like the other urban forms in the first three chapters of this book, then, industrial estates did certain kinds of political and economic work, and in doing so opened up new and more radical futures. However, many of the extreme, almost-utopian fantasies about the kind of economy that industrial estates might allow were never realized.

Trafford Park

As the nineteenth century was drawing to a close, the de Trafford family could almost see the city of Manchester coming over the horizon to meet them. Their ancestral home, a large manor house surrounded by hundreds of acres of parks and gardens, had belonged to the family for eight centuries, supposedly without a break in the male line of succession. Now it found itself encircled by the enormous, soot-drenched city that was creeping ever closer. In 1887, construction began on the Manchester Ship Canal, a project to link the city with the Irish Sea thirty-six miles to the west, bypassing Liverpool and turning the city into a self-sufficient port. When it was clear that the canal would pass immediately to the north of their estate, the family decided that the game was up. Anticipating the sale, the Manchester Corporation made the de Trafford family an offer of £260,000, intending to turn the country estate into a gigantic public park modeled on London's Hyde Park. At the last minute, however, the city was outbid by a self-made businessman named Ernest Terah Hooley.[6]

Hooley was a notorious speculator with an extravagant and shady business portfolio. In the 1890s, he made a fortune buying patents from small

FIGURE 1.1. Sketch of Trafford Hall on the de Trafford family estate at the end of the
nineteenth century.

companies, using his charm to promote the company and then reselling
the patents at a profit. His ventures included a Spanish copper mine and the
promotion of a new bicycle chain, which he claimed would enable "a mere
novice . . . to ride from 40 to 60 miles an hour with only ordinary exertion."[7]
By his death in 1947, Hooley had been jailed three times for fraud and was on
his fourth bankruptcy.[8] His involvement in Trafford Park, and the subsequent
development of the world's first industrial estate, came about as the result of
a clerical error. In 1896, Hooley learned of de Trafford's intention to sell the
estate when a letter meant for de Trafford's steward was delivered to Hooley's
secretary by mistake. At the time, the two men (both named Ellis) happened
to be staying at the same hotel. He moved quickly, purchasing the estate for
£100,000 more than the Manchester Corporation had offered and thwarting
the city's dream of a park.[9]

Hooley had no experience as a landlord. His early ideas for the land included an amusement park and a residential complex consisting of five hundred expensive villas surrounded by a woodland.[10] The decision to transform
the land into an industrial estate was inspired by the shipping magnate Marshall Stevens, the former general manager of the Manchester Ship Canal. Stevens was concerned that despite the new canal manufacturers were reluctant

to move to Manchester rather than Liverpool. He hoped that a new development, with access to energy and infrastructure networks, would act as a kind of subsidy, a logical extension of the canal's developmental aims. Lacking ideas, Hooley gratefully accepted Stevens's plans, and in 1897 Stevens was appointed general manager of Trafford Park Estates Ltd. The two men were about to become some of the most unusual landlords in the country.

Trafford Park was ideally situated for industrial development. The land occupied what was effectively an island, bounded on all sides by canals and perched on the edge of Manchester. Over the next ten years, Trafford Park Estates set about overlaying the land with a grid of infrastructure. Companies were invited to purchase a plot of land from the estate, after which they would pay for access to various services. These included gas and water as well as access to the Ship Canal via the new Manchester Docks, which were contiguous with the estate. An oil company established depots to be used by other factories. After an eight-year battle, Stevens succeeded in winning permission from parliament to build a small railroad network throughout the estate, thus connecting tenants with both the docks and national network. Tenants were also offered subsidized access to electricity via a small on-site power station—a rarity at that time.[11] Aside from a handful of speculatively built industrial developments, which the company named "hives," tenants were expected to plan and build their own factories.[12]

By providing electricity, Hooley and Stevens ensured that Trafford Park was at the vanguard of a new type of mass production organized around electrically powered assembly lines. Henry Ford, perhaps the estate's most famous tenant, built his first British factory in Trafford Park in 1911 and was an early pioneer of such methods.[13] Another of the estate's earliest and most significant tenants was George Westinghouse, the US electrical supplies magnate who had played a vital role in developing commercially available electricity in the United States. Westinghouse transferred a cadre of US managers from Pittsburgh to work in the plant. British visitors were reportedly shocked by the sight of spittoons and by Fourth of July celebrations. The Westinghouse Corporation split from its US owners in 1919 and was renamed Metropolitan Vickers. At its peak, the company occupied nine buildings spread over a hundred acres employing thousands of engineers arranged in a complex hierarchy of skill.[14]

As well as providing energy and transportation, Trafford Park also supplied its tenants with a reliable stream of labor. The first attempt to stabilize the labor supply was the construction of seven hundred houses on the estate in 1899. Known, ironically, as "the Village," the development was overseen by Westinghouse, who added a US touch by laying out the houses in a grid pattern along numbered streets and avenues. The houses were on tightly packed terraces abutting narrow streets. The development at first included a modest school, with the eventual addition of a church, swimming pools, and a handful of shops.[15] Until the Village's partial demolition and redevelopment in 1981, the inhabitants of this bizarre residential development enjoyed a close-knit community. A nostalgic poem published in the Village's "newsletter" in the late 1970s by an elderly resident allows us access to the strangeness and isolation of life there:

> Surrounded by great Industry, and all its many works,
> Peace at Sunday shut-down, the only workers' perks?
> But people from "Park Village" were happy hard-work folk,
> And environmental pillage was not a heavy yolk.
>
> In spite of smoke and chemicals, rubber smells and dust,
> Home were happy living cells,—the doctor was no must,
> Health was quite amazing, School health-men judged it good,
> And healthy happy children, played ball on croft-site mud.[16]

The Village was clearly too small to house all the workers of the various factories in Trafford Park. The development of the park stimulated house building in the rapidly growing suburbs of Stretford, Eccles, and Salford.[17] Most of the labor arrived via a network of electric streetcars built and managed by the company to carry workers to and from these suburbs as well as from Manchester.[18]

The factory owner tenants at Trafford Park were provided with energy, labor, and transportation, but they were offered more unusual services too. The park had its own banks, workingmen's clubs, and a strip of forty-four warehouses along the banks of the Ship Canal. These were tailored for specific commodities, with fireproof warehouses for storing cotton and refrigerated warehouses for storing perishable foods.[19] At its midcentury apotheosis, Trafford Park employed forty thousand people in 150 different factories.[20] By this time, almost every trace of the centuries-old country estate had been obliterated. In its place stood a vast, integrated, balletic machine in which each individual enterprise was subordinated to the greater infrastructural whole. To signify the park's unapologetic modernity, a giant banner was hung over its entrance: "Wake Up England—Trafford Park Is Awake!"

As an urban industrial complex, the park bore a superficial resemblance to company towns elsewhere in the world, such as the steelworks of Magnitogorsk in the Soviet Union or the automobile production complex in Flint, Michigan. However, while the latter examples were urban landscapes shaped by a single, powerful business or state enterprise, Trafford Park saw multiple different enterprises subordinated to a property developer. The park had only

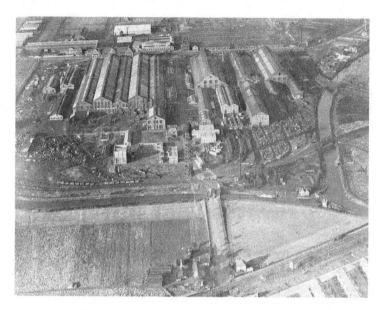

FIGURE 1.2. Aerial photograph of the Metropolitan Vickers (originally British Westinghouse) plant in Trafford Park, 1941.

FIGURE 1.3. The banner hung above the entrance of Trafford Park: "Wake Up England—Trafford Park Is Awake!"

a few global counterparts, all of which it preceded. These included "industrial districts" that leased land and provided services to manufacturers. Developed by US railroad companies in the first two decades of the twentieth century, these districts were built in midwestern cities along the railroad line between Los Angeles and Chicago, and included Chicago's Clearing Industrial District developed in 1905 and the Fairfax Industrial District in Kansas City developed in 1923.[21] In Germany, meanwhile, a handful of planned industrial areas were developed on either side of the First World War, including the Berlin Templehof Industrial Area and the municipally developed Cologne Industrial Area.[22]

In Britain, Trafford Park was the first and for a while only industrial estate. After the First World War, smaller, planned industrial developments began to appear, mostly in the south of England.[23] While Trafford Park was oriented toward the global market, with its fate tied to the Manchester Ship Canal, these subsequent developments were more modest and nationally focused. They tended to specialize in consumer goods and were usually more dependent on electricity rather than steam and road rather than rail transportation. For this reason, they typically were located in suburban areas, away from major coalfields and connected to Britain's burgeoning road network and domestic markets. Two of the biggest industrial estates to emerge during the 1920s, Park Royal and Slough, were developed in the western suburbs of London. The Slough industrial estate was created as a means of disposing of tens of thousands of surplus military vehicles produced during the war that were accumulating uselessly on the outskirts of the town. After the war, private developers bought the land and stock from the government and, with the help of prisoners of war, set about selling the vehicles. Once the vehicles were sold, the developers turned the land into a smaller, cleaner, and more suburban version of Trafford Park, with low-rise art deco factory buildings available for businesses to rent. Early tenants included the razor company Gillette, the French car manufacturer Citroen, and the US candy company Mars.

By 1930, the peculiar landlord-tenant relationship established at Trafford Park was spreading across the country. Industrial estates remained in the hands of private developers during this period. Businesspeople such as the eccentric Ernest Hooley or Noel Mobbs, the Conservative Party–supporting owner of Slough Estates who would become a vocal critic of Britain's postwar mixed economy, seem far removed from the politics of top-down, state-directed industrial development. Nevertheless, the new urban forms that these speculators were honing in places like Manchester and the suburbs of London had their own logic. This type of space preceded and prefigured the political changes of the 1930s. The portability and commensurability of industrial estates would soon allow some planners and politicians to believe that they could be agents in a reordering of the economic geography of Britain.

Landlord of Last Resort

By the early 1930s, out of sight of the rest of Britain, the North East of England was entering its second decade of economic crisis. Four hours on the train from London, the cities of Newcastle, Sunderland, Middlesbrough, Jarrow, Durham, and a host of smaller coal-mining towns and villages were sliding off the edge of the earth. Britain's relative decline in world trade, beginning in the last third of the nineteenth century, began to harm the economy of port cities. Countries such as the United States and Germany were catching up to Britain and raising tariff barriers in the process, meaning that Britain had less capital goods to sell. Shipbuilding, one of the area's primary industries, saw profit margins squeezed as the volume of goods leaving Britain decreased and the size and durability of ships improved.[24] It was in this context that the British state started to build its own industrial estates.

While some regions of the country were in terminal decline, others were booming. In the interwar period, Britain's industrial geography was changing, in some places taking new forms that would have been unrecognizable to most workers at the turn of the century. Instead of thunderous, awe-inspiring complexes, powered by steam and employing thousands, new interwar industries tended to be housed in low-rise suburban developments. In these places, "light" versus "heavy" industry predominated, and rather than producing ships, machine tools, textiles, or steel for export, these new factories were making consumer goods for the domestic market such as small electric items and processed foods.[25] The kinds of industry practiced on the Slough Trading Estate, for example, were becoming more common. These industries often employed mostly female workers on electric assembly lines performing rote tasks.[26] While old industries tended to gravitate toward ports and ship canals, the newer industries stayed as close as possible to domestic markets, mostly in the South East and the West Midlands—dominating the economy of places like Dagenham, Slough, Coventry, Oxford, and Letchworth.[27] While Northumberland and Durham's share of Britain's national net output fell by 21.4 percent between 1924 and 1935, Greater London's rose by 38.5 percent.[28] Geography, once the friend of the North East, a region that had depended heavily on coalfields and ports, had by the early 1930s become the region's worst enemy.

Initially the government had little means to combat this problem. With some high-profile exceptions, politicians on both sides of the aisle in the 1920s were still committed to the economic policies that had been ascendant since the mid-nineteenth century.[29] Free trade, balanced budgets, and a currency pegged to gold continued to be the established doctrine. Within these constraints, the state had little to offer beyond unemployment insurance, a smattering of public works financed by loans, and a handful of schemes to retrain unemployed workers in agriculture and construction.[30] The plight of the North East in comparison to areas with more advanced domestic industries became worse after 1930 as the Great Depression prompted an international crisis of finance and trade. Industrial production plummeted and unemployment surged, reaching almost three million. An emergency National Government, formed in 1931, brought to an end Britain's almost hundred-year commitment to free trade, uncoupling the pound from gold and introducing a general tariff of 10 percent. While by the mid-1930s Britain's economy was undergoing a tentative recovery, large sections of the country were still left behind.

In 1934, the *Times* newspaper sent a special correspondent to County Durham to write a three-part exposé of the crisis under the headline "Places without a Future." These articles initiated a two-year campaign that would eventually result in the construction of the first government-financed industrial estates. The *Times* journalist saw a crisis that challenged the orthodoxies of liberal political economy for two reasons. First, it was a crisis that was irreversible—one that went beyond the usual waxing and waning of the business cycle: "There are districts of England, heavily populated, whose plight no amount of general trade recovery can ever cure, because their sole industry is not depressed but dead. . . . [I]n places where the pits are not only closed but abandoned, the works are not only shut but dismantled, it is difficult to see any ground for hope, because there is no industry left there for recovery to revitalize."[31]

Second, it was a crisis of uneven geography, one that unfolded out of sight and out of mind for a London that was tentatively recovering from the Depression: "There are parts of Durham where one feels, strongly and sometimes angrily, that London has still no conception of the troubles that affect the industrial North. . . . Resentment exists among thoughtful people against the comfortable South because it is alleged that the South governs in ignorance."[32]

The *Times* articles were some of the first and possibly the most consequential (in policy terms) of a series of articles, books, and films written by southern journalists and intellectuals who traveled to northern towns to witness as well as publicize this uneven geography.[33] Among the most famous of these accounts were George Orwell's *The Road to Wigan Pier* and J. B. Priestley's *English Journey*, two texts that documented the desperate details of northern poverty while subjecting a fallen and lost working class, once the collective agents of industrial modernity, to a pitying anthropological gaze.[34] The explosion of literature documenting isolated and irredeemable pockets of northern poverty contributed to the end of a liberal framework for understanding the problem of unemployment and hunger. Where once the unemployed had been deemed as weak, incompetent self-saboteurs, now these communities were victims of humanitarian tragedies far beyond their control.[35]

It seemed to some commentators as if whole populations were becoming economically superfluous. Under these circumstances, the unemployed poor were reimagined in the aggregate as potential subjects for massive and swift acts of government intervention. In 1939, the think tank Political and Economic Planning recommended the wholesale and government-mandated deportation of the population of some parts of Britain to other, more productive areas. The think tank calculated that deporting the entire population of Merthyr Tydfil, a Welsh former mining town of more than sixty thousand people, would cost fifteen million pounds—a cheaper solution in the long term than continuing to pay unemployment assistance at the rate of one million pounds a year.[36] One planning officer reflected on the dilemma facing urban planners in such circumstances, writing that "as he puts the delicate bands of colour on his map . . . the thought suddenly occurs to him that the place has been damned for years, with no hope of resurrection." The only thing worth building, he concluded, were "cemeteries to hold the wretched people who had been left."[37] Short of mass deportation or managed decline, any attempt to redress the enormous problems facing the North East, South Wales, and other former industrial heartlands would involve rebuilding the region's economy from scratch.

In its final dispatch from the North East, the *Times* called on the government directly to appoint a handful of investigators to gather more information on derelict regions of the country.[38] This point was seized on by local members of Parliament and introduced as a topic of debate.[39] Under further pressure from the *Times* and Labour members of Parliament, the government announced the appointment of investigators tasked to this end. Euan Wallace, the Conservative member of Parliament appointed to investigate Durham and Tyneside, agreed with the *Times* in arguing that the collapse of industry in the North East had reached such catastrophic and irreversible proportions that many of the basic assumptions of liberal government had to be rethought. In language echoing John Maynard Keynes's famous quip that while economies may stabilize in the long run, in the long run we are all dead, Wallace wrote that "there is no likelihood that the same forces which have created the present situation will automatically readjust it, except after a lapse of time and at a cost in human suffering and economic waste which no modern government would care to contemplate."[40] His deposition was a call for direct state intervention to rebuild the economy of the North East.

The government's first legislative response, in December 1934, was to designate some of the worst-hit regions as Special Areas, which covered the

North East, South Wales, Cumberland, and parts of Scotland. Two commissioners, one for England and Wales and one for Scotland, were appointed the task of spending two million pounds each on development in the areas. At first the commissioners were barred from providing any inducements to industry, and for the first months of their lives the Special Areas mostly existed on paper only (it was telling that the name of the designation was changed from "depressed" to "special" in the final stages of its passage through Parliament).[41] One of the first acts of the commissioners was to circulate a promotional booklet to industrialists called "New Fields for Industry."[42] Without any positive inducements, the circulation received little response. For most small-time industrialists, moving to depressed areas was simply too risky. They were too isolated from consumer markets, rates were too high, and the areas were imbued with an intangible and off-putting feeling of decline.

By this point the solution was becoming obvious to many. The Special Areas commissioners needed to look no further than Trafford Park. Malcolm Stewart, the appointed Special Areas commissioner for England and Wales, took the initiative.[43] His 1936 report specifically praised both the Trafford Park and Slough industrial estates, and called for the government to finance similar projects in Special Areas. Stewart persuaded the Board of Trade that there was zero hope that a private property developer would be interested in such a project. The board approached Slough Trading Estates Ltd., which confirmed that it had no interest in such an undertaking.[44] It was under these circumstances that the government became a landlord of last resort.

Team Valley

In 1936, the government created a new body, North Eastern Trading Estates Ltd. (NETE), and furnished it with the money to build Britain's first government-owned industrial estate. NETE had an extensive remit, with permission to buy and sell land, lease buildings and plots, manufacture steam, sink wells, and construct and maintain railways and wharves.[45] Its finances were reviewed by the Special Areas commissioner for England and Wales and allocated by Parliament. The resulting development, Team Valley, was built between 1936 and 1939 in Gateshead, a town on the fringes of Newcastle. Two other industrial estates were built simultaneously in the other two Special Areas: the Treforest Trading Estate in South Wales and Hillington Industrial Estate near Glasgow. These estates were also funded and managed by new state-backed corporations—South Wales and Monmouthshire Trading Estates Limited and Scottish Industrial Estates Limited. Faced with an economic crisis that appeared unsolvable, the government embarked on a radically new kind of intervention, replicating the relationship between industry, infrastructure, and labor that had been modeled in places like Trafford Park.

Unlike the thunderous roar and chemical stench of Trafford Park, Team Valley left little impact on the landscape. The seven-hundred-acre estate was almost solely comprised of low-rise identical structures, laid out in a grid pattern along numbered streets and set behind privet hedges and wide pavements.[46] Twenty gardeners were hired to nurse the flowers and trees planted by the company.[47] The factories at Team Valley housed forms of production characteristic of the light industries that were more commonly found in southern England. Among the first twenty tenants were potato chip makers, confectioners, toy makers, lampshade makers, glazers, electrical engineering plants, laminated glass makers, and tailors.[48] What these diverse enterprises had in common was their use of electricity and their orientation toward a market of domestic British consumers.

While most of the occupants of Trafford Park bought a plot of land and built their own industrial buildings, NETE built, owned, and maintained all the buildings on Team Valley, and then leased them to tenants. Prospective tenants were offered three different sizes of factory (small, medium, and large), each fitted with first-floor office space and an open-plan shop floor.[49] The estate provided specialized services for small business owners with little initial capital by offering tiny "nest" factories, just forty-five by thirty-three square feet in size, for a pound per week.[50] The structures at Team Valley were designed to be flexible, with the anticipation that they would house multiple different industrial endeavors over the course of their lives. The idea was that the buildings could be torn down and easily replaced as manufacturing methods changed.[51] While Trafford Park's occupants built buildings to house specific industries, whether it was the vast Metropolitan Vickers complex or Ford's electric assembly lines, Team Valley made no such claims, providing only a space for industry in the abstract. If Trafford Park was like a classical sculpture, a fixed testament to turn-of-the-century industrialism that was intended to remain in place for hundreds of years, Team Valley was to be like a sketchbook—a blank slate to be populated with whatever was deemed to be productive at any given moment.

As at Trafford Park, Team Valley's planners ensured that tenants were plugged into a comprehensive energy and infrastructure network that was planned and constructed in advance of their arrival. The estate had its own railroads connected to the national network, and all factory units were provided with electricity, gas, and central heating as standard. NETE offered more bespoke forms of provision too. For an extra price, tenants could have their factories fitted with conveyor runways, gas tanks, built-in ovens, steam

FIGURE 1.4. Team Valley canteen. Kenelm C. Appleyard, "Government Sponsored Trading Estates," *Journal of the Royal Society of the Arts* 87 (June 30, 1939): 843–63. Reproduced with permission from the Royal Society of Arts.

boilers, and extra ventilation.[52] Amenities were also supplied for owners and managers at the Central Administration Building, which hosted upscale restaurants, meeting rooms, a clubhouse, banks, a hotel, and a handful of shops.[53]

Moreover, Team Valley was a space that many hoped would create new kinds of working subjects—the outcome of a faith that workers were raw materials who could be molded into a more productive form. The estate was a participant in the National Fitness Council (NFC), a body created in 1937 to improve the physical health and moral hygiene of the population. The NFC, with its attention to moral as well as physical human development, stemmed from a broader eugenic concern about the health and genetic stock of Britain's population and its workforce in the interwar period.[54] The NFC's instigators and boosters looked positively on comparable developments in Adolf Hitler's Germany.[55] In addition to providing grants to schools, children's clubs, and local communities, the NFC funded equipment to support physical recreation in industrial workplaces.[56] Team Valley was an early recipient of this funding in 1938, with an NFC grant allowing for the building of a large recreation center, which eventually boasted an ice rink, a swimming pool, and a sports field where interfactory football and cricket games were encouraged.[57] Diet as well as exercise were important means of augmenting the productivity of Team Valley's workers. NETE constructed a communal canteen where the employees of the various different factories were fed "scientifically balanced" meals available for five pence.[58] The 520-seat canteen was divided into sixty-five rectangular tables of eight, laid out symmetrically inside a long, narrow hall, mimicking the neat grid pattern of the estate outside.[59] Advocates for industrial canteens saw such spaces as instruments of social and nutritional reform, where sociability and civility would be fostered in the name of morale and human development.[60]

NETE prided itself on its pliant, malleable workforce, which included many long-term unemployed ex-miners. Pamphlets were distributed to southern factory owners, emphasizing the diligence of former miners who had been transferred into light industrial work elsewhere. The same promotional material included a chart showing the low number of days lost per person through labor disputes in the area (between five and six a year). Meanwhile, the Ministry of Labour offered incoming businesses a kind of consultancy service, conducting research into the supply of suitable labor before a factory was leased and paying for the traveling expenses of workers who needed to be sent elsewhere for their training.[61] Team Valley, then, was a machine for the rational and linear development of workers as well as goods. Its subjects were the long-term unemployed, an aggregate mass capable of being remade by large-scale government projects, whether it was Team Valley or the wholesale deportation schemes imagined by the Political and Economic Planning think tank.[62] In this sense, the estate operated with a belief that new kinds of people could be made by new kinds of built space.

While early publicity material was drawn up with the assumption that Team Valley's workforce would mostly consist of long-term unemployed men, the reality was that the estate's factories were mostly filled with women. In line with similar workplaces in the south of England, Team Valley saw comparatively high rates of female employment.[63] This was largely due to the relative cheapness of female labor, low rates of unionization, and an assumption that women were better suited for a job requiring maximum physical dexterity and lower levels of strength.[64] In 1938, it was calculated that women made up 61 percent of the workforce of the first three government-owned industrial estates in Team Valley, Treforest, and Hillington.[65] In some sectors, such as clothing manufacture, women made up as much as 88 percent of NETEs' workforce.[66] By 1958, it was still the case that more than half of Team Valley's workforce was female.[67] The high rate of female participation in Team Valley's labor force was arguably one of the primary reasons why the estates failed to dramatically reduce the high rates of male unemployment in the area.[68] Drawing on interviews with women who worked in light factories in London and elsewhere in the South East, Miriam Glucksmann allows us some access to what the working lives of women on these industrial estates would have been like. The overriding experience was one of extreme discipline. The pace of work was enforced either by overseers or the speed that the electric conveyor belt moved.[69] Women would stand or sit in fixed positions performing the same operation repeatedly,

FIGURE 1.5. Women working on an assembly line in a small electronics factory on the Whitehill Industrial Estate near Edinburgh, 1969. © Architectural Press Archive / RIBA Collections.

sometimes six days a week for ten hours a day.[70] Although talking was sometimes banned, some of Glucksmann's interviewees remembered a chatty environment and even smoking while working on the line.[71]

Industrial estates in Special Areas also played an important role in the resettlement of German Jewish refugees. It was estimated that a third of all German refugees applying for asylum in Britain in the late 1930s were manufacturers of some kind—a figure that likely reflects the prejudice of officials processing applications who were sympathetic mostly to refugees who had a track record of being economically productive. Although the Home Office lacked the legal means to compel new arrivals to set up businesses in Special Areas, it was made clear to applicants that their bid for safety would be more successful if they pledged to do so. Potential applicants were put directly in touch with Special Areas commissioners, who then provided them with information about settlement and how to access capital.[72] By 1941, there were more than a hundred German Jewish enterprises employing tens of thousands of British workers.[73] In 1939, 27 percent of all businesses on Team Valley were owned by refugees. During the war, many of these business owners fell victim to state internment policies.[74] Many refugee manufacturers specialized in producing ready-made women's clothing in fashionable styles that previously had been supplied only from imports.[75] One of these prewar refugees, Herbert Loebl, moved to England as a teenager after his father, the owner of an electrical engineering factory in Bamberg, was granted asylum. Loebl's father was advised by the commissioner to rent a ready-made factory in Team Valley. Loebl, who became a passionate advocate for government industrial estates and historian of NETE, recalled the days when, still learning English, his father had to hire his foreman to translate the thick local dialects of his workers for him.[76]

For NETE, Team Valley was only the beginning. Over the next two decades the company expanded rapidly, repeatedly requesting and receiving greater and greater sums of money from the government.[77] By 1960, NETE administered fourteen different industrial estates, many with their own canteens, leisure centers, and internal railroad networks. According to NETE's own figures, the estates employed fifty-three thousand workers with another fifty thousand employed in trades indirectly related to or stimulated by the estates (one in ten of all insured workers in the North East, NETE claimed, were dependent on the company in some form or other).[78] These promotional claims were perhaps exaggerated, and NETE was unable to solve the deep structural problems facing the economy of the North East—problems that persist today. Despite this, NETE orchestrated one of the biggest stimulus projects undertaken in the interwar period—a project that was grounded in a handful of spectacular spatial interventions.

A Slum Clearance of Factories

Observers of industrial estates were astonished by their radical potential. For many, these were sites where industry could be tamed, socialized, and beautified, marking a retreat from the sooty immiseration of the nineteenth century. Some even saw them as blueprints for a more collective, postcapitalist future. One of these prophets was Hugh Quigley, a senior planner tasked with managing Britain's electricity grid. He argued that industrial estates would usher in a new era:

> The development of the Trading Estate is a further indication of the general movement towards collective enterprise. The construction of immense blocks of residential flats, the elaboration of housing estates, the increasing size and concentration of office buildings—peculiar characteristics of the present stage in our economic civilization—all find their parallel and their complement in the factory or trading estate.[79]

Another early booster, Douglas G. Wolton, predicted that they would become a common feature of future cities:

> The germ of organisation embodied in the Trading Estate is the beginning of what may well become a growing force which may do much to transform the face of industrial Britain within the space of a few decades. The springing up of Trading Estates in various parts of the country is far from accidental. It reflects the steadily-changing conditions of industry, particularly since the beginning of the century.

He went on to predict that the industrial estate would initiate a "slum clearance of factories," and become "a centre of educational, artistic, sporting, entertainment and general cultural life . . . a central feature of our national life."[80]

No one was more enthusiastic about the radical potential of industrial estates in the 1930s, however, than those directly involved in NETE. NETE's general manager imagined that enormous industrial estates would coordinate supply chains on a massive scale, bringing together "on one estate . . . all the processes from the animal to the finished boot or glove," with the result that urban economies "would be planned as an industrial whole . . . rather than as a heterogeneous collection of unrelated enterprises."[81] Kenelm C. Appleyard, NETE's chair, was perhaps even more zealous. He was a passionate advocate for comprehensive forms of state-directed industrial planning. For him, the late 1930s were crucial years, when Britain risked falling behind in a global race for industrial development. "Industry is on trial," he proclaimed, "possibly even Capitalism is on trial."[82] For this reason, he anticipated that in the long run all small industry would eventually be housed on industrial estates.[83] He praised the totalitarian economies of Russia, Italy, and Japan, and argued that the British state should engage in similar projects of national planning, beginning with industrial estates.[84] More surprising, perhaps, was Appleyard's overt sympathies for Nazi Germany. In 1938, Appleyard toured Essen, Cologne, and Berlin, promoting Team Valley in talks to local industrialists, and delivered a high-profile speech in Berlin at the Anglo-German Fellowship, a society created under the direction of Joachim von Ribbentrop, then German ambassador to Britain, to foster good relations between Germany and Britain.[85] Meanwhile, a delegation of German manufacturers was invited by Appleyard to tour Team Valley, leading the industrial estate to be praised by the Nazi newspaper *Der Angriff*, founded by Joseph Goebbels in 1927. The paper called the estate a development for which Britain "need not be ashamed."[86] One can only imagine what the large numbers of German Jewish refugees who owned businesses on the estate would have made of this visit.

As collective, state-managed enterprises, industrial estates had become precocious modernist spectacles—ciphers for the new science of economic

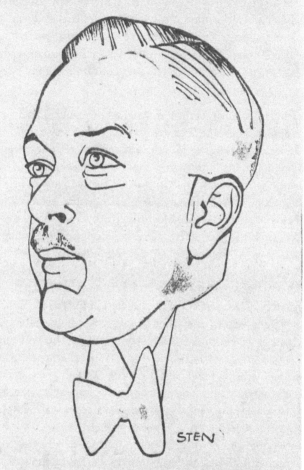

VÖLKISCHER BEOBACHTER

STEN

Oberst Kenelm C. Appleyard

hielt auf Einladung der deutsch=englischen Gesellschaft in Berlin einen vielbeach= teten Vortrag über „Die Lage in den industriellen Notstandsgebieten Englands"

FIGURE 1.6. A talk featuring Kenelm C. Appleyard as it was reported on in 1938 in *Völkischer Beobachter*, the official newspaper of the overseas branch of the Nazi Party.

planning. In Britain, these sites contributed to a broader rethinking of the relationship between government and industry. A major step toward a sustained industrial policy came in 1940 with the Royal Commission on the Distribution of Industry (known as the Barlow Commission) report. The commission was a concerted attempt to find reasons for and solutions to Britain's uneven industrial development. Information was solicited from more than a hundred business leaders, local politicians, and pressure groups to try to find out why cities and jobs had congregated in some places rather than others. The report argued that Britain's nineteenth-century industrial economy had frozen in place an urban and infrastructural arrangement that, like an unwanted tattoo, was awkwardly persisting.

The question was how to retrofit an economy built around roads, electricity, and consumer goods into a built environment shaped around steam, railroads, and capital-intensive forms of production.[87] Britain's population had gathered in large and unhealthy cities, which were prone to aerial attack and in many cases were hemorrhaging jobs. The solution was for the state to conceive of the nation as a totality, and take direct control over the settlement of people, jobs, and resources with an eye to long-term development. Along with the Beveridge report, the majority report of the Barlow Commission, published in 1940, is one of the founding documents of postwar British life. Its influence reverberates through the postwar town planning acts, the creation of new towns, and Britain's postwar industrial policy. One of the Barlow report's main recommendations was the creation of a central authority that would inspect and, if necessary, modify all future industrial undertakings, with the aim of rebalancing Britain's economic geography. Before this, to quote the report, industrialists had enjoyed "unfettered control" over where they could build factories.[88] These findings were backed up by the wartime government's 1944 "White Paper on Employment," which marked a major step in making full employment an aim of government policy. The white paper talked about the need for "the Government to exercise a substantial influence over the location of new industrial development."[89] Industry had to be drained, pooled, and channeled to different corners of the country to irrigate derelict cities and abandoned coalfields with jobs as well as capital.

It was under these conditions that the industrial estate ceased to be a regional curiosity. The Barlow Commission solicited evidence from both Trafford Park and Slough and reported on the progress of industrial estates in Special Areas. One of the commission's recommendations for dispersing Britain's industrial population involved the construction of more industrial estates across the country, in conjunction with new towns and suburbs to house their workers. These new estates, the commission suggested, would be managed by municipal authorities and funded by the central government, as "such

development is not likely to proceed successfully if left entirely to private enterprise."[90] One of the first serious legislative answers to the questions raised
by the Barlow Commission was the 1945 Distribution of Industry Act. This act
gave the government broad powers to stimulate industry in areas of high unemployment along with the power to limit development elsewhere.[91] Its first
two clauses empowered the Board of Trade and Treasury to fund the construction of industrial estates.[92] These estates were to be concentrated in Development Areas, a rebranding and expansion of the Special Areas designated in
1934. As a result, the five government estates companies—NETE, North Western Trading Estates Ltd., West Cumberland Industrial Development Company, Scottish Industrial Estates Ltd., and Wales and Monmouthshire Industrial Estates Ltd.—oversaw a rapid increase in their annual budgets and in the
number of industrial estates that they managed. NETE's own finances increased tenfold, from two to twenty million pounds, between 1940 and 1960.[93]
The 1947 Town and Country Planning Act and 1950 Distribution of Industry
Act furthered the state's power in this regard. By the 1950s, any industrialist
hoping to open a factory larger than five thousand square feet would need an
"Industrial Development Certificate," granted by the Board of Trade after an
extensive consultation. If the board had objections about a proposed location,
it would guide industrialists elsewhere, often to new industrial estates. What
was once an insurgent, meagerly funded, and highly experimental project
spearheaded by an activist government commissioner had become a substantial element in the state's holistic industrial strategy. If the government was
creating an irrigation scheme for jobs and capital, then industrial estates,
among other measures, were to be the pipes and wells through which new
industry would flow.

The next step in reorienting Britain's uneven geography was the creation of
new towns. The Barlow report spoke highly of the small new towns created by
charitable organizations in the interwar period to relieve congestion in Britain's main cities, such as Letchworth and Welwyn Garden City. These places
were referred to by the report in the same breath as industrial estates.[94] After
the war, a government commission that was convened to research the feasibility of new towns stated that each new development would have to be accompanied by an industrial estate, modeled on those already built in places like
Team Valley.[95] The subsequent 1946 New Towns Act allowed the government
to schedule land and fund the development of more than a dozen new towns,
each with a proposed sixty thousand residents. Many of these, such as Basildon, Harlow, Hemel Hempstead, Newton Aycliffe, and Crawley, were accompanied by industrial estates (or "advanced factory units" as they were sometimes known in a new town context) to employ their new residents. While
government factory building in distressed areas was tapering off by the 1950s

under a new Conservative government, industrial estates in new towns were just beginning to be built across the country.[96] Finally, some local governments also experimented with the building of comprehensively planned industrial estates in the immediate postwar period as part of efforts at urban renewal. Manchester and Liverpool, for example, both sponsored the construction of suburban industrial estates in their respective suburbs of Wythenshawe and Speke, and both cities drew up comprehensive redevelopment plans that featured more extensive use of industrial estates.[97]

As a result of these developments, industrial estates spread across the country after the war, appearing like points of light on a hillside as night falls. Within twenty years of the opening of Team Valley, they had become a familiar part of the British landscape. As we have already seen, by 1960 there were eighty-one industrial estates in Britain, the majority of which were funded and managed by the state in some form.[98] Estates in the five development areas alone employed more than a quarter-million people and represented a combined capital investment of eighty-five million pounds.[99] Despite the abundance of industrial estates conjured into being by Britain's postwar planning apparatus, however, the modernist dreams of figures such as Appleyard remained unfulfilled. While early prophets for industrial estates imagined that entire supply chains would be concentrated on single estates, the Board of Trade made decisions based mostly on short-term need rather than industrial strategy. What's more, instead of the gigantic, world-making endeavors envisioned by early pioneers, these new industrial estates tended to be smaller and more geographically dispersed.[100]

To make things worse, by the 1950s the relationship between industrial estate tenants and the government was fraying. In Wales in 1950, for example, a flash point emerged over the question of who was responsible for painting the outside of factory buildings. In industrial estates such as Swansea and Treforest, which were managed by the South Wales and Monmouthshire Trading Estates Company, tenants had been responsible for painting their own buildings and carrying out their own repairs. Now tenants were demanding that the company do this work as part of their rent. The company recognized it was in an almost impossible situation, observing that changing the terms would provoke resistance from those tenants who resented an intrusive landlord repainting their property.[101] In the Treforest Trading Estate in South Wales, the company had to take action against the shabby and neglected state of many of its buildings, forcing all its tenants to repaint their buildings at their own expense. The company noted that doing so resulted in "a certain amount of difficulty with the awkward type of tenant," and maintaining premises in the longer term would require "a good deal of inspection and in some cases acrimony to persuade them to face up to their responsibilities."[102] Acrimony turned out to be an understatement. Over the next two years, the tenants of industrial estates began to organize. Between 1950 and 1952, business owners formed tenants' associations that banded together into a national federation. The bodies circulated information about different kinds of leases and offered legal advice to all their members.[103] This unusual form of collective action came to a head in Wales in 1952, when tenants on multiple different estates formed a united front against a proposed reassessment of rents, threatening to withdraw en masse from government estates if the reassessment went ahead.[104]

When government industrial estates were first proposed, it was with extreme reluctance. Some expressed concerns about the way that industrial estates entailed the government entering into competition with other companies.[105] A committee convened to review the government's options for intervening in Special Areas warned that industrial estates would "involve the State in embarrassing questions of management."[106] Ten years later, these concerns would have seemed prescient indeed. By the 1950s, industrial estates had become an unusual terrain for a minor, corporatist battle between industry, organized as a collective, and the state, acting as landlord.[107] As a result, the Board of Trade archives are punctuated with legal squabbles over factory maintenance and concerned memos about the ratio of canteen size to factory floor space.

Imperial and International Development

By the 1950s, industrial estates had become a recognizable, go-to solution for dispersing industry around the country. Politicians knew what they looked like and what they could provide. It is no surprise, then, that shortly after the Second World War, industrial estates made an appearance in Britain's empire. Industrial estates entered the imperial stage during a turn toward colonial economic development that began in the 1920s. The focus of development during these decades tended to be in Britain's African and Caribbean colonies, with Britain seeking to shift the center of its imperial gravity away from India. With the aim of containing unrest, supplying markets for Britain's beleaguered manufactures, and solving labor shortages, colonial experts and administrators oversaw the building of infrastructure networks, scientific schemes for the improvement of agriculture and indigenous health, and plans to incentivize European settlement.[108] These policies were facilitated by a raft of colonial development acts passed between 1929 and 1959 that allocated large sums of money for various projects. In East Africa, development often took the form of road building and disease control as well as infamous, modernist, state-directed agriculture programs.[109] Meanwhile, the Colonial Office attempted to transform the agrarian economy of the Caribbean, hoping that the islands' sugar plantations would form the chemical basis for the industrial production of plastics and fuels.[110]

West Indian economist W. Arthur Lewis was an early advocate for the use of industrial estates in the British Empire. Lewis migrated from Saint Lucia to Britain in the late 1930s to study and eventually lecture in economics. He became a prominent theorist of development and won the Nobel Prize in Economics in 1979. While he began his career advising the Colonial Office, he ended it advising the postcolonial governments of Ghana and Jamaica on how to develop their national economies.[111] Lewis argued that rapid forms of economic growth were the result of a shift in labor from agriculture (characterized by a surplus of unproductive labor) to industry (where productivity is high). He claimed that low rates of growth were characteristic of undeveloped economies that were still entirely agrarian (and therefore unproductive) or highly developed economies where the process of transferal was already complete and there was no more surplus labor for industry to absorb.[112] In a handful of publications between 1944 and 1951, Lewis called on the British state to build industrial estates in the Caribbean in order to transition from rural to urban workforces in colonies.[113]

Shortly after the war, in a memo written for the Colonial Office, Lewis argued that "from the point of view of industrially backward areas," the industrial estate was "probably the most important development of the last fifty years."[114] The difficulty facing industrialists in agrarian colonies such as in the Caribbean, Lewis contended, was an overall lack of infrastructure and the absence of a multiplier effect caused by economies of scale. He maintained that in order for industry to survive, it was imperative that there were "large numbers of factories together" using "common services cheaply." While a single, isolated factory may fail, "a hundred factories side by side . . . even if each is producing something different," would be more likely to succeed. The industrial estate allowed factories to band together, sharing energy and infrastructure costs. Like the boosters of industrial estates in Britain, Lewis praised the cleanliness of these spaces and admired their rational ordering of space:

> The trading estate has also immense social advantages. Some people fear . . . industrialisation should convert the colonies into slummy, smoky, unplanned regions, á la [the] Industrial Revolution. The trading estate avoids this. The factories do not sprawl all over the place; they are concentrated in a single region which, as it is controlled by a single authority, can be properly planned.[115]

At different times, Lewis praised the private as well as the government industrial estates built in Britain between the wars, referring to the latter as a "happy invention."[116] In this sense, he was the imperial corollary of British

FIGURE 1.7. W. Arthur Lewis in 1979.

figures such as Appleyard who saw the industrial estate as a crucial point of mediation between the state and economy.

Lewis's calls for a network of industrial estates throughout the Caribbean went unheeded. Some of his ideas, perhaps unbeknownst to him, were nevertheless realized in East Africa in the 1950s. In 1953, a Royal Commission was appointed to look at the course of economic development in a handful of

FIGURE 1.8. The Guinness factory, built in 1959 with funding from the Commonwealth Development Council on the Ikeja Industrial Estate.

British African colonies including Kenya and Tanganyika. Like the Barlow report, the commission was appointed to discuss the geographic imbalance of industry and agriculture in the region, and, like the Barlow report, it recommended the use of industrial estates as part of a broader industrial strategy.[117] Three years later, this task was taken up in Kenya by colonial administrators, who created a committee to research the building of a handful of estates on scheduled native lands. The committee, composed of three native Kenyans and seven British administrators, was given funding to build industrial estates.[118] Proposed sites included Karatina and Nyanza Province, two remote regions in the south east of the country. Estates in these regions were to be fitted with railroad sidings, gas, water, and electricity, with tenants renting rather than buying factory space. As with estates in the metropole, they were to be sited in locations that would maximize the flow of cheap labor.[119] The Colonial Office also set aside funds for industrial estates in West as well as East Africa at the twilight of Britain's empire. In 1959, the Colonial Development

Corporation funded the construction of a 350-acre industrial estate in Ikeja on the outskirts of Lagos in Nigeria.[120] Industrial estates were built in Britain's present and former colonies in South and East Asia too. The development of estates in places like India, Ceylon, and Malaya in the early 1960s straddled the line between late imperial and international development initiatives. One driver for the construction of industrial estates in the British colonies and former colonies around the Pacific Rim that decade was the Colombo Plan, a regional development project agreed on in 1950 by a number of Common-wealth countries, including India, Pakistan, Ceylon, Malaya, Australia, and New Zealand. The plan encouraged its participants to draw up six-year devel-opment plans, many of which, by the early 1960s, featured industrial estates.[121] Finally, it is worth noting that there were private as well as public attempts to build industrial estates in the wider British world. Most notably, Mobbs, the owner of Slough Trading Estates Ltd., sponsored the construction of private estates in Melbourne, Australia, and Ajax, Canada, in 1949 and 1950.[122]

As Britain's empire collapsed, the task of promoting industrial estates as tools of economic development the world over was taken up by the United States. Indeed, although the Colombo Plan was initially centered on British colonies and former colonies, the United States contributed a significant amount of the plan's funds, and its creation must be seen within the context of the Cold War politics of the region, particularly the Communist insurgency against British rule in Malaya throughout the 1950s.

In 1958, William Bredo, a Stanford University economist with funding from the Ford Foundation, published a manual on how to construct and manage industrial estates, targeted at technocrats in newly industrializing nations. Like Appleyard or Lewis, Bredo saw the radical potential of industrial estates as spaces that could usher in a new and managed form of postwar developmental capitalism. His manual drew heavily from British examples and cited Trafford Park as the form's first iteration. While the United States had seen the develop-ment of a handful of planned industrial areas since the beginning of the twen-tieth century, often owned and managed by large railroad companies, publicly owned estates were rare, and only a small number provided tenants with ready-made buildings and services. In 1952, the US mainland had just five munici-pally planned industrial estates—a tiny number compared with the fourteen government estates in North East England alone. While US agencies such as the Ford and Rockefeller Foundations advised developing postwar economies to build industrial estates as part of their industrial policy, the United States' biggest venture in this regard was much closer to home. In the 1940s and 1950s, the federal government initiated and funded a rapid industrialization program in Puerto Rico in an attempt to encourage US capital to settle on an island with almost no history of industry. Operation Bootstrap, as the program came to be known, offered a mix of supply-and-demand incentives, turning Puerto Rico into a tax haven while simultaneously peppering the island with more than sixty industrial estates, providing a now-familiar package of infrastructure, energy, and plant to tempt US capitalists.[123]

In the first half of the twentieth century, industrial estates passed from the hands of private speculators to government planners, spreading from the banks of the Manchester Ship Canal and Tyne to sub-Saharan Africa and the Pacific Rim. As the intensity and scope of economic planning expanded, they became a mainstay, first of regional, then national, and then international economic development. By 1960, there were industrial estates in Mexico, Jamaica, Brazil, Ireland, Nigeria, Ghana, India, Pakistan, and many other places.[124] By the 1970s, industrial estates were becoming something different, mutating the world over into science parks, business parks, and other nodes of emergent knowledge and service-oriented economies. This mutation is the story of a later chapter.

Writing about the emergence of welfare policies at the turn of the twentieth century, Daniel T. Rodgers has argued that communities of intellectuals on both sides of the Atlantic produced a "large external stock of working solutions"—ideas that were ready and waiting, biding their time for the moment when, during the emergency of the Great Depression, they could be pulled off the shelf by politicians and planners.[125] Similarly, when faced with economic crisis in select regions of the country, the British government seized on a type of space that had been forged decades earlier. In reconceiving of factory owners as "tenants," and offering them access to cheap and comprehensive systems of energy, transportation, labor, and advertising, Hooley and Stevens created in Trafford Park a portable tool for industrial development that would come to be used by developmental states across the world. Modular, replicable, and functional, the industrial estate was one of the first large-scale urban forms to be utilized by the government in the service of national economic development. There was something almost utopian about these spaces—a fact that is easily forgotten as one passes by the drab remains of the industrial estates that still litter the outskirts of British towns and cities. For their boosters, they offered the opportunity to replace broken economies with identical single-story factories, carefully tended hedgerows, swimming pools, football matches, and canteen-made pies. Some believed that they had the potential to remake the historical geography of Britain and the world, taming and rationalizing the explosive chaos left behind by nineteenth-century industrial development. This radical potential, inherent in the space itself, was not foreseen by either the property speculators who created industrial estates or Conservative politicians who reluctantly agreed to fund their construction in Special Areas.

The reality, of course, is that industrial estates had a more limited historical footprint. In Britain, postwar industrial estates were stunted by changes in government along with a shortage of capital and materials. Tenants were restive, buildings were shabby, canteens were overcrowded, and assembly-line production was often miserable and backbreaking. The tendency for estates to employ unskilled, frequently female labor and house the subsidiary locations of enterprises that were based elsewhere meant that they were poor instruments in the eyes of many planners. Unemployment and dereliction persisted in the areas where industrial estates clustered. Those like Appleyard, Lewis, or Bredo who argued that planned industrial estates would remake the industrial landscape of Britain, its empire, and the world were always marginal voices. The earliest of the three urban forms that make up the first half of this book was also the least able to fulfill its developmental promise.

2

The Shopping Precinct

ON AN UNUSUALLY cold summer evening in 1946, a young architect named Donald Gibson met a London-based artist at Coventry's train station.[1] With a bottle of whiskey, some blankets, eggs, bacon, a frying pan, and a stove, the two men set off north by car into the night, bound for a remote slate quarry in the Lake District. The city they left behind was still in ruins. Six years earlier German bombers had torn through Coventry, killing hundreds and leaving a landscape of singed bomb craters and hollowed out buildings interspersed with emergency hostels and makeshift tin shacks serving as shops.[2] Gibson, a didactic modernist, had watched the destruction of his city with a mixture of horror and excitement, writing that "like a forest fire the present evil might bring forth greater riches and beauty."[3] He advocated for a new kind of city— clearing away the tangled and congested medieval streets and replacing them with wide pedestrianized plains, office blocks, and a self-contained multistory precinct that would envelop all of the city's shops. Gibson was nervously granted permission by the city council to implement these ideas. The morning before his midnight drive, he had attended a council meeting called to discuss how the city would celebrate the first anniversary of the war's end. Some suggested fireworks, and others suggested a public banquet, but Gibson proposed a ceremonial laying of the foundation stone for what would become his shopping precinct. The occasion would be a bold public statement about the new kind of city that would emerge from Coventry's ruins in the postwar era. The council gave Gibson a small budget and three-week deadline to find the stone. The two men set out from the station, driving all night through narrow country lanes. As the sun rose and the towering Lake District hills came into focus, the two men stopped by the side of the road and cooked their breakfast on a fire made from a bed of gorse leaves. It was nine in the morning by the time they arrived at Westmorland Green quarry, where the manager led them on foot to a vast, delicate sheet of slate, shaped like the wings of a butterfly. Three weeks later, as crowds of demobilized soldiers celebrated the first anniversary of peace in Europe, the stone was transported by a local farmer to Coventry and unveiled to designate the construction of the city's new shopping precinct. This chapter is about the emergence of the shopping precinct as a distinct urban form in the mid-twentieth century and how it would come to reshape Britain's urban environment. If ever this story needed a poetic mythology, then the image of these two men cooking eggs by the side of the road at the dawn of the postwar world is better than any.

Britons often use the words "shopping precinct," "shopping center," and "shopping mall" interchangeably. These terms are used to refer to the hundreds of comprehensively planned developments housing multiple different shops that punctuate British towns and cities in a way that is both banal and familiar.[4] In this book, I dispense with the term "shopping center," and preserve an important distinction between the "shopping precinct" and "shopping mall." I do so to make a historical argument about the way in which the spaces where British people shop have developed over the course of the twentieth century.[5] Shopping precincts were the children of a mid-twentieth-century developmental state.[6] They tended to be small (meaning tens rather than hundreds of shops) and centrally located. The state, usually in the form of either local municipal councils or new town development corporations, initiated the construction of precincts, typically by having some role in funding, commissioning, designing, or owning them. Shopping malls, conversely, tended to be large, suburban, and fully enclosed developments, whose existence was shaped by private versus public capital, and whose look and feel was tailored to international standards. I am trading here in ideal types, of course. Many developments in Britain share elements of each of these two forms. But as ideal types of space, the latter displaced the former over the course of the twentieth century. While this chapter is a history of the shopping precinct in Britain, chapter 5 shows how precincts were reimagined in the later twentieth century, mutating into the private shopping mall.

When they emerged in the mid-twentieth century, shopping precincts, like the one that Gibson envisaged, were vested with a developmental mission. It was hoped that they would restrict the free play of market forces and rein in the haphazard spread of shops along suburban arterial roads. By allowing state authorities to control the number and size of shops, they enabled towns and cities to connect urban planning with consumer demand, calculating exactly how many and which type of shop to build. What's more, planners saw shopping precincts as a means of recentralizing sprawling towns and segregating pedestrians from vehicles. Once these spaces became vectors for private property speculators, this early vision was forgotten. I seek, therefore, to recover a lost moment. In doing so, I hope to contribute to a rich literature on consumerism in postwar Britain by showing that shopping had a spatial and infrastructural logic—one that was tied to the politics of urban renewal and national economic development.[7] Shopping precincts allowed British planners and politicians to imagine a new kind of town along with a new kind of consumer economy. Just as industrial estates provided a mechanism for reordering British industry as well as channeling jobs and capital to different corners of the country, shopping precincts supplied a mechanism by which consumers could be planned for. Just as industrial estates involved the state in intractable and unforeseen disputes over tenancy and management, however, shopping precincts entailed a new type of expertise, as economists and planners tried and eventually failed to plan in advance for the consumer desires of a fickle urban population.

While government-managed industrial estates were easily identifiable and countable, shopping precincts are harder to pin down. Some were small pedestrianized squares while others were complex multistory structures that dominated skylines. This chapter draws on the example of Gibson's precinct in Coventry—one of the first and arguably most extravagant of the wave of postwar shopping precincts. It ends in the 1950s United States with the birth of a new kind of space: the suburban shopping mall. The shopping mall would eventually spread to the United Kingdom, displacing the shopping precinct and transforming the developmental promise of mid-twentieth-century retail space. While the spread of malls to Britain is explored in chapter 5, this chapter will end by dwelling on the strange historical conditions surrounding the birth of the US shopping mall. Its inventor, Victor Gruen, was a self-described socialist and Viennese refugee who, like Gibson, imagined that shopping malls would be instruments for reining in suburban sprawl and engaging in more precise forms of state-led economic planning. If political battles rage today between the chain supermarket and boutique, locally owned market, then the vision of planners like Gruen and Gibson were both and neither.

A New Kind of Marketplace

Throughout the nineteenth century, urban marketplaces were enclosed and reformed, and residents of British towns and cities began shopping indoors. Prior to this process, urban markets had varied wildly in size and permanence, and performed a variety of different social and ritual functions. Early modern markets were spaces known for their openness. Social interactions were visible, and transgressions could be punished in public.[8] In some late medieval and early modern markets, this publicity verged on the riotous, and these markets played host to festivals, fairs, and executions.[9] These spaces have held a privileged place among twentieth-century modernization theorists. Thinkers such as Max Weber and Karl Polanyi saw medieval and early modern marketplaces as sites of exchange between strangers that prefigured the emergence of a modern condition, characterized by anonymity, capitalism, and contractual social relationships.[10] Other historians and theorists have seen premodern markets as spaces of reciprocity and liminality. For E. P. Thompson, they were sites for the enactment of a "moral economy," where a primitive form of distributive justice made sure that the basic needs of all were satisfied.[11]

As industrialization, urbanization, and technical improvements to agriculture liberated millions from subsistence farming, medieval and early modern markets had to be remade.[12] Once-small towns such as Manchester, Sheffield, and Bradford were growing rapidly in the early nineteenth century, and as a consequence, their small markets were becoming congested and chaotic. In 1851, for instance, Doncaster's ten thousand inhabitants were served by a market of twenty-five saleswomen with baskets.[13] One by one, most major cities in Britain reclaimed and reorganized their markets, enclosing them behind grand facades, banning street vending, licensing vendors, and segregating traders by type. Between 1750 and 1945, 626 market halls in 392 cities and towns in England were constructed, not including those located in London.[14] The vast majority of these markets were built in the nineteenth century with the construction of new markets peaking in the 1830s, 1840s, and 1850s.[15] They were part of a broader liberal project to sanitize and reorder British cities, replacing blood-soaked squares with hygiene, order, and internalized pedestrian discipline.[16] This reordering of public space came as a blow to some nineteenth-century political radicals who were dependent on urban markets for demonstrations and speeches.[17] By the end of that century, the market hall had become a conspicuous and often-ornate municipal presence—a consumerist counterpart to the town hall, train station, and courtroom.

These forces are perhaps best seen at work in Smithfield Market in London. Until the 1850s, Smithfield was London's primary livestock market, and had been since the Middle Ages. Early sketches show a wide urban square riven by a dense latticework of wooden pens brimming with animals. Visiting the market in the 1720s, Daniel Defoe was awestruck by what he saw, calling it "without question the greatest market in the world; no description can be given of it, no calculation of the numbers of creatures sold there can be made."[18] By the mid-nineteenth century, however, assessments of the market were much gloomier and calculations were more exact. At this point it was estimated that 1.5 million sheep and 0.5 million cattle passed through the market each year. In 1848, one observer described how "the environs of Smithfield are poisoned by blood and garbage," harming the health of the urban poor who were forced to depend on its meat.[19] Four years later, Parliament acted to shut down the market, relocating it to the outskirts of the city, and began the work of creating a grand new municipal structure on Smithfield's heavily trampled ground. Funded and owned by the Corporation of the City of London, the new

FIGURE 2.1. The old Smithfield Market. *Illustrated London News*, 1855.

FIGURE 2.2. The new Smithfield Market. *Illustrated London News*, 1872.

building, which still stands, was an ornate and decorous hangar, organized around four towers adorned with copper domes. Inside, 162 identical and discrete trading spaces were arranged alongside two major thoroughfares. Rather than selling livestock, the new market sold meat. Each shop had a back room with a separate countinghouse and toilet.[20]

Smithfield was the first in a new network of municipal markets in London, many of which were designed by the corporation's architect, Horace Jones, including Billingsgate Fish Market built in 1875 and Leadenhall Market designed in 1881.[21] This wave of new markets prompted a switch from wholesale to retail within the central areas of the city, with the sale of livestock and bulk farming produce relegated to the outskirts.[22] Markets such as Smithfield contributed to the municipalization of urban food networks in the nineteenth century. Prior to their enclosure, most urban markets were owned by private individuals or trusts that gathered income from tolls. Ownership rights were mostly granted on a case-by-case basis by royal charter.[23] After the reopening in 1868, Smithfield's annual accounts were audited by the City of London.[24] Following a half century in which London's population almost tripled, Smithfield allowed the City of London to secure and monitor the city's food supply, coordinating distant markets across the globe. The market's accounts show its expanding scale and scope toward the later nineteenth century as Smithfield began storing and selling meat from the United States, Australia, Canada, and New Zealand.[25]

Rapid urbanization in the nineteenth century coupled with liberal reform had a transformative effect on British market spaces. Markets were expanded, enclosed, and rearranged into orderly and legible shapes, and these became focal points for booming towns expanding in every direction. By the turn of the century, these municipal spaces were being complemented by more private and sophisticated retail operations. Department store chains, such as Lewis's, Debenhams's, and Selfridges, tailored toward elite shoppers, opened in most major towns and cities, aided by new building techniques that allowed spacious interiors and elaborate glass displays facing the street. These retail chains were at the forefront of a new consumer culture. With their lavish interiors, complete with domestic furnishings and well-dressed shop attendants, they were spaces for the tentative introduction of middle-and upper-class women into urban public space—a limited form of mid- to late nineteenth-century emancipation fraught with sexual danger and moral concern.[26] These trends continued in the early twentieth century as electric light increased the possibilities for shopping and street life. By the 1920s and 1930s, Liverpool and Manchester, with their department stores, gallerias, and fashionable clothes shops, started to resemble the bourgeois urban landscapes depicted by Émile Zola and Walter Benjamin.[27] At the same time, places like Regent Street in

London, traditionally symbols of monumental and imperial display, were being reordered for elite shoppers.[28]

This is the point at which historians and theorists of modernization have lost interest in the marketplace, however. For scholars such as Thompson and Polanyi, the triumph of urban industrial capitalism had resulted in the superseding of marketplaces by *the market* in the abstract. The kinds of disembodied, contractual social relations that these scholars argued had been contained in premodern markets had become the rule.[29] The subsequent literature on consumerism in Britain has, with some extremely important exceptions, been de-spatialized.[30] The rest of this chapter will pick up where these scholars left off.

Britain and the Octopus

There is an argument to be made that the first shopping precinct appeared in the fantasies of the anarchistic urban planner Ebenezer Howard. In 1898, Howard suggested that congested towns and rural villages should be dissolved and recomposed as "garden cities," small, self-sustainable, and utopian communities that would bring Britain's Industrial Revolution to an end by collapsing the distinction between urban and rural life. In a famous pamphlet, Howard speculated about how these cities would function. At the heart of his imaginary community, he described the following urban form:

> Running all round the Central Park . . . is a wide glass arcade called the "Crystal Palace." . . . Here manufactured goods are exposed for sale, and here most of that class of shopping which requires the joy of deliberation and selection is done. The space enclosed by the Crystal Palace is, however, a good deal larger than is required for these purposes, and a considerable part of it is used as a Winter Garden—the whole forming a permanent exhibition of a most attractive character, whilst its circular form brings it near to every dweller in the town—the furthest removed inhabitant being within 600 yards.[31]

In Howard's vision, the trader in the Crystal Palace will "depend upon the good-will of his customers."[32] If the trader fails in this duty, the residents of the town can vote to elect a competitor to discipline or replace the lapsed trader. This was the nineteenth-century market hall, reimagined for the coming age of mass politics. It combined the glamour and delight of department store shopping with the multiplicity and functionality of the modern market hall. Howard's overall vision for garden cities was partially realized in the cities of Letchworth and Welwyn, founded in 1903 and 1920, respectively. Disciples of Howard were also heavily involved in building new towns in the United

States and across Britain's empire. New Delhi, Canberra, and Radburn, New Jersey, were all consciously inspired by Howard's writings. Yet nothing like the Crystal Palace was ever attempted in these towns, and it is often forgotten that Howard had also proposed a radical new relationship between shopping and the built environment.

By the First World War, liberal reform, which had reordered towns and cities in the name of public health and seen activist local authorities in cities like London, Birmingham, and Glasgow municipalize water and sewerage systems, energy networks, and transportation systems, was giving way to the increasingly ambitious and institutionalized discipline of town planning.[33] The 1909 and 1919 town planning acts, by compelling local authorities to reorder their housing stock, meant that architects and planners were more and more engaged in the day-to-day business of government. Planning towns and cities in the name of economic and spiritual development became a cause that united diverse factions of Britain's political elite. The *Town Planning Review* was founded in 1910, and the Town Planning Institute was formalized in 1914. They built on the more ad hoc and philanthropic movements that had been gathering pace throughout the nineteenth century and had found a home under the umbrella of the Town and Country Planning Association founded in 1899. This period saw the tentative emergence of a new kind of expertise, whose practitioners charged themselves with the task of governing and reordering British urban space. As town planning became increasingly formalized and nationalized after the First World War, women were systematically excluded from a discipline in which many had played an important role at both the local and voluntary level.[34] These new, primarily male experts and their ideas moved across borders, as intellectuals, activists, and politicians on both sides of the Atlantic as well as across Britain's empire pooled their knowledge.[35]

One of the key ways in which this new expertise intersected with debates about shopping and consumerism concerned the issue of urban sprawl. By the early twentieth century, the edges of British cities were beginning to coil and fray. As the extraordinary population growth of towns and cities started to taper off, slum clearance, council housing, and a wave of low-rise private house building resulted in vast and largely unplanned tracts of suburbia. The suburban bourgeois enclaves that had emerged on the fringes of cities during the nineteenth century were growing quickly and becoming more diverse in terms of class.[36] As early as 1880, the four fastest-growing areas in Britain were London railway suburbs for the poor or lower-middle classes.[37] This process accelerated into the twentieth century. While urban planners in the early twentieth century were chiefly concerned with problems of density and overcrowding in large industrial cities, some commentators were worried that this new urban landscape was soulless and emasculating.[38] The Council for the Preservation of Rural England, founded in 1926 by urban planner Patrick Abercrombie, railed against the haphazard mingling of town and country and argued for a clear separation of the two, enforced by national planning structures.[39] Two years later, architect Clough Williams-Ellis compared the tendrils of the arterial roads that were flailing outward from towns and cities to the limbs of a grotesque, thrashing octopus.[40]

The decentralization of towns and cities was initially made possible by the growth of streetcars and light-rail networks. From 1915 on, for example, parts of the Home Counties near London came to be branded by boosters as "Metro-Land" in anticipation of the extension of the Metropolitan Railway's commuter service. It was the arrival of the automobile, however, that provided the biggest impetus for urban decentralization in the interwar period. Between 1918 and 1939, the number of licensed cars in Britain increased from just over a hundred thousand to over two million.[41] The result of millions of new drivers crowding onto underregulated roads was carnage. According to one calculation, 68,248 people were killed on Britain's roads in the ten years leading up to the Second World War.[42] Almost half these fatal accidents concerned pedestrians.[43] It is worth remembering how this chapter began: with a young man, driving drunk at night along dark rural roads with no sleep. While department stores and market halls had acted as powerful centralizing forces, reviving the centers of towns and cities in the service of shopping, the new sprawling suburbs were a countervailing force, as retailers started to gather along the wide arterial roads that ambled through the outskirts of towns and cities. This was a state of affairs that was deemed dangerous and aesthetically unappealing. Wilfred Burns, an urban planner who worked on the postwar redevelopment of both Coventry and Newcastle, reflected on the experience of shopping under such conditions, complaining of rows of shops "stretching almost continuously for miles on either side of a dangerous road."[44]

A solution to this problem came from an unusual source: a senior police officer and traffic scientist named Alker Tripp. In a series of pamphlets published between 1938 and 1942, Tripp argued that the bloodbath unfolding weekly on British streets necessitated a complete transformation of urban planning.[45] Rather than blaming drivers, Tripp blamed narrow roads and poorly planned cities.[46] He opposed, for example, measures for curbing instances of drunk driving.[47] Tripp called for interventions that would make cities as "accident-proof" as possible. Curbside snack bars would have to go, and intersections would have to be rethought. Crucially, Tripp proposed a new kind of urban form to do this work. He contended that dense pockets of urban space belonging to a particular use, be it residential, industrial, or commercial, should be isolated from the road network and set aside for pedestrians. After suggesting a variety of different "ornamental" terms for this new type of space, including "purlieu," "circuit," and "enclave," Tripp settled on the ecclesiastical term "precinct." In a precinct dedicated to shopping, Tripp maintained that shops should have their backs facing major roads and their front entrances facing pedestrianized footpaths, out of sight of cars.[48] To implement his vision, Tripp called for the reining in of "private interests" in towns and cities along with a massive extension of state power in the name of his own expertise. As we will see later in this chapter, the segregation of vulnerable pedestrians from speeding cars by fracturing cities into discrete, pedestrianized zones would have a profound effect on a subsequent generation of British and US urban planning.

By the 1930s, there were both centrifugal and centripetal forces transforming the landscape of British shopping. While ancient markets were being sheaved beneath municipal iron domes, new shops were spreading outward, facing off for many miles along arterial roads. The postwar shopping precinct was an urban form that tried to solve these contradictions by combining the novelty and structural permanence of the roadside dry cleaners with the urbanity of the civic market hall.

The Coventry Shopping Precinct

Gibson was just twenty-nine years old when he became the first head of Coventry City Council's new planning office in 1938, eight years before his drive through the night to the Westmorland slate quarry.[49] He had already studied architecture at Manchester University, lived briefly in the United States, and worked as the sole architect in the Building Research Station, a government body whose remit was to conduct technical research into the design of homes. Gibson arrived to find a city in the throes of a feverish interwar boom. Coventry's expanding car-building and engineering plants produced a 75 percent increase in the city's population between 1921 and 1939—a rate of growth seven times faster than the country as a whole.[50] During these years, the city was characterized by a "Klondike" atmosphere, with an affluent and atomized working-class population still finding its roots in the city.[51] Gibson came with a ruthless and modernist mind-set, describing the clock tower in the center of the city as "a very ugly piece of Late Victoriana" and noting that "it stood in the way of the redevelopment which I envisaged."[52] Unfortunately for Gibson, his first years as planning officer were mostly spent designing benches and lampposts.[53] His narrow remit left him with lots of time to think and plan, and in May 1940 he hosted an unofficial exhibition called the Coventry of Tomorrow: Towards a Beautiful City. The exhibition showcased Gibson's fantasy for the future redevelopment of the city—a future that he possibly imagined would never come. His new city plan featured a forty-acre space for shopping as its main event, to be planned and owned by the local authority. Using the same language as Tripp, Gibson referred to his proposed center as a "precinct."

For Gibson, shopping and sound urban planning were inextricably linked. He railed against previous generations of British retail architecture and promised to begin anew: "Commercial buildings, even when well designed, can still be as 'dull as ditchwater' and produce a negative backdrop to the daily city life. . . . I fought for something different, something better."[54] The pamphlet drawn up by Gibson to advertise his quixotic exhibition opened with a vicious attack on Coventry's prewar shopping environment and dense web of medieval streets:

> Something is wrong with our city. This is as plain as a pike staff. . . . We resent the nightmare of shopping during the week-ends; the crowded pavements; the impossibility of being served quickly in our shops; the irritation of being elbowed and jostled by each other. Why is this so? And then the thought forms itself that these things are symptoms of an illness—our City is ill and not functioning correctly. Yes, let us say it—it is badly planned and ill-made [with an] irrational mixture of shopping, industrial and residential areas."[55]

Six months after the exhibition, the bombs fell, destroying two-thirds of the city's buildings. Gibson's imaginary shopping precinct was about to become a reality.

Within months of the bombing, the city hastily assembled a committee for redevelopment. Gibson's first task was to design forty prefabricated shops with cement sheeting and tiny windows that could withstand future bombing raids.[56] Pretty soon, however, he turned his attention back to building a shopping precinct. Like any infrastructural project, Gibson's precinct required large amounts of both land and capital. His first problem was ensuring that he had total planning control over his chosen area of redevelopment. In an interview conducted before the bombing, Gibson had made the case that the rationalization and modernization of Britain's cities could only be achieved once all land had been nationalized.[57] These were effectively the means by which Gibson was able to build his precinct. As the German bombing campaign intensified in different parts of the country, the government began to tacitly hint that the cost of redevelopment would be shouldered by the Treasury rather than the affected local authorities. John Reith, minister of works, visited Coventry shortly after the bombing, letting it be known that he favored bold, government-financed redevelopment schemes and that Coventry would be a test case for these measures.[58]

As plans for a new Coventry were being assembled, the government was undergoing a shift in thinking about the relationship between land use, planning, and the state. Alongside the Barlow report, discussed in the last chapter, two other reports, Scott (1941) and Uthwatt (1942), recommended a national extension of the government's powers to control urban space. The most significant legislative response to these reports was the 1947 Town and Country Planning Act, which encouraged local authorities to draw up ambitious redevelopment plans and provided mechanisms for streamlining the purchasing of private land.[59] Meanwhile, war-damaged towns and cities were given emergency powers to establish complete planning control over approved areas. Coventry was the first city to be approved for these measures and was given permission to replan a 452-acre swath of its bombed city center. Despite objections from the chamber of commerce and large department stores such as Woolworths that were staunchly opposed to the development, the council and government approved the broad parameters of Gibson's plan for a shopping precinct.[60] With the permission and finances to carry out his plans, Gibson set off to the Lake District to inspect potential foundation stones.

The precinct was built in stages beginning in 1946, in a process slowed down by labor shortages. The idea of using forced prisoner-of-war labor to construct the precinct was floated but never acted on.[61] The finished precinct consisted of multistory arcades connected by internal steps, and contained a mixture of small shops and larger department stores. As well as increasing the amount of space for rent, the precinct's density allowed for a mix of high- and low-end shops, with the council charging substantially more for ground-floor rents.[62] The public spaces of the precinct—the courtyards, walkways, and parking garage—were owned and managed by the council, with the council acting as landlord for the shops and market traders using the space.

While shopping centers in the coming decades would come to be seen as the epitome of suburban, automobile-centered anomie, Coventry's shopping precinct was founded in order to re-center the city and to diminish the danger and pollution caused by increased car ownership. Journalists and visitors marveled at what they saw as an avant-garde and thoroughly metropolitan urban form. Both *Architectural Design* and the *Architects' Journal* devoted special editions to Coventry, with the latter praising the shopping precinct's "warm, human qualities."[63] The pedestrianization of the precinct was championed by the local newspaper, which stressed the novelty of "dry shopping," while noting that for many older residents, the redeveloped town center felt "unfamiliar and strange."[64]

Gibson's precinct offered a solution to the interwar problem of traffic and sprawl. It was a means of reining in the small retail and department stores that were marching off toward the horizon on the outskirts of cities and reordering congested medieval town centers. Most of all, it allowed pedestrians to be

FIGURE 2.3. Christmas card sent to residents of Coventry by the city council in 1946 to advertise the new shopping precinct. Image reproduced with kind permission of Coventry Archives for the full period of such publication rights.

FIGURE 2.4. Photograph of Coventry Shopping Precinct in 1960. © John McCann / RIBA Collections.

segregated from dangerous and lead-clouded streets. The precinct, however, looked backward as well as forward. As we have seen, the enclosure of market space was nothing new in Britain, and Gibson's inclusion of market stalls under a domed roof as part of his development had much older precedents than its modernist surroundings would suggest. As with early industrial estates, the precinct showcased a set of infrastructural and economic relationships between the state and private firms—one that was portable, and would be replicated in urban redevelopment schemes and newly planned towns across the country.

Comprehensive Redevelopment

In the decades after the war, shopping precincts became a familiar feature of Britain's urban landscape. They appeared in three different planning contexts. First, a handful of precincts were built in war-damaged towns like Coventry in the 1940s and 1950s. Second, shopping precincts became an organizing feature of the dozens of new towns built in the 1950s, 1960s, and 1970s. Finally, shopping precincts became key components of the hundreds of comprehensive redevelopment plans instigated by towns and cities during a wave of rebuilding in the 1960s.

The bombing of British cities by German planes mostly occurred in a concentrated burst between 1940 and 1941 and saw the destruction of seventy-five thousand shops as well as forty-two thousand commercial properties, twenty-five thousand factories, and almost a half-million homes.[65] Coventry was the first of sixty-two declaratory orders awarded to towns and cities in the first six years after the war that gave authorities the power to remake the urban environment of bomb-damaged or blighted areas.[66] In Plymouth, for example, an ambitious postwar redevelopment plan was proposed by Abercrombie, a planner who would become famous for his master plan for London. Plymouth's plan, implemented in stages throughout the 1950s, featured a symmetrical fifty-three-acre shopping precinct bisected by a wide thoroughfare encircled by grand civic buildings.[67] Many of the other plans for rebuilding blitzed cities, however, were only half realized or shelved entirely. The fantastic visions of urban reconstruction, promoted through exhibitions, film reels, and radio advertisements, became ensnared in realpolitik—stymied by shortages of labor, capital, and building materials and slowed by bureaucratic infighting.[68] In Southampton, for instance, the city drew up far-reaching proposals during the war for a semi-enclosed, multilevel, and fully pedestrianized "circus" to replace its bombed city center. Although the city received a declaratory order from the government, these plans were rolled back due to financial constraints, opposition from traders, and general apathy among the population.[69]

FIGURE 2.5. Artist's impression of the shopping precinct in Harlow new town.
J. R. James Archive, University of Sheffield.

As with industrial estates, many shopping precincts were built in the new
towns planned in the 1940s and 1950s. The 1946 New Towns Committee,
which laid out the abstract requirements for these new postwar settlements,
emphasized their importance from the outset.[70] More than being merely functional and peripheral sites for the efficient distribution of products, new town
shopping precincts were to be the centerpieces of urban life.[71] In Harlow, a
handful of pedestrianized public squares were fronted by shops beneath aw-
nings. Frederick Gibberd, Harlow's chief architect, likened the town's new
precinct to a Renaissance plaza.[72] Stevenage saw something similar: a wide
tiled plain orbited by shops with an angular modernist clock tower at its heart.
The second wave of British new towns built in the 1960s and 1970s boasted
more extensive shopping facilities. Washington in Tyne and Wear, initiated in
1966 in the North East, featured a municipal system of pedestrian shopping
streets sheltered by glazed arcades.[73] Cumbernauld, built on the outskirts of
Glasgow between the late 1950s and early 1970s, went further still, housing its
shopping precinct within a vast, modernist megastructure that would also include pubs, a library, a hotel, and a bowling alley.[74] While they varied in size,
shape, and architecture, the new town shopping precincts were all built,
owned, and for the most part funded by development corporations whose
boards were appointed by the government. Like sewers and gas pipes, they
were part of the infrastructure of new towns.

Outside of blitzed cities and new towns, the transformation of town centers in Britain proceeded at a slow pace until the early 1960s. After 1960, however, booming land values along with a new cross-party consensus at both the national and local level led to a renewed enthusiasm for planned redevelopment, often spearheaded by a cohort of radical architect planners employed by local authorities.[75] In 1959, fifteen holistic redevelopment schemes were under consideration by the Ministry of Housing and Local Government. This figure rose to seventy in 1963 and a reported five hundred by 1965.[76] These proposals were usually accompanied by a comprehensively planned shopping precinct of some kind. Much of the construction of these centers was outsourced to property developers, although many remained "public" once built, with the local authority owning the building as an asset and acting as landlord for the shops inside. This was the case for Sheffield's Castle Market (1965), Portsmouth's Tricorn Centre (1966), Hartlepool's Middleton Grange (1968), Oxford's Westgate Centre (1972), and Banbury's Castle Shopping Centre (1977), among many others. Definitions vary, but according to one estimate fifty-nine shopping precincts were built either by local authorities or by new town development corporations during this period.[77]

These schemes were built at the high-water mark of a renewed anxiety about the destructive impact of traffic in British towns.[78] Between 1955 and 1965, the number of British households with access to a car doubled.[79] As millions of new cars flooded onto Britain's outdated road network, various national and local authorities busied themselves once again with stemming the rising number of road deaths and decongesting city streets. In 1963, a Ministry of Transport working group, headed by architect planner Colin Buchanan, published a shocking and widely read report on the problem. Named *Traffic in Towns*, the report warned that the social and environmental problems resulting from mass car ownership were pressing in from all sides. Drawing partly on the designs of the new National Health Service hospitals built after the war that sought to control the flow of patients and staff through wards, Buchanan argued that British cities should be segregated into discrete "environmental areas" to limit through-traffic.[80] These were effectively larger and more complex reiterations of Tripp's precincts. Although Buchanan's ambitious proposal that these environments should include elevated decks separating pedestrians from traffic was rarely implemented, the idea that towns should be divided into protected zones provided further intellectual fuel for the construction of shopping precincts.[81] What it meant to be a pedestrian in a city had to be reimagined in the wake of mass car ownership. While the suburban shopping malls described in chapter 5 were a product of the motor age, postwar shopping precincts were conceived of as a means to restrain and temper the tedium as well as potential violence of busy, unplanned roads.

FIGURE 2.6. Colin Buchanan's plan for multistory city centers that would segregate pedestrians and cars.

Managing Demand

The shopping precincts built in the first two decades after the war came hand in hand with a new kind of spatial science, as planners attempted to figure out how many shops needed to be built and where they should be located. In the 1940s, 1950s, and 1960s, enthusiasm about the possibility of discovering abstract laws that would determine where shops and workplaces should be built in relation to housing and transport permeated universities and planning departments in Britain, mainland Europe, and the United States. In the latter, economists such as Walter Isard and William Alonso, with generous funding from bodies such as the Ford Foundation, started using computer simulations in university laboratories to design new urban and regional systems. These thinkers set the tone for a highly quantitative turn in postwar urban planning, leading many to believe that with enough data, cities and their hinterlands could reach new, undreamed-of levels of efficiency and happiness.[82]

With the British state increasingly involved in planning, designing, and owning retail space, officials at both the local and national level began to search for ways to tailor the size and content of new shopping precincts to the populations they were due to serve. Some planners also hoped that shops would serve a social as well as economic function, forging neighborly communities at the local level by fostering face-to-face interactions.[83] The authors of a 1953 survey of Southampton summarized this novel problem, noting that while in the past the number and location of shops were left to the free market to determine, the increasing role of the state in planning and managing British cities meant that authorities "cannot avoid making decisions on the number, size and distribution of shopping centres and sites, and even on the trades that should be represented."[84] As with the construction of industrial estates, the involvement of the state in planning spaces for consumption threw up a host of unforeseen technical and logistical problems that were solved in different ways throughout the 1940s, 1950s, and 1960s.

When it came to shopping precincts, the 1946 New Towns Committee report offered an early, crude attempt at calculating the number of shops needed per resident—estimating that shopping precincts should have one shop for every 100 to 150 people. The report pointed out that if precincts were too small, monopolies might emerge among those lucky enough to be renting space, while if the precinct were too large, bankruptcies and redundant space might result.[85] The figure of 100 to 150 was quickly contested because it was seen by some as being too low.[86] By the 1950s, attempts to establish a fixed ratio of residents to shops began to give way to more sophisticated and abstract models of predicting demand. Critics pointed out that these figures made no allowance for the kinds of shops that would be built or, more crucially, their size, at a time when over-the-counter shops were morphing into larger self-service operations.[87] Indeed, between the late 1940s and late 1950s the number of "self-service" stores in Britain increased from a few dozen to more than five thousand.[88] Academics turned to mathematical models developed in the interwar period in the United States that sought to predict the movement of shoppers between shops. This line of research was influenced by the work of US mathematician Harold Hotelling. His "principle of minimum differentiation" posited that rival businesses selling the same product at the same price would, over time, gravitate toward one another at the point with the biggest market share. For Hotelling, this was an inevitable social force. "Our cities become uneconomically large and the business districts within them too concentrated," he wrote. "Methodist and Presbyterian churches are too much alike. Cider is too homogenous."[89] This "social law" was developed further by economist William J. Reilly. In his 1931 *The Law of Retail Gravitation*, Reilly claimed that different shopping centers of different "mass" (defined by the number of shops, size of the population, size of the center, and so on) would have a larger catchment area for potential shoppers. While a shopper living between two shopping centers might be slightly closer to a smaller center, they would be likely to invest in the slightly longer trip to visit the larger center. Shops in this sense act like cosmic bodies, exerting a finite and measurable amount of gravitational attraction determined by their size.[90]

Reilly's law was refined and challenged by planners and economists in the subsequent years, but the basic idea that, given the correct inputs, the number and type of shops that any given town should build could be deduced from data collected on its residents, came to dominate postwar thinking about the relationship between shopping and urban planning. In the late 1950s and 1960s, town planning departments were awash with increasingly complex models for doing this work. Practical use of these models was made by new town planners, once the 1946 projection of one shop for every 100 to 150 people was found to be inadequate. With real household earnings increasing by 35 percent between 1945 and 1975, and the end of rationing in 1954, planners found themselves anticipating abundance rather than alleviating scarcity.[91] The authors of the master plan for Washington in Tyne and Wear, for example, used a modified version of Reilly's law to calculate the shopping floor space required by the town and assess how far those living nearby would be willing to travel to shop in its new shopping precinct.[92] Meanwhile, the Cumbernauld planners gathered data on a hundred towns with populations between 25,000 and 100,000 people and used that information to estimate the necessary size of the new town's shopping precinct.[93]

These calculations were used most intensively, however, by a series of working groups that the Ministry of Housing and Local Government formed in the wake of anxieties that a commercial property boom in the 1960s was creating too many shops—more than could possibly be used by Britain's population at that time. Planners and developers feared that Britain's cities would be littered with deserted or underused shops. One property journalist calculated that if all the shops being planned in 1963 had been built, then Britain would have the retail capacity of a country four times its size.[94] In 1961, the government appointed a Working Party on Shopping Centres to study data gathered by the Board of Trade with the intention of advising towns and cities about how many shops they should build. The working party discussed the merits of a host of complex models for assessing the desired size and location of shopping precincts and eventually concluded that even more data would need to be collected.[95]

The election of a Labour government in 1964 and renewal of enthusiasm for planning on a national scale provoked another hunt for a perfect model. The new government appointed a handful of economic development committees to assess different aspects of Britain's economy in order to form a national economic plan. One of these, appointed in 1966, was tasked with trying to understand and control the geography of shopping. The committee, which was chaired by the head of a department store chain, John Lewis, commissioned an economist named Robert Bacon to study the movement of shoppers in a state-built shopping precinct in Cowley in the suburbs of Oxford. This was perhaps the most comprehensive attempt to develop a social law that could be used as the basis for planning the future of British shopping spaces. Informed by Reilly's gravitational law of retail, Bacon conducted more than two thousand interviews with shoppers and local residents to determine a complex list of the variables affecting the choice of shopping location. His data varied substantially on whether shoppers were visiting Cowley for food shopping or other goods, how large their family was, and rates of car and refrigerator ownership. The idea was to divine a set of universal processes that could be used by future government planners, "to establish the patterns of shopping at the Cowley Centre and then *attempt to find the principles behind these patterns*."[96] What emerged was a more sophisticated set of modifications to the law of retail gravitation—a complex equation that took into account the distance that a shopper would have to drive, the frequency of their trips, and the type of household that the shopper came from.

The early 1960s arguably marked a retreat of the state from the business of urban planning, as cities and towns began to use comprehensive redevelopment schemes as a means of attracting private property developers.[97] While this may have been the case at the local level, there were still sustained attempts by national governments to use town planning as a mechanism to plan precisely for consumer demand. As we will see later in this book, consumer psychology would play a major role in the internal design of shopping malls in the last third of the twentieth century. Yet it is important to remember that much of the early attempts to discover the hidden laws guiding the behavior of shoppers came not from private developers but rather from state technocrats and planners. Once the state started building shopping precincts, it became ensnared in complex questions about consumer demand that it was unable to answer. Indeed, after soliciting a number of reports from academics such as Bacon and from private researchers, the economic development committee's final report was forced to admit that "what we know is far less impressive than what we do not know."[98]

Shopping precincts were built in their dozens during a period when British technocrats were developing nuanced statistical measures of economic life. Although measurements of national income, output, employment, and the balance of trade and payments predated the mid-twentieth century, these measurements took on a new significance for both Labour and Conservative governments in the 1950s and 1960s. During these decades, detailed measurements of the economy became central for economic planning, propaganda, and making international comparisons.[99] In fact, the Census of Distribution, the measure on which many of these spatial calculations was based, was first taken only in 1950. Attempts to calculate Britain's shopping capacity were therefore part of a broader project undertaken by experts in the 1950s and 1960s to gather and process information in the service of national economic management and state-directed development. Shaped by infrastructural rather than political imperatives, these attempted calculations were made under both Labour and Conservative governments in the postwar period. The shoppers imagined by these models resembled the workers imagined by the planners of industrial estates. They were subjects whose needs could be satisfied or productivity enhanced by new types of urban space. In the end, though, the models were radically insufficient. They were dependent on a set of unspoken assumptions about the subjects that were being planned for—a faith that people's desires were bounded and finite, and that they would remain the same decades into the future. It wouldn't be long before this faith would begin to wane.[100]

In 1974, eight years after Bacon's report was written, writer Jonathan Raban was walking through a fashionable part of North London that had been relatively untouched by the top-down transformations described in this chapter. On his walk, he came across a shop that sold only imported Moroccan birdcages. Raban recorded this discovery in his memoir of urban life:

> No urban planner, puzzling out the rational requirements of a new city development would ever have arrived at the Moroccan birdcage shop. . . . The market in fashion is omnivorous in this improvisatory, make-do-and-mend way; it transforms junk into antiques, rubbish into something rich, strange, expensive and amusing. It is solely concerned with effecting arbitrary changes of value; its raw material is the continuous stream of waste products which we leave behind us in our crazes.[101]

By the time these words were written, the moment of British politics in which planners believed that consumer desires could be calculated and planned for as part of a project of national economic development was beginning to pass away.

The Strange Birth of the Shopping Mall

In 1938, the same year that Gibson unveiled his redevelopment plans for a city that was still untouched by war, Gruen, the inventor of the modern shopping mall, arrived as a refugee in New York City.[102] Gruen had traveled from Vienna, where he had lived in the final desperate decades of a country heading for catastrophe. He was the child of an upwardly mobile Jewish family and became a socialist in his youth. Gruen trained as an architect and worked as the director for a left-wing satirical cabaret troupe called the Red Players.[103] Before fleeing Austria, shortly after the Anschluss, Gruen had designed large housing projects for the city during a period of municipal socialism that became known as Red Vienna. After the municipal socialist regime fell from power in 1934, Gruen began designing the interiors of fashionable shops on the city's Ringstrasse. In New York City, Gruen joined a group of architects who had been forced by the Depression to work as store designers during a nationwide drought in construction contracts.[104] During that time, Gruen became fascinated with department stores. Modeled on Parisian arcades, chain department stores had proliferated across the United States (as they had in Britain) in the years after the Civil War, and by Gruen's arrival they were a permanent feature of the US urban landscape.[105] Actively competing for foot traffic, these stores prided themselves on the lavish and total nature of their interior space, often boasting tea shops, rotundas, courtyards, smoking rooms, libraries, art galleries, and dazzling, almost theatrical window displays. In the words of historian Alan Trachtenberg, they offered US pedestrians a "pedagogy of modernity."[106] In Gruen's storefront designs, both speculative and realized, he played with the capacity of such spaces to create sealed worlds in which the division between inside and outside was ambiguous, enclosing the entrances to stores in arcades and vast canopies.[107] Gruen's work on Fifth Avenue was noticed by chain stores looking to attract motorists in the United States' nascent suburbs, and by 1940 Gruen was working mostly in California, designing storefronts for the women's clothing chain Grayson's that would appeal to passing traffic.

In 1943, Gruen and his business partner and new wife, Elsie Krummeck, were invited by *Architectural Forum* to propose a shopping environment for the postwar United States as part of a series of speculative articles called 194X (with the X referring to the year that the war would end). Having worked for both upscale department stores and suburban chains, the two architects had spent the last few years wrestling with questions of aesthetics and function such as, How could the circulation of customers and stock be segregated from each other in an environment that was decorous and humane? Their answer was one of the first instantiations of the suburban shopping mall:

Shops could be grouped in one building surrounding a landscaped area. . . .
With the exception of the main entrance the outside is modest in character. . . . Each end of the block has parking space and loading and unloading
are carried on behind screen walls. For the shoppers there is a covered walk
connecting all the stores, a restful atmosphere and protection from automobile traffic.[108]

Over the next eight years, Gruen's marriage to Krummeck and their joint
architecture business fell apart. Krummeck's coauthorship of the first proposal
for a shopping mall is often forgotten, although she continued to have a pres-
tigious career as a sculptor and landscape architect. Meanwhile, in a series of
subsequent articles and exhibitions, Gruen would continue to call for various
top-down means of controlling the United States' haphazard suburban
growth.[109] While his socialism had faded, his zeal for planning had only intensified. Using language redolent of Tripp and Gibson, Gruen called for a reordering of suburban sprawl in the name of efficiency and development, con-
demning "the . . . strip developments which choke traffic on our suburban
highways," and the "anarchistic conglomerations of shopping facilities which
vary in size and character."[110] Elsewhere, he proposed separate "reservations
for the human race and reservations for the automobile race."[111]

Gruen's call for the enclosure of suburban strips and their isolation from
traffic came in the wake of an attempt by Clarence Stein and Catherine Bauer,
two urban planners, to calculate the United States' shopping capacity in
1934.[112] Stein and Bauer developed a plan to rationalize the unplanned and
haphazard shopping environment in the United States. Previously, Stein had
worked as lead planner for Radburn, New Jersey, the new town founded in
1929 that, as we have seen, was inspired by Howard's garden city. Despite
Stein's claim that Radburn was a city for "the motor age," Stein and Bauer's
research called for the building of hundreds of small, open-plan, walkable centers embedded in urban neighborhoods.[113] Interwar US shopping centers, to
the extent that they had been considered by planners at all, had been seen as
addenda to residential developments and placed at their core within walking
distance of most residents.[114] Gruen's designs, as they took shape in the 1940s
and 1950s, were a major departure from this tradition. As in Britain, their new-
ness was partly a response to the emergence of mass car ownership. Gruen and
Krummeck's 194X article advertised the mall as a solution to dangerous road
crossings, inadequate parking spaces, and the awkward overlap between stock
delivery and arriving customers.

    While Gibson was rethinking British shopping under a sky pealing with
German bombers, Gruen was reaching some of the same conclusions in
the dry desert air of Southern California. For both architects, shopping

FIGURE 2.7. Victor Gruen. Victor Gruen Papers, American Heritage Center,
University of Wyoming.

centers were instruments of rational planning, a way of re-centering the "anarchistic wilderness" of British and US urban sprawl.[115] The nationalization
of Britain's planning apparatus after the war meant that the vision of Gibson
and his contemporaries could be implemented quickly in blitzed cities, new
towns, and, eventually, under different regimes of ownership in 1960s redevelopment plans. Gruen's state-directed consumerist palaces, however, were
forced underground for another decade before resurfacing as private suburban boxes. In the years between the 194X article and his contract with the
J. L. Hudson Company to build the first shopping mall in the United States,
signed in 1954, Gruen honed his idea. He hoped that shopping centers would
usher in a new kind of urban society. Gruen imagined that they would be

community centers, art galleries, town squares, and civic monuments all rolled into one. In a traveling exhibition created for the American Federation of Arts called Shopping Centers of Tomorrow, his firm put forward a utopian vision:

> From the time bartering was done under a tree the market has been a meeting place where people afoot could mingle leisurely, discuss business, exchange gossip. . . . After the Industrial Revolution, with its advancing technology, narrow 19th century streets were lined with towering skyscrapers, congested with an ever growing volume from city streets. Obsolete practices failed to transform late technology's promise of a fuller way of life into a cultural reality. . . . The human scale was lost. . . . The Shopping Center of Tomorrow will fill the vacuum created by the absence of social, cultural and civic crystallization points in our vast suburban areas.[116]

He hoped that the shopping mall would act as a kind of leviathan, diminishing the power wielded by individual enterprises and subordinating them to a cooperative endeavor. His description of the relationship between shopping mall owners and their tenants is almost Hobbesian: "The shopping center is one of the new building types created in our time. It also represents one of the rare instances in which a number of individual business enterprises, in banding together, are ready to submit to certain over-all rules in order to further their common welfare." He compared the organization of a shopping mall with the United States' federal system of government.[117]

In the articles and exhibitions churned out by Gruen and his firm in the 1950s and 1960s, the shopping mall was coded as a space for women, children, and the elderly. Because men traveled daily from the suburbs to the downtowns of major cities, Gruen reasoned, they had frequent access to the pleasures of urban public space. Yet "our children . . . the aged and housewives," groups that "together represent a majority of the population," travel downtown "once or twice a year."[118] For women, these new spaces were to be "pleasing to the eyes and soothing to the nerves." Shopping malls would offer recognition from urban planners that women were "the pivot around which the family's domestic and economic life centers."[119] In this sense, Gruen imagined that the shopping mall would codify the patriarchal geography of US suburbia, segregating public space along the lines of gender and age. Just as late nineteenth-century department stores remade the city as a safe space for shopgirls and elite women to be seen in public, Gruen hoped that his malls would provide an alternative city for the 1950s US housewife.[120]

Gruen was finally given an opportunity to implement these ideas in 1952, when his firm began constructing a large suburban shopping center on the outskirts of Detroit commissioned by J. L. Hudson, a local department store

FIGURE 2.8. Fashion show at Victor Gruen's Southdale shopping center in Edina, Minnesota.
Victor Gruen Papers, American Heritage Center, University of Wyoming.

magnate. The Northland Center opened two years later, consisting of a stretch
of geometrically planned open-air arcades that encased fountains, sculptures,
courtyards, and even a theater, ringed by more than eight thousand parking
spaces.[121] The development was a major commercial success and propelled
Gruen to nationwide fame. Two years later, he would open Southdale on the
outskirts of Minneapolis, the first indoor, climate-controlled shopping mall in
the United States. True to his vision that malls would become hubs for civic
gatherings, Gruen filled Southdale with $50,000 of public art and built an au-
ditorium for outdoor plays, meetings, and even extravagant circuses.[122] In 1958,
the auditorium hosted the Minneapolis Symphony Ball.[123]

It was shortly after the opening of Southdale that Gruen began to lose control of his vision. The same year that Southdale opened, the federal government introduced a change in the way that real estate was taxed. While US real
estate owners had for decades been allowed to claim tax exemptions each year

FIGURE 2.9. Public art on display at Victor Gruen's Southdale shopping center in Edina, Minnesota. Victor Gruen Papers, American Heritage Center, University of Wyoming.

to compensate for their property's depreciation, the new change front-loaded these annual exemptions, giving huge tax advantages to developers that built new commercial buildings and then sold them after a few years. By turning shopping malls into tax shelters, this change in the tax code precipitated a boom in shopping mall construction that by the 1960s saw more than one hundred built each year.[124] The US suburbs became swamped with malls that resembled Gruen's Southdale (many of which were built by Gruen's own rapidly expanding firm). It was not long before these developments became ensnared in the toxic race and class politics of US suburbanization. Shopping malls, along with the construction of highways and racially discriminatory mortgage practices, enabled millions of white Americans to secede from large cities, draining them of capital and contributing to generations of urban crisis.[125] Although Gruen and his firm continued to design malls throughout the 1950s and 1960s, he did so at a time when national economic planning and democratic public assembly, his two lifelong passions, were being destroyed in a process aided by his own mutant creations. In 1968, sick of watching his developments being transformed by property developers looking for tax deductions, Gruen moved back to Europe, where, with almost dizzying irony, he discovered that his childhood second home in Eutin in northern Germany had been demolished to make way for a shopping mall.[126] Toward the end of his life, when asked about shopping malls, Gruen reportedly said that he "refused to pay alimony for those bastard developments."[127]

At different times in the 1950s, two British architects, Sydney Greenwood and Paul Boissevain, traveled to the United States, where they noted with awe the new malls that were sprouting in the suburbs.[128] After their return, the two architects would design Britain's first two private indoor shopping malls: the Bullring Center in Birmingham (1964) and the Elephant and Castle Shopping Centre in South London (1965). Shorn of their social promise, Gruen's bastard children, like Gruen himself, made their way back across the Atlantic. The spread of shopping malls built by private developers in Britain in the 1960s and 1970s marks a collision between the world of Gruen and that of Gibson—a collision that brings this chapter to an end. The displacement of shopping precincts by shopping malls, and the subsequent implications for planning and public space, will form the story of a later chapter.

Between the mid-nineteenth and mid-twentieth centuries, the spaces where Britons shopped were transformed, as ramshackle market stalls gave way to formalized stores set behind glass frontages in department stores, municipal market halls, or planned shopping precincts. The premodern market was centralized, enclosed, and municipalized, first by liberal reformers and later by postwar urban planners, producing a new kind of urban space that acted as a conduit between state power and individual consumers. In new towns and blitzed cities, the shopping precinct became a conspicuous part of Britain's mid-twentieth-century developmental state. The uniqueness of these precincts is made all the more striking by their erasure in recent years. Almost all the state-built shopping precincts constructed after the war were sold off to property developers starting in the 1980s. What remains of Gibson's precinct is currently owned by a holding company called Mall Solutions Europe.

Many have drawn attention to the ways in which Western states encouraged consumer spending in the aftermath of the Second World War, wedding consumerism and citizenship through full employment measures, demand-side economic adjustments, and public spending programs.[129] By the end of the 1970s in Britain, the government had acknowledged the power of consumerist political movements and passed a raft of consumer protections.[130] As well as stimulating demand and regulating products, however, the state had a hand in building many of the physical environments in which people consumed. Britain's postwar consumer economy came with a new type of space—one that had its own compelling logic, allowing planners to reimagine town centers and lulling technocrats into the false belief that the needs of city dwellers could be perfectly satisfied, given the right kinds of inputs. While recent histories of Britain and elsewhere have seen consumers enter the stage as agents, fickle, demanding, and with cash in hand, the history of shopping precincts points in a different direction, showing one way in which their agency was anticipated by urban planners and circumscribed by a developmental infrastructure.

3

The Council Estate

TO ANYONE who has ever lived in a British city, council estates are instantly recognizable. Take any train leaving London's Victoria Station and look out the window as it the crosses the river heading south. On your right, you will see the Winstanley, Doddigton, and Rollo estates, a spine of symmetrical white and gray tower blocks that recede into the horizon. Despite the glittering, half-finished luxury towers that swarm around Battersea Power Station and stretch along the banks of the Thames, these public housing projects still, for now, dominate the skyline of this part of London. The view is the same along the exurban corridor between Edinburgh and Glasgow, beside the South Wales coast, and on the outskirts of Manchester, Southampton, Leicester, Newcastle, and Belfast. This chapter concerns the history of the council estate in Britain. A council estate is a group of homes, usually in one or many buildings, planned as a totality that was owned and leased by municipal authorities. Although many council estates were low-rise suburban developments, this chapter will focus on the urban, high-density iterations of this form, which usually comprised a handful of high- and medium-rise apartment buildings connected by a mesh of public walkways, courtyards, playgrounds, and parking lots. It was in these types of estate that Britain's postwar developmental political formation was most visible. While they vary wildly in quality, architecture, size, height, and age, council estates are a distinctive and inescapable part of Britain's built environment—perhaps even the *most* distinctive and inescapable.

Although many council estates have been demolished, these developments still exist in almost every British town and city, most now under the ownership of charitable trusts or private property developers. The residents of these spaces once paid subsidized rents and utility charges (usually combined in a single fee) to municipal authorities who also acted as landlords, changing lightbulbs in lobbies and hallways, fixing elevators, and cleaning windows. Council estates had their global counterparts among the *Khrushchyovka* of Moscow, the *superquadras* of Brasília, the Unités d'Habitation in Marseille, and the projects of Chicago, all of which were constructed in the mid-twentieth century to bring order to cities that were rapidly and haphazardly expanding.[1] Those in Britain varied in size. The Ossulston Estate, for example, is a small block of flats nestled next to the British Library in London, while the vast Holme Wood Estate in Bradford is an expansive zone of mixed-density buildings, housing ten thousand. It is almost impossible to believe that within the lifetimes of close to half the current population, some of the most famous architects in the world were commissioned by the housing departments of local governments to fill British towns and cities with enormous, comprehensively planned developments for working-class people to live in. Even more so than the industrial estate or shopping precinct, the council estate is tainted by the strangeness of history. To stand in a stairwell on the twenty-seventh floor of a tower block, next to a communal garbage chute, beneath a fluorescent light, and look out through thick glass at the skyline of a British city is to be reminded of the suddenness and completeness of historical change.

High-density council estates were built in a concentrated burst, mostly between 1955 and 1975.[2] They were the shock troops of the British state's massive house-building project in the twentieth century—a public housing drive that saw almost one in three households become tenants of the state by 1980.[3] Almost a third of all council housing built after the war was located in municipal apartment buildings in estates of various shapes and sizes, and by 1980 local governments in England alone owned more than 1.6 million flats.[4] The high-density council estate was therefore by far the most conspicuous and arguably most consequential of the urban forms that comprise this book. Perhaps for this reason, unlike the industrial estate or shopping precinct, the council estate has generated a rich historiography. It has been the main protagonist in recent histories of working-class community formation, policy and political culture, gender, consumerism, and architecture.[5] This chapter is not an intervention in the high politics of British housing policy, nor is it particularly concerned with the aesthetics of modernist architecture. I am also not concerned here with the multiple, perhaps infinite, number of different ways that their millions of residents experienced living on estates, and whether these experiences qualify estates as successes or failures. The question of how the council estate came to be so fraught with problems, so denigrated, and so inexplicable to many twenty-first-century Britons will be answered in the next chapter. Instead, I will try to historicize the subjects that council estates attempted to call into being and look at the vision of developmental modernity that these spaces instantiated as well as consider those who were excluded from this vision.

Here I will explore the two most striking and historically distinctive features of postwar, high-density council estates: their capacity to modernize domestic life and the hope that they could forge community out of proximity.

The opportunity for architects to build entirely new housing developments allowed municipal authorities to provide new services in ways that were hitherto unimaginable. Beyond electricity, indoor plumbing, and hot water, things that would been novelties to many of the first tenants of new housing estates, planners were able to supply playgrounds, community centers, laundry rooms, forms of employment, waterborne garbage disposal systems that sucked waste into the basements of tower blocks, and new types of heating systems that were powered through the by-products of nearby industry. Meanwhile, as council estates assembled together individuals and families who were strangers to each other, bringing them into close quarters in a new environment planned apart from the rest of the city, they made it possible for planners to construct and manage the twentieth century's most elusive kind of body politic: the community. As we will see, however, at a time when British cities were being transformed by migration from its disintegrating empire, these spaces frequently operated in ways that had the effect of excluding people of color.

Housing the Urban Poor before the Estate

In 1842, Friedrich Engels stumbled on a newly built gathering of houses on the south bank of the River Irk in Manchester—a set of courts that, he wrote, contained "unqualifiedly the most horrible dwellings which I have yet beheld." It is worth pausing briefly on his description of this space:

> In one of these courts there stands directly at the entrance, at the end of the covered passage, a privy without a door, so dirty that the inhabitants can pass into and out of the court only by passing through foul pools of stagnant urine and excrement. . . . Everywhere half or wholly ruined buildings, some of them actually uninhabited, which means a great deal here. . . . Everywhere heaps of débris, refuse, and offal; standing pools for gutters, and a stench which alone would make it impossible for a human being in any degree civilised to live in such a district . . . a planless, knotted chaos of houses, more or less on the verge of uninhabitableness, whose unclean interiors fully correspond with their filthy external surroundings.[6]

What Engels saw was a nightmarish inversion of the twentieth-century council estate. He described the residents of this new kind of urban housing as feckless and fleeting, crowding intimately together with no privacy, with boarders and lodgers sharing beds with married couples and people "mixed indiscriminately." Here was proximity without community, a "society wholly composed of atoms," strangers to each other who were randomly colliding in courtyards and still-warm beds.[7] Here too was density without order, a haphazard jumble of homes, unconnected from each other, whose residents were forced to source their own water, heat, and toilets. Before we arrive at the mid-twentieth-century council estate, it is worth thinking about what came before. My task here is not to rehearse the well-told story of urbanization, liberal housing reform, and the origins of council housing.[8] Instead I want to offer some brief, and necessarily incomplete, reflections on how conscious attempts by reformers, philanthropists, and planners in the later nineteenth and early twentieth centuries theorized these twin problems of density/planning and isolation/community.

These two problems haunted James B. Russell, a physician appointed by the city of Glasgow in 1872 as its first medical officer. Glasgow's late nineteenth-century urban fabric was dense and distinctive. Like Edinburgh, its urban poor were mostly crammed into small apartments in multistory tenements. By the 1880s, more than 40 percent of families in the city were living in a single room, and as late as 1917, 93 percent of one-room tenements were still dependent on an outdoor bathroom.[9] Overcrowding in the city's tenements had been such a problem that the corporation had introduced a system of "ticketing": fixing a metal plate on the doors of each home stipulating the number of people allowed to sleep there and enforcing the limit with midnight police raids. These sandstone buildings were remarkable in Britain for their tall height as well as their provision of both private apartments and public stairwells and courtyards. In this sense, they bear a distant formal resemblance to the council estates that would be built across Britain half a century later. While Russell was concerned about the chaotic squalor of such spaces, his biggest worry was density itself. In an influential and widely circulated speech, "Life in One Room," delivered in 1888, Russell offered a vivid portrait of these overcrowded spaces, emphasizing the excess of physical proximity suffered by their residents, "the racket and thoughtless noise . . . the heat and smells . . . the steam and disturbance combined in a house of one room." Russell wrote that "a man may learn to exist without air for several minutes. . . . [A] man may live for several days without food. . . . [B]ut *space* to live on and in is an absolute necessity." Worst of all from Russell's perspective, some of these residents were strangers to each other. They were a transient community of lodgers, "strange men and women mixed up with husbands and wives and children within the four walls of small rooms."[10]

In London during the same period of time, philanthropists attempting to reimagine urban housing for the working poor were also wrestling with questions of overcrowding and proximity.[11] In East London starting in the 1860s, a group of charitable trusts such as the Peabody Trust, East End Dwelling Company, and Four Per Cent Industrial Dwellings Company purchased land and built new tenements, which were made available at subsidized rents through a process streamlined by new permissive powers granted by the 1875

FIGURE 3.1. Nick Hedges, "Mother and Baby in Gorbals [Glasgow] Tenement Courtyard," 1970. Reproduced with kind permission of Nick Hedges.

FIGURE 3.2. Nick Hedges, "Tenement Courtyard, Mayhill, Glasgow 1," 1971. Reproduced with kind permission of Nick Hedges.

Public Health Act. These constructions enjoyed the financial patronage and political support of wealthy industrialists and bankers such as Charles Booth and the Rothschild family, and were built to replace some of the most notorious slums in the city. The acute moral concerns posed by fleeting families of strangers living in close proximity—concerns that haunted both Engels and Russell—were addressed by attempts to carefully monitor and police the deportment of the buildings' tenants. The Katherine Building, a wide, five-story block owned by the East End Dwelling Company, made a point of employing only female rent collectors when it opened in 1885, hoping that respectable young women would have a civilizing effect on its tenants, who would learn new practices of domestic management from their weekly visits.[12] The company struggled at first to impose the levels of discipline required to manage the social problems that resulted from density. Within a year of its opening, the management were expressing dismay about the high levels of vacancy in the building due in part to the eviction of tenants whose "habits and behavior were found incompatible with the maintenance of order and comfort."[13]

Limits on the ability of the dwelling companies to impose order on these large tenements were set by the absence of efficient systems of distributing water, heat, and energy into people's homes. Residents of philanthropic tenements had to look beyond their private apartments when it came to sourcing fuel and water or disposing of waste. Housing reformer Octavia Hill commented that plumbing was unnecessary in philanthropic tenements as it was "no hardship to carry a pail of water" from a communal tap.[14] One of the early rent collectors in the Katherine Building was future Fabian reformer Beatrice Potter Webb. Webb recalled the problems that arose from this arrangement:

> Right along the whole length of the building confronting the blank wall ran four open galleries, out of which led narrow passages, each passage to five rooms identical in size and shape. . . . Within these uniform cell-like apartments there were no labour-saving appliances, not even a sink or a water tap. . . . [T]he sanitary arrangements taken as a whole, had the drawback that the sets of six closets used in common by a miscellaneous crowd of men, women and children, became the obtrusively dominant feature of the several staircases, up and down which trooped, mornings, noon and night, the 600 or so more inhabitants of the buildings.[15]

Meanwhile, in the Rothschild Buildings, built in the same year about a mile to the north of the Katherine Building, the residents, primarily Jewish migrants from eastern Europe, were governed by a complex set of numbered rules that sought to impose order on the ways that amenities and common spaces were shared. Most notorious was rule 5, which stipulated that the communal passages and stairs were washed and whitened by each resident in rotation. Although some of the homes in the Rothschild Building had sculleries with taps, wastewater was infrequently emptied and bathing was a challenge. Most residents chose to bathe communally in the nearby public baths. All the philanthropic tenement buildings in East London were heated by individual open fireplaces, for which residents often struggled to source coal, with tenants of the Rothschild Buildings complaining that the coal suppliers refused to deliver to upper floors of the tenement.[16]

By the time that activist local governments began to build the first iterations of what would become known as council housing, little had changed. London's first municipal housing estate, the Boundary Estate, was completed in 1900, as one of the earliest acts of the London County Council (LCC), London's first citywide organ of local government. The Boundary Estate was located less than a mile from the Rothschild tenement buildings and featured almost a thousand homes organized into six-story apartment buildings radiating out from a central bandstand. Almost half these homes still shared a toilet with others on their corridor, and all the apartments had open fireplaces, for which residents had to source their own coal.[17] Limited by the house-building and urban-planning technologies of the age, then, neither the philanthropic tenement nor the turn-of-the-century council estate offered much in the way of domestic amenities. For many of the tenants of these buildings, life was spent sourcing their own fuel and water, washing their own stairwells and courtyards, traipsing along corridors to use the bathroom, and bathing elsewhere.

In the late nineteenth century, the link between density and the construction of community or the modernization of domestic life was not an obvious one.[18] During this period, the language of modernity and community was the preserve of those who were building low-rise company towns or garden cities—spaces that were also funded by philanthropists and charitable trusts. In the last decade of the nineteenth century, at the same time that the Boundary Estate was under construction, LCC politicians were already looking toward low-rise suburban expansion as an alternative to dense tenement building.[19] This had been the predominant conclusion of the 1885 Royal Commission on the Housing of the Working Classes, which recommended a combination of suburban homes and new transit lines for London. Howard, in his famous pamphlet outlining his vision for new, utopian towns, described his plans for freestanding cottages built in concentric rings.[20] These low-rise cottages made up the housing stock of Britain's first two garden cities, Letchworth and Welwyn, founded in 1903 and 1920, respectively. Raymond Unwin, a radical town planner who was heavily involved in the construction of Letchworth Garden City, argued vociferously that low-rise cottages were the ideal solution to the requirements of shelter, privacy, and health. Unwin was a disciple of the Arts and Crafts movement, pioneered by William Morris and John Ruskin,

FIGURE 3.3. Communal toilet in the interior of the Boundary Estate before its renovation.

which celebrated ornament and craftsmanship over industrial production and standardization. He called for towns and cities to be organized on the basis of individuated cottages arranged in quadrangles of no more than thirty around a common green space. Each quadrangle would have its own laundry and common baths.[21]

These were the ideals that underpinned the massive expansion of house building immediately after the First World War. Between 1919 and 1939, more than four million homes were constructed, roughly a quarter of which were council homes built by municipal authorities.[22] The 1919 Housing Act compelled each local authority to survey its housing stock, calculate its future level of need, and, with hefty subsidies, build to meet it. This act was the first peacetime recognition that Britain's housing stock was a national concern and a resource to be tended and managed by the state. Of the more than one million public homes built between the wars, just 5 percent were flats in high-density housing estates, and most of these were concentrated in just two cities: London and Liverpool.[23] Most council houses were built in sprawling suburban developments such as Beacontree in Essex or Wythenshawe in Manchester. It was in these suburbs, both public and privately built, that a new type of domestic suburban modernity began to take shape—one characterized by scientific household management, new technologies for performing domestic labor, and a renewed emphasis on familial intimacy.[24] Recommendations for the layout of new council estates and the design of dwellings were set for local authorities by the 1918 Tudor Walters government report that preceded the 1919 act. Unwin heavily influenced the report, which recommended the construction of two-story houses with a living room, scullery, toilet, and three bedrooms. Electricity did not yet feature in the proposed designs; the cottages were to be heated by coal and lit by gas. Paramount was the economization of space in order to streamline domestic labor and childcare for working-class housewives.[25]

I hope to have shown some of the ways that density posed a problem for planners and reformers who were seeking to remake the housing conditions of the urban poor. In rapidly urbanizing industrial cities, multiple families sharing courtyards, toilets, rooms, and even beds resulted in a shocking combination of anonymity and intimacy. Even in the philanthropic tenements built solely for the "respectable" poor, communal toilets, taps, and baths along with strict cleaning rotations resulted in confusing ambiguities about the relationship between public and private space. Under these conditions, it is not surprising that radical attempts to use the built environment to remake society, whether undertaken in garden cities or on interwar council estates, took the form of squat, low-rise cottages symmetrically arranged on the outskirts of large industrial cities.

The Networked Home

In 1954, five officials from Sheffield Council's Housing Department walked through Bellahøj, a partially completed housing project on a windy hill overlooking Copenhagen. The delegation, led by Sheffield's city architect, John Lewis Womersley, was researching large modernist housing estates in a variety of different European cities. Bellahøj was to be a flagship of Danish social democracy, consisting of a thicket of twenty-eight tower blocks with communal laundries, ground-level garages, a theater, and a shopping precinct. A few months earlier, the Sheffield delegation had written to the Ministry of Housing for a list of suitable developments in France, the Netherlands, Belgium, Denmark, Germany, and Switzerland, from which they created an itinerary that they dutifully followed. The delegates liked what they saw. In their report to the city council, the officials argued that the density and comprehensive nature of the developments they visited allowed for new kinds of residential services that could satisfy every human need. Their report glowed with enthusiasm for the ways in which density could produce new standards of living:

> For families who do not desire life in a suburban house with a garden, the multi-storey flat can give exceptional amenities in the form of open space, community buildings, services and equipment—amenities which, it is considered, may have a particular appeal to the younger generation of parents. All the evidence obtained . . . points to the fact that multi-storey housing schemes, which are essentially of a communal nature and of modern construction, should exploit these . . . inherent features to the full if they are to be completely successful.[26]

Comprehensively planned high-density developments offered an opportunity to reimagine the relationship between the individual, state, and household. Specifically, they supplied the means to centralize the provision of goods such as energy, water, and sewage disposal as well as spaces of recreation and assembly in ways that bound residents together as a collective. US economist Robert Gordon has written of the "networking" together of homes between 1870 and 1940, as once isolated and self-sufficient nodes were connected to infrastructure grids providing access to water, electricity, transportation, sewage disposal, and communications.[27] For Gordon, this was one of the most significant transformations of everyday life to have ever occurred. By the mid-twentieth century, this infrastructure network, along with electric elevators, cheap construction methods, and new heating technologies, had expanded the possibilities for planned, high-density housing developments. The difference between the freestanding interwar cottage and a flat on a postwar council estate was analogous to the difference between the individual factory and the industrial estate.

The delegation's visit to mainland Europe was part of reenergizing the British state's house-building program after the war. With few local precedents to draw on in Britain, Sheffield, along with other housing departments across the country, was looking east—fascinated by dense municipal housing projects in Scandinavia and western Europe. Indeed, this was a well-trodden path. Architects and politicians from many major British cities, including Birmingham, Leeds, Glasgow, and London, had toured central and western Europe in the 1930s, 1940s, and 1950s with an eye to emulating the grand high-density housing programs of cities such as Vienna, Marseille, Berlin, and Copenhagen.[28]

By the war's end, German bombing had destroyed hundreds of thousands of homes, precipitating a desperate housing crisis. Meanwhile, 1945 saw the election of a Labour government committed to economic development and postwar reconstruction. In new towns as well as expanding or bomb-damaged cities, Britain underwent an exceptional period of state-backed house building that continued for more than a generation. Unlike the boom in house building between the wars, which saw low-rise estates trooping over the horizon into rural areas, this second, massive wave of building took place under a tight new planning apparatus that protected greenbelts around cities and restricted the options available to both local authorities and private developers. Some municipal authorities dealt with these restrictions by building upward.[29] In 1956, a Conservative government, committed to mass house building, passed the Housing Subsidy Act, tying the provision of government housing subsidies to height—the higher the tower block, the greater the subsidy. Many of the new tower blocks built during this period were hastily erected using a method called "system building," where components of tower blocks were mass-produced elsewhere and then assembled on-site.[30] At the same time, a younger generation of architects and planners employed by councils was rethinking the aesthetics and function of housing, coming to associate density with futurity.[31] Quadrangles of two-story cottages ceased to be the normative blueprint for working-class housing. As a result, the skylines of British towns and cities began to change, and residential tower blocks of more than ten stories became a familiar feature of urban life.

When the delegation returned to Sheffield from its European tour, it set about commissioning two of the most well-known and ambitious council estates in Britain: Park Hill and Hyde Park. The council was faced with the task of clearing two slums to the north of the city, and Womersley, the city architect, was adamant that high-density housing, along the lines of the developments that he had seen in Europe, must replace them. Park Hill, completed in 1961, comprised 992 dwellings spread among multiple four- to thirteen-story structures. The development was billed as a "city within a city," located on a hill, isolated from Sheffield's major roads, and containing its own network of paths and small streets.[32] The buildings were connected by three-meter-wide decks suspended in the sky, big enough for a milk delivery vehicle to drive along.[33] The estate's architects, Jack Lynn and Ivor Smith, imagined that the access decks would serve as "streets in the sky," re-creating what they understood to have been the vibrant and communal street life of the demolished slums on internal walkways shielded from weather and traffic.[34] Hyde Park, meanwhile, was completed in 1966 on a plot of land adjacent to Park Hill. It was comprised of small maisonette blocks and big towers—the largest of which was more than nineteen stories. As with Park Hill, these structures were connected by sheltered walkways and elevators. Besides heating, plumbing, electricity, and indoor toilets, the two estates offered a range of more unusual services to their residents. Both estates shared a waterborne refuse system imported from France called the Garchey system, in which refuse, including ashes, tins, and bottles, could be placed into a chute fitted into the kitchen sink.

FIGURE 3.4. Park Hill from a distance, 1960. © John Donat / RIBA Collections.

FIGURE 3.5. Children playing on Park Hill's internal streets, 1961. © Architectural Press Archive / RIBA Collections.

The waste would then flow out to a centrally located incinerator, where it was burned and removed in ash form. The system worked by filling a large hole in the sink with water and refuse, and using a plunger to initiate the suction.[35]

Park Hill and Hyde Park were also planned with a number of amenities that allowed the estates to exist in relative autonomy from the rest of the town. In its central courtyards, Park Hill included a handful of shops, four pubs, and a public health clinic for expectant mothers. Hyde Park featured a clothing factory, rehoused by the council, which provided work for two hundred women. The common spaces of both estates—stairwells, courtyards, walkways, and elevators—were to be cleaned and maintained by a team of staff employed by the council. Social activities among the residents were run by an informal tenant's association. A full-time sociologist was employed to live on the estate and monitor the formation of its community as time passed.[36]

Less conspicuous than the estate's wide-access decks or imposing height, but no less historically significant, was Park Hill's provision of central heating. Heating for all 992 dwellings on the estate was provided by a single boiler at the lower end of the development and included as part of each household's rent. In the mid-1950s, when Park Hill was under construction, central heating was almost nonexistent in Britain.[37] Open fireplaces and spaces reserved for storing coal were key features of both London's philanthropic tenements as well as cottages in garden cities and interwar estates. While a small number of apartment buildings experimented with communal boilers in the interwar period, particularly in Scotland, these often had to be supplemented with open fires in order to maintain a bearable temperature.[38] When the Sheffield delegation visited housing developments in Europe, they noted that coal fires would be "an anachronism" in high flats, and central boilers would conserve the nation's coal supplies and improve the city's air quality.[39] The shift to new sources of domestic heat was also catalyzed by concerns over deteriorating air quality in British cities, with millions of open fires triggering periodic winter smogs, such as the famous Great Smog of 1952 in London that resulted in thousands of deaths. The 1956 Clean Air Act restricted the kinds of fuel that could be used in open fireplaces, further incentivizing the spread of alternative forms of indoor heating.[40] Within twenty years of the opening of Park Hill, hot water central heating would feature in more than half of all British households.[41] The majority of high-density council estates built after the war provided heating for their flats.

For a brief moment, mass central heating, enabled by density and public ownership, allowed planners to imagine a radically new relationship between individuals, energy, and the state. As with many other new domestic technologies for the home that emerged in the mid-twentieth century, contemporaries imagined that central heating would reduce the amount of time and energy spent on domestic labor by housewives.[42] Plumbed hot water complemented the arrival of fitted kitchens, which, during the interwar period, promised to reduce the burden of domestic work in both public and private housing. Fitted kitchens with cupboards, sinks, working surfaces, and draining boards were standard on postwar high-density council estates, and municipal authorities proudly advertised their own standardized designs (there was, for example, a "Birmingham Kitchen" and a "Coventry Kitchen").[43] These designs would have been a novelty to most women who were moving into council estates for the first time. Central heating and hot water meant that women were no longer tasked with sourcing energy for and cleaning fireplaces. When it came to heat, this new domestic modernity ran up against countervailing and gendered forms of nostalgia. There were concerns that central heating, by distributing heat evenly through the home, would disrupt the cohesiveness of the family unit, allowing different family members to retire to different rooms rather than gather by the hearth.[44] Starting in 1943, the coal industry sponsored the creation of the Women's Solid Fuel Council, which spent decades campaigning against central heating and in favor of open fireplaces. As late as the 1980s, the council distributed publicity material with titles like "The Magic of a Real Fire" to its many local and regional branches, and it encouraged its members to tour collieries and set up stalls at consumer expos with slogans such as "Open Fires Can Run Radiators round the House."[45]

Despite this opposition, central heating became tied to modernity and national economic development in the postwar period. During the war, a new method of collectively heating thousands of homes flashed tantalizingly into view for planners and architects—a technique called "district heating." District heating referred to a system in which multiple different homes—sometimes hundreds, sometimes thousands, and sometimes entire neighborhoods or towns—were heated from one or a handful of the same boilers. In the vast majority of these instances, the users of such systems were tenants of the state in large housing estates such as Park Hill and paid for their heat as part of their rent. Pioneered in the United States in the late nineteenth century, these systems would depend on vast municipal boilers, preferably fueled by the excess heat generated by nearby industry, to pipe heat into multiple homes. As huge, mostly invisible energy networks, district heating systems were the antithesis of the private coal or wood-burning fireplace. Although there were scattered uses of district heating in US cities in the late nineteenth century, the technology was most prominent in states with cold climates where urban and infrastructural networks were controlled by the state. The USSR was, unsurprisingly, district heating's biggest adopter. The Soviet state saw the construction of multiple new industrial cities as a means of simultaneously remaking the national economy and the lives of its citizens.[46] In the many new cities built in the USSR in the mid-twentieth century, it was common practice for large tenement buildings to be heated by the surplus energy generated by the factories in which their tenants worked. Residents often had no control over the heat that was pumped into their homes—the quantities of which could only be altered by petitioning the local authorities in charge of the building. These schemes were also popular in Germany and Sweden, where by the late 1960s there were twelve district heating networks operating in eight cities.[47] Crucially, in the early decades of central heating, these schemes were providing domestic heat as a necessary public good rather than a salable commodity.[48] By integrating industry, high-density public housing, and the provision of heat, they created a hermetically sealed energy circuit that was beyond the control of market forces.

Although collective heating on this scale was never used in Britain to the same extent, there were still a handful of experiments in this direction. In 1943, during a moment of war-induced cooperation between Britain and the USSR, a committee in the government's Building Research Station began gathering information on the technical aspects of district heating schemes in Moscow, Rostov, and Leningrad.[49] Reams of articles in Russian-language engineering journals were translated for British officials, who were investigating the feasibility of heating entire British cities with vast subterranean boilers or the run-off energy from industry.[50] In 1947, the committee reported back, broadly in favor of similar schemes in Britain. The report cited the opportunities created by wartime damage for rebuilding British cities as well as the new impetus for efficiency caused by shortages of coal.[51] Based on some of this research, the "Final Report of the New Towns Committee" recommended an experimental trial of district heating in new towns.[52] A handful of large district heating schemes were experimented with. The Wythenshawe Estate, built in the inter-war period, was fitted with a heating system that also serviced a local police and fire station, cinema, church, and three hundred acres of industrial buildings.[53] The Great Hamilton Street Estate in Paisley boasted a similar arrangement. One of the most ambitious schemes was Gilley Law in Sunderland, a suburb that was heavily redeveloped into a large council estate in the 1960s. Gilley Law was perhaps the closest thing Britain saw to a collectively heated Soviet company town. The estate's boiler was located in the nearby Silksworth Colliery, owned by the National Coal Board, and this pumped hot water to three thousand residents at a cost of ten shillings a week for a two-bedroom flat. The hot water was metered and charged to the Sunderland Corporation.[54] More ambitious plans were discussed but never implemented. In 1949, one planner even proposed that a speculative tunnel built under the English Channel could pool heat and hot water between the two countries during energy shortages.[55]

Britain's largest and most conspicuous district heating scheme serviced Churchill Gardens, a housing estate in Pimlico in West London that was developed in stages between 1946 and 1962 to replace a coil of terraced homes that had been partially damaged during the war. Heat and hot water for the scheme were provided by Battersea Power Station, an iconic municipal development built on the southern banks of the Thames in 1933. Surplus heat generated by the station was piped under the Thames in the form of hot water, which was stored in a 140-foot glass and steel silo that rose many feet above the tallest buildings on the estate. It was then piped out to the ten thousand residents of Churchill Gardens and Dolphin Square, a smaller private block of flats nearby. Prior to this arrangement, the power plant's surplus heat had been channeled directly into the river. The heating system amounted to a sealed circuit of energy shared between two state agencies: the nationalized British Electrical Authority, which owned the power plant, and Westminster City Council, which built the estate. The estate itself comprised a geometric row of nine-story buildings angled perpendicular to the Thames in order not to impede views of the river.

Like other large council estates built in the immediate postwar period, Churchill Gardens came with a raft of ancillary services, including four pubs, a handful of shops, a restaurant, a community center, playgrounds, a day nursery, and even a mortuary.[56] The development also included a large children's library, the shelves of which were heated by the system.[57] Residents paid a fixed weekly sum for heat and hot water, initially estimated to be eight shillings for a three-bedroom home, with the heat coming mostly from underfloor ducts. The system was active between 6:00 a.m. and 11:00 p.m. during the winter months and provided for a temperature of 65°F in the living rooms and 60°F in the bedrooms.[58] Residents had no way of controlling the heat that came into their homes—a fact that was occasionally a source of tension with the Westminster City Council. During a particularly cold May in 1960, a delegation of residents complained to the council that their heating had been turned off. The council refused to reactivate the heating, telling them that turning on the heat after it had been turned off was a slow and technical process.[59]

District heating schemes similar to Churchill Gardens were built throughout the country. Although few were connected so efficiently to nearby industry or municipal power plants, large centralized boilers that piped heat into tens, hundreds, or even thousands of households were commonplace in housing estates in the 1950s, 1960s, and 1970s. While the use of municipal heating systems such as those in the USSR that liberated entire cities from coal fires or individual boilers were never built in Britain, the experience of having heat pumped into your home from a distant source that you couldn't always control was something experienced by many of those who lived on large,

FIGURE 3.6. Churchill Gardens Estate. In the center of the picture you can
see the heat accumulator. Behind you can see Battersea Power Station, whose
surplus energy heated the estate. © RIBA Collections.

comprehensively planned housing estates. By the early 1980s, it was estimated
that two hundred thousand households on council estates had this arrangement in England and Wales alone.[60]

The high-density housing estate was a technical device for streamlining the
delivery of urban municipal services—an efficient means of plugging millions
of Britons into networks of plumbing, waste disposal, and energy. As the delegation from Sheffield's housing department quickly realized, the escalation
of scale had qualitative as well as quantitative effects. For nineteenth-century
social reformers, density was a major problem. They were haunted by fetid
shared toilets, cluttered stairwells, heavy bundles of coal dragged up multiple
flights of stairs, and long, freezing queues to access outdoor taps. For this reason, the utopias of early twentieth-century planners were mostly low rise. Yet
with the municipalization of housing and "networking" of homes came new
possibilities. The pooling of services, made possible by the density of planned
housing estates, allowed engineers and planners to imagine a new future where
the twin problems of domestic heating and industrial energy waste could be

solved in a vast, efficient network of subterranean pipes. Heat could be equally distributed beyond the control of any individual tenant. At its most extreme, this fantasy imagined that housing and industry would be mutually dependent, tied together for generations in a municipally enforced compact underwritten by abundant reserves of cheap energy. Like the subjects who were called into being by the shopping precincts described in the previous chapter, the consumers of this energy had needs that could be precisely anticipated. Decisions about when and how much their homes would be heated were proscribed from above. Although this future was never fully realized, a handful of spectacular spaces such as Churchill Gardens were built in the hope of its attainment. The most distinctive feature of the services provided on high-density estates, however, was that they were shared. Unlike the porous use of municipal services in transient inner-city neighborhoods or limitless suburban sprawls, the services on council estates were distributed among a fixed constituency of residents. It is to the communities that shared these services along with how they were conjured and imagined that this chapter now turns.

Community Building and Its Limits

In 1968, David Llewellyn, a former police officer of thirty years, traveled to a marshy construction site on the eastern fringes of London to begin his first day of work as a community development officer. His employer was the Greater London Council (GLC) and his place of work was the vast Thamesmead Estate, one of the largest and last high-density estates to be built in Britain. Thamesmead was a gigantic, theoretically self-sufficient development consisting of a three-dimensional tangle of soaring high-rise blocks, flat-roofed terraces, and geometrically planned lakes, built on a patch of wetland that used to house an arsenal belonging to the Ministry of Defense. Working out of a makeshift information center, Llewellyn's job was to organize the residents of this enormous behemoth into a functional and diverse community—a discrete and harmonious social unit that would effectively manage the dazzling array of services at its disposal. Having recently obtained a degree in social studies, Llewellyn had the qualifications to exercise this new kind of expertise.[61] With housing planned for sixty thousand residents, Thamesmead was to be one of the biggest experiments in residential community building undertaken in Britain. A year later, with the first forty families now living on the estate, Llewellyn hosted the inaugural meeting of the estate's community association, reportedly telling the assembled crowd, "There is no one waiting with open arms to greet you . . . you've got to be able to make friends with people." Pressed up against a remote bend in the Thames, poised atop the submerged remains of a rotting nineteenth-century arsenal, and surrounded by cranes and half-built towers, the first families to arrive must have felt profoundly dislocated. One tenant described the move as like "landing on the moon without a life support system."[62]

Thamesmead was positioned somewhere between a housing estate and a new town. It was a housing estate in that it was planned and implemented entirely by the GLC, with the majority of its housing stock made available to council tenants, but it was a new town in that it was intended to be a self-sufficient, almost autarkic settlement. The GLC attempted to provide employment for as many of the residents as possible within Thamesmead itself, mostly in a new industrial estate built by the council that was to employ as many as fifteen hundred people in light engineering and small-scale manufacturing jobs.[63] The GLC also built a small shopping precinct on the estate, simultaneously a source of employment and a further incentive for residents not to stray beyond Thamesmead's borders. Thamesmead was given its own primary and secondary schools, playgrounds, pubs, library, health clinic, churches of multiple denominations, nurseries, and many other services, clubs, and amenities. Some of these were provided by council planners; others were organized by groups of residents in houses, garages, churches, or function rooms dotted among the lakes, towers, and overhead walkways. For many in the 1960s, Thamesmead would have felt shockingly modern. A survey of the first 328 families to move to the estate showed that 17 percent had come from housing that had no indoor toilet.[64] True to form, Thamesmead came with an ambitious district heating system that provided heat and hot water, which was included in every household's rent and piped in from six subterranean gas-fired boilers, each the size of a double-decker bus.[65] As in Churchill Gardens, the residents had no control over how much heat was coming into their homes (although each household was given a booklet with advice on how to clean the taps and heated floor tiles).[66] The challenge facing Llewelyn and the GLC was how these waves of new families would live together in isolation on their patch of the riverbank.

Communities in twentieth-century Britain have been coveted, mysterious, and uncontainable entities, constantly slipping through the fingers of those who have tried to produce them. The term "community" has been forced to do wildly different kinds of work, from describing a preexisting, self-generating, and anthropologically discoverable bundle of social relations to being a functional means of representing corporate interests, something that can be planned for or constructed out of thin air. Nikolas Rose captures this tension between community as made or community as discovered, calling it a "third space" that "must . . . become the object and target for the exercise of political power whilst remaining, somehow, external to politics and a counterweight to it."[67] In the postwar decades in Britain, "community" was often the site where the universalist claims of welfare and citizenship were challenged along the lines of race or neighborhood.[68] There are abundant intellectual histories of the shifting meanings and political valences of "community," the term's application in nineteenth-century imperial ethnography, its contested mobilization by the New Left, and its use in Cold War international development, for example.[69] For the purposes of this chapter, I am interested in something quite specific: the relationship between "community" and the built environment, or, more specifically, the idea that isolated and comprehensively planned new estates could animate a richer form of associational life.[70] The use of new municipal housing estates to construct, manage, and agonize over new communities did not, of course, begin at Thamesmead. But Thamesmead is a useful case study because it marks the culmination of optimism about the production of community on housing estates and allows us to glimpse some of the ways that it began to unravel.

Early intellectual links between community and physical space appeared at the turn of the twentieth century amid concerns that the Industrial Revolution had produced a rootless society of strangers. We have already seen in this chapter how the mix of families, lodgers, and transient workers that populated the slums of the nineteenth century triggered the anxiety of social reformers. Howard's speculative garden city offered an early means of rationalizing, redistributing, and accounting for these strangers, allocating each one a cottage in an isolated and self-sufficient new town.[71] Unwin, who, as we saw in the previous chapter, was responsible for planning Britain's first garden city at Letchworth, imagined that his quadrangles of cottages would be accompanied by shared allotments, laundry rooms, bathhouses, and even kitchens so that tenants would learn "the advantage of association in domestic work."[72] Arguably the most influential theorist of the relationship between community and urban space between the wars, however, was Clarence Perry, a US architect and planner who worked for the city government of New York. Perry's most famous invention was the "neighborhood unit": the idea that planners should mold their towns and cities around discretely planned and self-sufficient pockets of houses and stores. Perry was critical of the large, sprawling, and intangible neighborhoods that appeared in places like New York City—spaces whose grid-patterned streets flowed ambiguously into adjoining neighborhoods and existed only in the minds of residents. He contended that neighborhood units had to be small and physically self-contained.[73] Perry's neighborhood unit became a feature of new town planning across the globe, chiming perfectly with the coming world of the automobile, with large arterial roads well suited for drawing the boundaries of these units. It was incorporated in many of the foundational planning documents of the 1940s, featuring in Abercrombie's *Greater London Plan*, the

"Final Report of the New Towns Committee," and the Ministry of Health's *Housing Manual 1944*.[74]

While Howard, Unwin, and to a lesser extent Perry were all haunted by the crowded courtyards and stairwells of rapid nineteenth-century urbanization, the new low-rise housing estates that spread throughout Britain between the wars produced a different timbre of anomie and loss. These new suburbs were seen to have torn slum dwellers from their familiar worlds and deposited them in formless neighborhoods where they were surrounded by strangers. The same journalists that decried interwar sprawl—writers such as Williams-Ellis and Priestley—looked at these new estates and saw two-story homes strung out like silent, lonely pearls for miles along empty roads. The potential social problems facing the millions of working-class former slum dwellers who were drafted into the large, new, low-rise suburbs were flagged by Britain's increasingly professionalized charitable institutions.[75] From 1919, the National Council of Social Service, a professional body that encompassed a variety of different voluntary organizations, began to pressure the government to provide communal services for the residents of these estates. Ten years later, this body would create the National Federation of Community Associations (originally named the New Estates Community Committee), a body that used various tactics to organize the residents of new working-class housing estates into communities. While this organization lamented the sterility of interwar estates, it was also optimistic about their capacity to produce rich communities. One report noted that "the New Estate is not merely a street of houses or a collection of streets of houses: it is a unit of social life. It may have been planned as a physical thing: it soon became . . . a spiritual thing."[76] By 1939, it was estimated that over seventy community schemes were in operation across the country.[77] One of the federation's biggest concerns was with the state-funded provision of community centers—multipurpose function rooms that would form the nucleus of communal life. To the body's delight, the 1936 Housing Act permitted local authorities to build such centers, although their uptake was relatively slow, and most centers continued to be built by churches or voluntary organizations. In 1944, the Ministry of Education renewed calls for municipal community centers. It argued that the recruitment of millions of Britons into the military during the war had naturalized a way of living that was collective and sociable and that could be replicated on peacetime housing estates.[78] While many postwar estates were built with function rooms for the community's use, the grand civic dreams of many campaigners who imagined giant palatial complexes were never fully realized—not least because investment in such centers was curtailed in 1948 due to a shortage of capital.[79]

By the early 1950s, the "neighborhood unit" was already being challenged by sociologists and new town planners who were increasingly skeptical that planned pockets of urban space could assimilate different classes or replicate the organic sociability of urban slums.[80] Nevertheless, a belief that human association could be encouraged by the physical properties of space continued to influence the construction of high-density estates throughout the 1950s and 1960s.[81] As we have seen, the Park Hill estate's wide-access decks and playgrounds were designed to re-create the vibrant street life and chance encounters that planners imagined existed in urban slums. As well as the new kinds of street life found in corridors or stairwells, high-density estates bound residents together with shared services, as they used and paid for the same heating pipes, elevators, playgrounds, and laundry rooms. Many of the modernist architects tasked with designing postwar council estates believed that the provision of generous amounts of communal space had a democratic function, supplying poor people with access to amounts of open space that had previously been the preserve of the rich.[82] The architects who won state building contracts boasted of their sociological talents, with an architect from one brutalist firm noting, "The moment the man or child steps outside his dwelling, here our responsibility starts."[83] As late as 1967, with language strangely resonant of contemporary critical theory, one government report on urban planning and community building summed up these ideas by stressing that "we are particularly critical of the view that 'the social' is a separate sphere which can be considered independently of physical planning and development."[84]

Meanwhile, communitarian voluntary organizations continued their work on council estates after the war. By 1964, the National Federation of Community Associations estimated that there were more than two thousand community organizations of some kind in Britain organized at a neighborhood level. On large council estates, these organizations existed to aid the work initiated by architectural determinism. The federation, with an almost Habermasian assurance, prided itself on its ability to construct organizations whose sole collective grounds for membership was proximity: "a community association is . . . a democratic fellowship of individuals and organizations bound together by one purpose—the common good." Despite these claims for inclusivity, the activities and spaces produced by community building were gendered in ways that reflected the divisions of household labor immediately after the war. A 1950 guide to the construction of community centers, for instance, recommended that they have two entirely separate functions: one for men engaging in "heavy crafts" and one for women engaging in "light crafts."[85] A 1954 advice manual for creating a women's club within a community organization recommended a list of activities that included crafts, cookery demonstrations, and "talks and discussions on methods of washing clothes."[86]

What's more, the communities that were to take shape on new high-density estates were mostly white. The modernizing promises of Britain's midcentury developmental state operated selectively. Many of the hundreds of thousands of nonwhite migrants to Britain from its former empire who arrived in the decades after the Second World War were either partially or fully excluded from its privileges—especially when it came to education, health care, social services, and housing.[87] Commonwealth migrants in the 1950s and 1960s, coming mostly from Britain's former colonies in the Caribbean and South Asia, tended to find housing by following networks of friends and family living in already-established urban communities. Many first-generation Commonwealth migrants settled in lodging houses owned either by private landlords or by their employers. Those who tried to rent on the private market were often at the mercy of white landlords, many of whom refused to accept black lodgers or tenants. Overwhelmingly, this migrant generation lived in precarious and overcrowded conditions, shaped by poverty and exclusion from other types of housing. In the early 1960s, compared with other city dwellers, Commonwealth migrants were five times more likely than nonmigrants to live in overcrowded housing without exclusive access to a stove or sink.[88]

Many planners were pessimistic that stable communities could be forged in mixed-race neighborhoods. This was particularly the case after the summer of 1958, which saw unrest among the black residents of Nottingham and in West London, provoked by violence from a hostile white population.[89] Two years after the disturbances, sociologist Ruth Glass published a high-profile study of London's West Indian population. Glass emphasized the antagonism faced by black migrants from teachers, employers, landlords, and trade unions and expressed concerns about the future of integration.[90] While mixed-race neighborhoods such as Notting Hill became subject to a raft of community development programs led by white welfare officers in the 1960s, these mostly attempted to manage preexisting tensions rather than construct fresh, interracial communities on brand-new estates. In this climate, "community" became the space in which racial antagonisms could be revealed and justified. In the words of Camilla Schofield and Ben Jones, community was "the organizing principle through which racism came to be written into British progressive thought and action after 1958."[91] The allocation of housing was an important area in which community was circumscribed by race. The idea that the presence of black tenants on new council estates would disrupt the production of stable, respectable communities was baked into the allocation policies of many local authorities in the 1960s and 1970s. Many housing departments were unwilling to test the "tolerance" of white residents on new estates. As one housing manager in the West Midlands put it, "I wouldn't put coloured people on a new estate mixed up with all the young couples. It's got to go slowly."[92]

Partly as a result of these attitudes, migrants to Britain struggled to gain access to newly built council estates in the first three decades after the Second World War. In 1961, just 4.3 percent of all Commonwealth migrants in the six largest cities in England and Wales were living in council housing, compared with 23 percent of all households.[93] Some of this disparity can be put down to an unwillingness to apply for housing, with many not wanting to leave the relative safety of their neighborhoods. In other instances, Commonwealth migrants found themselves at the bottom of waiting lists structured on a first-come, first-serve basis or or around family connections, or they were simply excluded by residency criteria imposed by municipal authorities.[94] Often, however, more direct forms of racism barred people of color from access to council housing. A 1965 government report on housing found that housing officers working in London were deliberately moving white Britons up on housing lists at the expense of people of color.[95] Migrant families were frequently discriminated against by white council officers, who would inspect families to ascertain their fitness for council housing. Reports by housing investigators were one of the most important factors deciding where an applicant would be placed on a waiting list for council housing in the 1960s. According to one investigation in the mid-1960s, these officials were often "baffled" and "biased" when faced with people of color and would "play it safe" by giving applicants low marks.[96] Those who were able to secure council housing were less likely to be housed in the new, modern, high-density estates that this chapter describes. People of color were disproportionately housed in dilapidated pre–World War II flats. As late as 1977, the proportion of nonwhite tenants living on estates built since 1961 was only half the figure for council tenants as a whole. In an investigation into housing practices in the East London borough of Hackney, the Commission for Racial Equality found that while 25 percent of white applicants were being awarded new housing, the equivalent figure for black applicants was just 3 percent.[97]

When black residents did secure housing on one of the new high-density council estates built between the mid-1950s and mid-1970s, they were often forced to live precarious, isolated lives surrounded by hostility. In the mid-1980s, the Commission for Racial Equality, a public body created by the 1976 Race Relations Act, began to gather evidence of racist violence on council estates. The commission's report, called *Living in Terror*, revealed that this was part of everyday life for many living on large estates; more than half of nonwhite tenants on estates in Glasgow, for example, were found to have been victims of racist graffiti. This violence was frequently enabled by the ignorance or sometimes complicity of housing officials and the police. Significantly, the report claimed that the architecture of the estates themselves, with their mix of public internal spaces, exacerbated the potential for violence.[98] Indeed, when people of color were housed in council housing, it tended to be in flats rather than homes.[99] The walkways, corridors, and courtyards that many architects believed would aid the production of communities instead left nonwhite residents visible and vulnerable.

In the first three decades after the war, then, new council estates were agents, sometimes unwittingly, in the reproduction of white supremacy.[100] When it came to housing, the production of new communities through the shared use of space had limits that were implicitly and explicitly enforced by white residents as well as housing officials. A series of race relations acts in 1965, 1968, and 1976 attempted to mitigate the housing crisis facing people of color in Britain, banning discrimination by private landlords and local councils. In the late 1970s, the Commission for Racial Equality began to call on local authorities to at least keep reliable statistics on race in the context of housing, as a starting point for improving access for nonwhite Britons to newer and better types of homes.[101] At this point, however, Britain's developmental state was beginning to ebb away, and mass council housing was on the verge of being dismantled by a Conservative government elected in 1979. As the next chapter will show, people of color began to be housed in significant numbers on high-density housing estates at around the same time that these estates started to be seen as spaces of last resort for Britain's poorest and most precarious citizens, rather than long-term homes for a broad segment of the population.

Thamesmead is an ideal place to see planners experiment with the alchemy of community, proximity, and race. In 1974, the GLC produced a brief film, *Living at Thamesmead*, to advertise life on the new estate. The film follows the movements of a young teenage couple, dressed in flares, as they move around the estate, visiting social clubs, football games, and the politely staffed "information centre," and watching the arrival of new residents. Along with a more straightforward informational film produced in 1970, *Living at Thamesmead* shows the residents, recently strangers to each other, forming a bustling community on the development's soaring walkways and stairwells.[102] Those in charge of Thamesmead hoped to use the estate's material fabric to, in the words of one report, "prove that a living, organic community could be produced from the drawing board."[103] Its self-sufficiency as well as relative isolation from the rest of the city would enhance what the planners optimistically referred to as a "sense of belonging." Despite the enormity of the development, it was envisioned that the estate would act as a single, identifiable unit "by linking together areas that might otherwise become separate neighborhoods with spines of flats."[104] It was a community that was engineered to span time as well as space. The GLC experimented with keeping a separate list of homes on reserve for the children or elderly parents of residents, aiming to establish a continuity of residency across generations. In the final scene of *Living at*

FIGURE 3.7. New residents congregate on an elevated walkway at Thamesmead, 1971. London Metropolitain Archives (City of London).

Thamesmead, the young teenage couple arrive at the estate's information center and tentatively ask to have their names put down for a flat of their own on the estate.[105]

The communal features of Thamesmead's physical environment were helped along by an exhaustive array of community organizations, some funded directly by the GLC and others spontaneously forming among the estate's residents. The most significant and official of these groups was the GLC-funded Thamesmead Community Association (TCA), emerging in 1969 among the initial group of residents. In its first year, the TCA's organizers would canvass door-to-door several times a week to greet new residents and invite them to meetings. At its peak, the TCA recruited approximately five thousand dues-paying members, making it one of the largest estate-based community groups in the country. The centerpiece of Thamesmead's communal infrastructure was the Pyramid social club, whose popularity among residents was enhanced by the installation of a pub at Llewellyn's behest—an

FIGURE 3.8. Thamesmead canteen, 1973. London Metropolitain Archives (City of London).

apparently controversial decision for some members of the GLC who equated good estate management with temperance.[106] Another important space for community building was the club room, which hosted diverse activities. A collection of photographs of the club room taken in 1973 shows groups of women predominantly involved in sewing and pottery classes, while groups of young men were taught car repair and woodwork.[107] The club room also had a canteen where residents could eat meals together. Moreover, the estate had a newspaper, *Insight*, with multiple pages of news, adverts, and letters. Thamesmead's most ambitious collective endeavor, though, was perhaps its radio station, founded in 1978 and operating out of a small spare room in one of the estate's churches. The station was one of seven experimental community radio programs sponsored by the Home Office.[108]

Thamesmead's developers consciously equated community with diversity. A 1974 report expressed a hope that the estate would "reflect the structure . . . of London as a whole" by providing housing for "a fair cross section of society."[109] In this instance, "diversity" referred only to family size, age, and class.

FIGURE 3.9. A dance class in Thamesmead's club room, 1973. London Metropolitain Archives (City of London).

To this end, a handful of apartments were reserved for tenants who were will-ing to pay higher rents, and some were even made available for outright pur-chase from the council. Although most of Thamesmead's residents were mov-ing from London boroughs with high concentrations of Commonwealth migrants, this fact did not feature in early attempts at community building.[110] Indeed, based on reports from elsewhere about the subtle racism exercised by housing departments, we can perhaps speculate that some nonwhite appli-cants to Thamesmead may have fallen afoul of the rigorous way in which po-tential residents were vetted. Those who applied to be on the waiting list to move to Thamesmead were subjected to systematic inspections to make sure that they had a good housing record. One GLC officer is quoted as saying, perhaps with some hyperbole, that he would visit "their home, to see whether by 10 o'clock in the morning the washing up was done, the beds were made and the baby's nappies rinsed."[111]

Like many other housing departments, the GLC did not keep any statistical records on the racial composition of Thamesmead in its early years. In 1971, the GLC conducted an extensive survey of the first thousand residents of the estate, gathering data on employment, family size, age, and previous address. Absent was any information on race.[112] By the early 1980s, there was some evidence that the demographic composition of Thamesmead was shifting, with implications for the kinds of services provided by community groups. During that time, the Thamesmead Multi-Cultural Funfield organization was founded by a group of young residents to, in their words, "promote better community relations and foster racial harmony" on the estate. Thamesmead was also used to settle Vietnamese refugees, who on arrival, reportedly suffered from language problems and high rates of unemployment. Although the initial data collected on the estate neglected to count the numbers of nonwhite residents, an early, albeit extremely partial glimpse into the racial composition of Thamesmead comes via a 1986 survey conducted by the estate's new librarian. Of 312 self-selecting respondents, just 6 percent identified as an "ethnic minority."[113] As on other council estates, the early years of Thamesmead were marred by racist violence. In an interview, Robert Dyer, a black resident of Thamesmead, remembered being the only black person in his school year in the mid-1970s and talked of a conspicuous National Front presence on the estate.[114] Racist violence on the estate reached its peak in 1991 with the horrific murder of Rolan Adams, a fifteen-year-old black boy who was stabbed to death by a white gang as he was leaving the estate's youth club.

Thamesmead's planners were reluctant to imagine or construct a successful multiracial vision of the social. What's more, by the time the first families began settling in Thamesmead, the idea that planners could construct community out of little more than proximity and enthusiasm was in retreat across Britain. A new definition of "community" as something organic and spontaneous, something to be discovered rather than made, had started to emerge. As opposed to constructing new communities out of thin air, the role of experts and planners was increasingly to encourage the participation of preexisting communities of residents in planning decisions.[115] Meanwhile, the 1960s and 1970s saw the arrival of community arts, community publishing, community organizing, and community architecture, each of which in different ways emerged as a democratic critique of state power. This period also saw black residents of places like Notting Hill reclaim the language of community to become synonymous with black political autonomy.[116] Council estates were another instance in which race tested the limits of the universalist claims of the postwar developmental state. The social, no longer imagined to be a homogeneous totality, could not be planned for in quite the same way.[117]

In 1968, when Llewellyn first set foot in the estate's show home, he heard an ominous squelching noise underfoot. It was raining heavily outside, and water was seeping into the house, saturating the brand-new gray carpet.[118] This was the first recorded instance of a problem that would haunt the earliest residents of Thamesmead and form the basis of a new conception of community on the estate. Chronic dampness blighted the lives of the estate's first settlers, with more than a third of the residents reporting some kind of rain penetration. The residents widely believed that their complaints to the GLC about this problem went unheard. Taking advantage of the hordes of architectural tourists who visited the estate each year, residents printed out and distributed a thousand placards reading "we've got damp" to be publicly displayed. The posters provoked an immediate response, forcing the GLC to hire a technical crew to study the causes of the dampness. In the words of one journalist, this campaign, "paradoxically . . . may have been the making of Thamesmead as a living community." More so than the expansive public space, regular community meetings, or boozy social club, the "we've got damp" campaign was cited by the editor of *Insight* as the reason why Thamesmead has "more community spirit than any other GLC estate."[119] While Thamesmead was arguably one of the most intensive experiments in residential community building ever conducted by an organ of the British state, its outcome was ultimately spontaneous and unknowable, making unanticipated claims on the fabric of its new environment.

Like a snowball rolling downhill through the twentieth century, increasing in size and density, the council estate became an ever-more-complex arrangement of architectural, infrastructural, and sociological parts. Like the industrial estate and shopping precinct, it was an urban form that offered new technical and social possibilities for Britain's midcentury developmental state—possibilities that were latent in the qualities of the space itself. In 1963, a few years before he would become a lead consultant for the master plan of the new town of Milton Keynes, US urban theorist Melvin Webber argued that the world had entered an age of "community without propinquity," and space and physical proximity were an increasingly irrelevant aspect of the daily lives of city dwellers.[120] In tracing the emergence of the British council estate and showing the work that this unique type of space came to do by the end of the 1970s, this chapter suggests otherwise. The high-density council estate was an experiment in physical proximity, conducted under carefully controlled conditions among a mostly white social body. The estates provided housing for millions, but they also went a step further, making possible the provision of new kinds of residential services while allowing architects, the state, and voluntary organizations to imagine new ways for people to live together. As council estates networked their residents into municipal systems of provision, the line between public and private space became increasingly fixed. No longer would flat dwellers traipse upstairs to pee or downstairs to gather water. No longer would they have to carry bags of coal and ash up and down flights of stairs, clear clogged chimneys, or sweep and mop tenement corridors under threat of eviction. Under these circumstances, the social relationships between tenants could be fostered rather than feared, and the shifting human lava unleashed by the volcanic disturbances of nineteenth-century urbanization could cool into igneous islands of community.

Reading the publicity material for estates like Thamesmead, Park Hill, or Churchill Gardens, it is easy to fancy that these spaces solved, once and for all, problems of deprivation in a blaze of modernity. It is impossible to imagine that they could have failed, just as it is impossible to imagine that they ever existed. Their success, however, depended on a delicate blend of aggressive municipal strength, economic growth, racial exclusivity, and an optimism that communities could be produced by politics, rather than the other way around. Without these four elements, as we will see in the next chapter, housing estates were like ancient and delicate works of art that appear impressive from a distance yet crumble immediately to the touch.

4

The Private Housing Estate

COUNCIL HOUSING arrived after decades of gestation. It emerged over the course of more than sixty years, as philanthropic tenement blocks gave way to suburban new towns and tall tower blocks, built in carefully planned estates. Its death was comparatively fast. In the 1960s and 1970s, local authorities were building an average of 157,000 new council homes each year. By the first decade of the 2000s, this figure had fallen to just 23,000.[1] In 1980, roughly one in three English households was owned by local authorities.[2] By 2017, this figure had fallen to less than one in ten.[3] Much of this collapse was due to the 1980 Housing Act, passed in the first full year of Thatcher's premiership. The act simplified the ability of council tenants to purchase their homes from the state and financially incentivized those who did. While the tenants of state housing had been able to purchase their homes before 1980, doing so had been a lengthy and expensive process. In the six years after the act was passed, close to 800,000 council houses were purchased by their occupants.[4] This chapter looks at what became of the council estate as the sizable class of people renting their homes from local councils ebbed away.

We have already seen how the council estate streamlined the provision of new kinds of residential services in ways that transformed the relationship between housing, the state, and the individual. After 1980, housing estates continued to exist in massive numbers, but they were no longer expected to produce these technical and social outcomes. As the Housing Act enabled residents to purchase their flats from the council, it became commonplace for council tenants to be living next door to private residents who owned their flats, sharing elevators, corridors, and heating systems. Many new homeowners demanded the right to audit the service charges that they were paying to councils, refusing to pay for services that they personally felt did not benefit them and in the process undermining the collective logic that guided council estates in the first place. It became clear that council estates were architecturally unsuitable for private ownership. They were networked into the city in ways that could not be undone overnight. In order to sell off the hundreds of thousands of flatted homes on housing estates across Britain, local authorities went to war with reluctant mortgage brokers, collective heating systems, and an urban fabric of high-density public space that was engineered to produce a feeling of communal ownership. The first argument that I want to make in this chapter, therefore, is about the relative *endurance* of the council estate and the way that it marked the outer limit of Britain's emerging property-owning democracy. With the stubborn persistence of thousands of high-density housing estates, places that were designed for public ownership and communal management, the British built environment became like an orchestra whose instruments were all playing different tunes.

Meanwhile, faith in the ability of the built environment to automatically create, under the correct material conditions, tight-knit new communities began to wane. In the 1970s and 1980s, a new kind of criminology of the built environment started to emerge. Increasingly, on both sides of the Atlantic, it was argued that high crime rates were the result of opportunity rather than inequality, and thus cities could be planned in ways that "design out" crime. The large courtyards and walkways intended to form communities out of the raw material of strangers were suddenly suspect. In the name of crime reduction, these spaces were fenced off or demolished, their communal promise coming under intellectual and political fire. By the late 1980s, many were maintaining that council estates were not just shabby, aesthetically displeasing, or a waste of government money. They also ran contrary to an innate aspect of our human condition—one that strives permanently toward privacy and security. This chapter will follow the career of Alice Coleman, an urban planner who critiqued council estates along these lines and in doing so caught the attention of the Thatcher government, winning funding in the 1980s to redesign many large estates. Relatedly, the second argument I want to make in this chapter is that the denigration of council estates, something that feels commonsensical to many Britons alive today, was partially the outcome of a realignment among psychology, criminology, and urban planning that occurred in the 1980s.

The final part of this chapter looks at the birth of a new urban form in Britain: the private housing estate. I use this term to refer to any large residential building or group of residential buildings that are owned by the same private developer, planned as a totality, and to which access is available only to residents. This includes gated residential communities, private blocks of flats, and the skeletal remains of former council estates that have been transformed beyond recognition. These spaces became common in the last two decades of the twentieth century. Here, the council estate was reimagined to suit a new political, technical, and criminological settlement. They were, and continue to be, spaces intended to design out crime, where the provision of services is individuated and audited, and where buildings are constructed, owned, and policed by property developers instead of by the state. The chapter will explore the growth of these developments in East and South London in the 1980s along with the records of private residents' associations to see the new ways in which "communities" were imagined to exist in such spaces. My final argument, then, is about how we should understand privatization in the context of housing. Unlike the spectacular overnight sell-offs of state-owned infrastructure companies such as British Gas, British Telecom, and British Rail by successive Conservative governments in the 1980s and 1990s, the privatization of council estates was a messy and drawn-out affair. While legislation was crucial, privatization was also dependent on the day-to-day tactics of residents and planners who were securing as well as surveilling public space, disaggregating communal charges and lobbying for mortgages, in both public and private developments.

Only Disconnect

On a spring morning in 1968, Britons awoke to images of the Ronan Point tower block in East London, framed against the dawn sky, with a thick stripe of smoking rubble running along its exterior. A gas explosion in a resident's kitchen had torn through a load-bearing wall, leading the above flats to concertina downward, killing four and injuring seventeen. In the years that followed, the event became a synecdoche for the failures of cheap, system-built residential tower blocks, prompting a government inquiry that in turn cast doubt on the safety of the construction methods. Although Ronan Point is widely remembered as marking the end of high-density estate building in Britain, this isn't quite the case. While construction of tower blocks peaked in Britain in the late 1960s, some local authorities continued to build high-density housing until well into the 1970s.[5] By the early 1980s, there were perhaps as many as 1.6 million flatted council homes in England alone.[6] While some of these flats would have been above shops or in older, stand-alone blocks, a significant number were located on estates that by the time of Thatcher's election in 1979 were only a few years old.

The 1980 Housing Act gave almost every possible incentive for council tenants to purchase their own homes. This policy marked the culmination of a generation of strategic and philosophical debates within the Conservative Party about its response to increasing working-class affluence and owner occupation.[7] Those who had been tenants for more than three years were given a 33 percent discount on their home's market rate—a discount that rose to a maximum of 50 percent (increasing to 70 percent in some cases after 1986). Tenants were also offered a 100 percent mortgage and the option to have the value of their homes fixed for two years if they wanted to defer purchase.

While Thatcher's government struggled to reduce the overall size of the state, this is one area where she succeeded, effecting a 34 percent cut in capital spending on housing during the first six years of her administration.[8] The "right to buy" was offered to the tenants of council flats as well as those in freestanding homes—something that Thatcher herself would emphasize in the House of Commons during her first year in office.[9] All of a sudden, many of the large council estates, the spaces whose emergence was described in the previous chapter, were split between private owners and tenants of the state. Some local authorities, seeking to unload large amounts of housing stock, launched aggressive campaigns to market flatted homes to council residents. Wandsworth, a borough in southwest London, for example, which was governed by a right-wing Conservative leadership from 1978, oversaw one of the biggest sales of council flats anywhere in Britain.[10] In 1988, Paul Beresford, the Conservative leader of the council, bragged that his borough had sold over ten thousand of these dwellings, with 60 percent of them in high-rise flats.[11] In 1984, the five thousandth sale of a Wandsworth council home was marked by a highly publicized event, attended by a minister from the Department of the Environment. The council used various methods to facilitate the sale of flats, including establishing a "Home Ownership Unit" that held regular meetings with residents on large estates.[12] Targeted letters were sent to individuals living on estates that were earmarked for sale. One example read:

> Like a lot of Wandsworth tenants you've probably always wanted to own your own home. . . . Just take a look around you—already 21% of tenants on the Chatham Estate have taken up our offer and bought their own homes. . . . You will be joining the happy band of owner-occupiers on the Chatham Estate, each secure in the knowledge that their growing numbers are raising the standard of the area—and the value of their investment.[13]

The sale of flats was a messy affair, revealing the limits of the new culture of homeownership that emerged in the late twentieth century. By the mid-1980s, places like the Ethalburga Estate in Wandsworth, where roughly a hundred privately renting households shared tower blocks and courtyards with more than five hundred tenants of the local authority, became a silent front in a war between two different visions of the British state.[14] Although these problems touched the face of almost every British city, they were particularly prevalent in London, where high-density council estates were common. The main battle lines, as we will see, were fought over heating networks, service charges, and access to mortgages.

As the previous chapter of this book showed, high-density housing estates allowed for novel systems of distributing heat and hot water. Most residents of large council estates were plugged into large heating networks over which they sometimes had little control. These ranged from the vast, neighborhood-wide systems of central heating that were linked to nearby industry or utility plants, such as those servicing the Churchill Gardens estate in Pimlico or Gilley Law in Sunderland, to the more common method of using a handful of central boilers, maintained by the council, to provide heating for all flats on a single estate. As we have seen, one report estimated that in the early 1980s, close to two hundred thousand local authority homes were served by such methods in England and Wales alone.[15] While many tenants on estates with district heating had their flats fitted with individual thermostats, allowing them to have control over their heating, others had no control over the supply. Therefore, when residents purchased their council flats under the right to buy, many were buying homes that were integrated into complex district heating networks that continued to serve council tenants.

Many of the first generation of private occupants immediately demanded the right to disconnect their newly purchased flats from these networks and install their own boilers. This prompted a crisis that was solved in different ways by different local authorities. The London boroughs of Hounslow and Islington, for example, favored allowing new homeowners to disconnect from collective heating systems and install their own. Indeed, Hounslow even offered to remove council-owned heating equipment free of charge. This was unusual, however. In housing developments managed by the Greater London Council, residents who had exercised their right to buy were forbidden from disconnecting from communal systems and forced to continue to pay charges for heating (and in many instances were unable to control the flow of heat to their homes). There were even fears that mass disconnection from collective heating systems could be dangerous, with added pipes leading to structural problems in tower blocks. Faced with such high numbers of flat sales, Wandsworth Council, for example, was compelled to ban most private tenants from disconnecting from collective heating systems because of the impracticality of running large boilers serving decreasing numbers of tenants.[16] In the contracts drawn up between Wandsworth and purchasers of flats, residents were required to sign a document agreeing not to waste heat and hot water.[17] Despite Wandsworth's zealous commitment to private ownership in the 1980s, the council still found itself taking on managerial roles for heat provision as well as other aspects of maintenance and repairs on estates in which home-owning residents were becoming the majority.

The same was true for the Churchill Gardens Estate. As we saw in the last chapter, Churchill Gardens, a large housing estate built in the mid-1950s in South London, was heated by the surplus energy generated by the nearby Battersea Power Station. Despite an almost 40 percent increase in the system's cost due to the effects of the 1973 oil crisis, the district heating network was still in place by the early 1980s. Although the City of Westminster's council, like Wandsworth's, was zealous in its attempts to sell its housing stock to tenants, the council was unable to justify the replacement of Churchill Garden's heating system with individual boilers. Even in 1983, when Battersea Power Station closed, the council made a decision to retain the system and built a new coal-fired boiler to generate its heat. The system is still in place today.[18]

What's more, a subsequent problem with the sale of flats on large council estates emerged when it came to charging residents for collectively provided services. While most council residents in mass housing estates would have paid a fixed "service charge," including the heat, maintenance, and cleaning (among other services) provided across the estate, the sale of individual flats disrupted the collective logic that made these charges possible. Would a theoretical private tenant have to pay for maintaining the elevator services in adjacent tower blocks, for example? Speaking to an audience of local government officials around the time of the 1980 act, a Department of the Environment official declared that this was "a new problem to all Local Authorities" and noted that they were entering uncharted territory.[19] This question was analyzed at length by a legal team commissioned by the London borough of Southwark. The team concluded that service charges had to be adjusted for each circumstance.[20] In other words, local councils would have to reassess the cost of heat and maintenance on a block-by-block, floor-by-floor basis—a challenge to the way that most housing departments had operated since the mid-twentieth century. This fact was greeted with dismay by housing department authorities faced with the task of reassessing the service charges paid by tens of thousands of residents on an individual basis.[21]

On many part-privatized estates, management issues became topics of dispute between councils and residents of different tenure status. In Wandsworth, it was reported that some private owners had formed their own "leaseholders" association representing only the interests of the private tenants on the estate and acting independently of the tenant associations that organized council residents.[22] One family on an estate in the new town of Crawley who had bought their flat wrote to the Department of the Environment to complain that management of their estate was falling between the cracks:

> Where there is a block of flats (such as here) where there are tenants and purchasers, should not the purchasers have a say in the running of the site? In my particular case the whole place has changed from a "show place" to a dirty untidy site with the minimum amount of attention given by the Council. No longer have we a permanent Caretaker or regular ground worker, but "casual Council labour."[23]

This problem was compounded by the fact that under the 1980 Housing Act, private tenants had the right to audit the service charges that they were subject to and mount a legal challenge if what they saw was unsatisfactory. As well as applying to the inhabitants of private blocks of flats, this right was enjoyed by those who purchased flats on housing estates on the private market (or those renting from those who had done so). As many pointed out, including Labour members of Parliament, this meant that property owners by virtue of their tenancy alone had greater rights than their next-door neighbors living in identical apartments. George Cunningham, the Labour member of Parliament for Islington South and Finsbury, a constituency with many large, semi-privatized estates, campaigned for council tenants to be given the same right as their homeowner neighbors to audit the service charges that they were paying to local authorities.[24] It is likely that Cunningham's objections were intended to defend the interests of an increasingly subordinate class of council tenants. Yet the demand for the right of tenants to audit as well as contest each item on their service charge further contributed to the unbundling and segmentation of once-collective services on high-density estates during this period. By the mid-1980s, the political compact between tenants and housing departments, where services were provided en masse for fixed rates that were standardized across local authorities, was breaking apart under these new pressures.

Meanwhile, the Housing Act was creating bigger problems. While the act stipulated that council tenants exercising the "right to buy" would be offered mortgages worth 100 percent of the value of their home, it quickly became clear that building societies, the financial institutions that provide mortgages in Britain, were unwilling to lend to those living in tower blocks. To the government's frustration, this proved a major early obstacle to the sale of council flats. By 1982, there were reports that some mortgage providers were refusing on principle to offer mortgages to those living in blocks where council tenants also lived.[25] The leader of Tower Hamlets Council expressed his annoyance that despite government pressure to sell flats, building societies were refusing to lend to flat dwellers in his borough unless they had proof that the flat would be sold again on the private market.[26] This problem persisted throughout the 1980s. As late as 1987, Halifax, a large building society, wrote to the Department of the Environment to note that even though Halifax had "supported Right to Buy since its inception," in its opinion, "high rise and deck access blocks . . . would not necessarily form satisfactory securities for mortgage purposes."[27] Their objections were grounded in a critique of the physical environments of estates, with Halifax citing "a lack of desire to live in high rise estates," "the high cost of maintenance of common parts," and "difficulty of maintaining security in common parts." Halifax's report claimed that "as a home owner, the occupier becomes master of his own environment whereas a flat owner is dependent on outside factors."[28] Despite the fact that housing loans from banks increased tenfold in the decade after 1978, a period that saw an increasing overlap between the roles of building societies and banks, many of those living on council estates did not have access to this new glut of capital.[29]

While the hostility of mortgage lenders to those who wished to buy flats on high-density council estates depressed the numbers of sales, an even bigger problem emerged when the first generation of tenants who bought homes in council flats tried to sell them. Even as late as the early 1990s, these former tenants found it almost impossible to locate building societies willing to provide potential new buyers with a mortgage. In 1992, one frustrated government official, using language taken from the racially discriminatory mortgage practices that produced segregated urban neighborhoods in the United States, implied that mortgage lenders were "redlining" high-density estates.[30] Shortly afterward, there were reports that the Chelsea Building Society was automatically turning down any applications from residents of a block that was not more than 60 percent owner occupied.[31] Later that year, a fleet of coaches full of right-to-buy owners on large estates who had been unable to resell their flats and were facing escalating service charges descended on Hammersmith Town Hall to draw attention to their situation.[32] It was estimated that there were three thousand flat owners in Wandsworth alone who were in a similar bind.[33]

For all the above reasons, the government faced intractable problems when it encouraged local authorities to sell off their stock of high-density council housing. Throughout the 1980s and into the 1990s, sales of flats under right to buy were a tiny percentage of the overall sales. Of the hundreds of thousands of flatted homes in England, just 49,000 had been sold by the end of 1987, compared with 865,000 houses. Flats therefore comprised just 5 percent of all sales, despite making up more than a third of English council homes.[34] What's more, these sales were concentrated mostly in a handful of London boroughs such as Wandsworth. By 1985, for example, Birmingham City Council had sold just 314 of its 55,372 flats.[35]

There were moves to address the poor sales of flats with subsequent legislation in 1986 and 1988, which gave councils the power to rehouse the residents of a single estate and paved the way for entire developments to be off-loaded. Sometimes these estates were sold to property developers, many of whom spent more than the purchase price on renovations such as new heating and security systems that would turn flats into desirable assets safe for homeownership.[36] More often, however, what was left of Britain's public housing stock was transferred to housing associations: nonprofit organizations that blurred the line between state and nonstate ownership. These organizations could borrow money to fund desperately needed repairs without the debts showing up

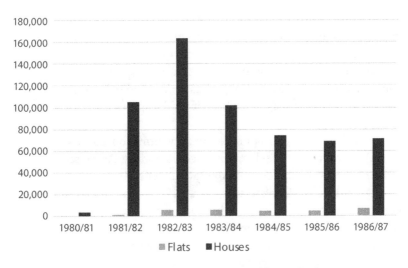

FIGURE 4.1. Local authority homes sold in England.

on the balance sheets of local authorities. In 1985, housing associations owned just 13 percent of Britain's nonprivate housing. By 2007, they owned more than half.[37]

Various attempts were made to dismantle the thousands of vast, state-owned housing complexes that had emerged over the previous thirty years. In the first instance, local authorities and residents, with the political and legal support of the Conservative government, attempted to cleave individual flats from their collective fabric and transform them into financial instruments. The results were largely a failure. With their generous amounts of public space, communal heating systems, and undifferentiated service charges, dense council estates resisted the logic of private ownership. If one of the aims of Thatcher's government was to create a "property owning democracy" that tied new homeowners to the low-tax and small-state policies of the party, then council estates marked the frontier of this experiment.[38] Or to put it another way, while the last third of the century witnessed a massive growth in private debt, ranging from mortgages to credit cards to student loans, these spaces were beyond the horizon of this newly liquid world.

Secured by Design

Council estates were built during a brief period of optimism, shared by politicians and planners, that groups of strangers, uprooted from slums, could be turned into communities of friends and neighbors. As we saw in the last chapter, this hopefulness was reflected in the architecture of many large council estates, whose inward-facing courtyards, wide-access decks, and shared amenities were intended to enable the work of community formation. As new methods of allocating housing from the late 1970s onward clashed with right-to-buy initiatives, these attempts to theorize and repackage the social body floundered. The collective social promise embodied in high-density estates became increasingly suspect, and their public spaces were carved up and reassembled.

As vehicles of modernization, community formation, and social mobility, council estates operated selectively, excluding many. As we saw in the last chapter, many state-sponsored attempts to generate communities out of strangers in shared residential space operated with an implicit expectation that these communities would be mostly or entirely white. A new Race Relations Act in 1976, along with high-profile investigations into housing departments carried out by the Commission for Racial Equality, compelled local authorities to begin remedying the unequal way that people of color had been treated by housing departments.[39] This important civil rights victory occurred just a few years before council estates were privatized and reimagined under a new Conservative government. It also took place at the same time as new legislation in 1977 forced local authorities to house people who had previously been deemed too young, old, or ill for council housing. These measures meant that by the late 1970s and 1980s, council housing was increasingly being allocated on the basis of need rather than the length of time spent on waiting lists. The result was an intensification of the "residualization" of Britain's remaining council estates—a term used to describe the process by which council housing became an option of last resort, housing only those deemed to be in precarious living situations owing to extreme poverty or other issues such as illness.[40] Residualization was most likely to happen on high-density council estates that, for reasons described above, were difficult to privatize and thus increasingly formed the sole remnants of council housing stock after the 1980 Housing Act. Thus, within ten years of legislation aimed at redressing the structural exclusion of people of color from modern housing estates, high-density council estates had come to be redefined as a safety net for the poor instead of a long-term option for a significant portion of the population.[41]

In a controversial study of early 2000s council housing in East London, Geoff Dench, Kate Gavron, and Michael Young blamed needs-based housing allocation for disrupting the supposedly stable working-class communities that council housing was meant to serve. Their argument was predicated on the notion that high-quality state housing was a gift to white working-class communities as part of an implicit midcentury social contract to reward them for their contribution to the Second World War. They contended that the change in allocation strategies, which improved the access of people of color to council housing, had "ridden over the existing local community's assumptions about their ownership of public resources."[42] As other commentators have noted, this is an argument that overlooks the informal exclusion of Commonwealth migrants from different parts of the welfare state as well as the substantial contributions that were made in the war effort by imperial subjects.[43] It also fails to account for the added pressures placed on housing departments by the introduction of right to buy. As we have already seen above, the mass sell-off of low-rise homes coupled with the difficulty faced by councils that attempted to sell individual flats meant that high-density housing estates were increasingly all that remained of the public housing stock. In the rest of this chapter, I will show how the supposedly stable communities that Dench, Gavron, and Young claimed were being threatened by the opening up of council housing to people of color were in fact being undermined by a set of processes that were both more technical and more profound.

While there was no shortage of those making arguments against high-density housing in the 1960s and 1970s, most of these assertions were specific and partial. There were many who, for example, accused particular estates of being shabby or ugly, or maintained that they were isolating their residents in urban peripheries.[44] While many recognized specific problems of provision, upkeep, and safety, few were contending that high-density social housing per se was to blame. Indeed, some early surveys of residents were mostly positive. At Park Hill, for instance, only 7 percent of those asked were critical of the appearance of the estate. In a 1955 survey of families in a London tower block, 90 percent of people living above the fifth floor said that they liked living there and did not wish to go lower.[45] When planners and early residents expressed doubts about the suitability of tower blocks, these questions tended to apply more to particular groups, such as families with young children.[46] In the 1970s and 1980s, however, a new avenue of critique emerged that served to denigrate all forms of mass public housing and further enable privatization. This critique was initiated by a new generation of criminologists and psychologists whose attacks on housing estates were not grounded in politics but rather in biological determinism or rational actor theories of human behavior.

The intellectual origins of this critique lie with a New York–based urban planner named Oscar Newman. In 1972, Newman published his research into the living conditions of the tenants of the New York Public Housing Authority. Framed within the context of a perceived transatlantic crime wave, Newman argued that the high levels of crime recorded in US cities was a result of the uprooting of neighborly communities and their placement in hostile and artificial urban environments:

The crime problems facing urban America will not be answered through increased police force or firepower. We are witnessing a breakdown of social mechanisms that once kept crime in check and gave direction and support to police activity. The small-town environments, rural or urban, which once framed and enforced their own moral codes, have virtually disappeared. . . . In our society there are few instances of shared beliefs or values among physical neighbors. Although this heterogeneity may be intellectually desirable, it has crippled our ability to agree on the action required to maintain the social framework necessary to our continual survival.[47]

These ideas had resonances of the assertions of the influential 1960s US urbanist Jane Jacobs. Jacobs argued that urban crime could be abated in situations where crowded streets produced informal forms of surveillance—"eyes on the street"—among concerned neighbors and passersby.[48] Newman's contentions also echoed British sociologists Michael Young and Peter Willmott, who criticized 1950s slum clearance programs in London for breaking up traditional working-class communities.[49] What was lost as a result of this uprooting, according to Newman, was not a sense of community but rather a sense of individual ownership over space. Without this feeling, the collectively managed stairwells, corridors, and courtyards of high-density housing projects were concrete incubators of crime, alienation, and mutual suspicion.[50]

These problems could be ameliorated by a variety of architectural interventions, from decreasing the number of entrances shared by large developments to subdividing communal walkways and placing them under the ownership of a small number of apartments. To fully solve the problem, however, Newman maintained that the entire concept of high-density living would have to be jettisoned. Citing examples from ancient Rome and sub-Saharan Africa, Newman argued that "defensible space" was not unique to the urban environment of 1970s New York; instead, it was something ancient and essential.[51] Problems with large housing projects, according to Newman, were not due to the shabbiness of construction techniques. Nor were these spaces only suitable for those without children (as 1960s and 1970s researchers feared). Rather, such projects were fundamentally *unnatural*. Breaking with theories of residential planning in the United States and Britain that stressed "habitat" as an ecological system capable of molding and reforming its inhabitants, Newman was among the first and most influential to suggest that humans' relationship with space was governed by "territoriality"—a term, originating in zoology, that described a prevalence for the construction and defense of parcels of private space.[52] Britain was first exposed to Newman's ideas through a 1974 BBC documentary, *The Writing on the Wall*, in which Newman visited the Aylesbury

THE PRIVATE HOUSING ESTATE   119

Estate, still under construction in South London, and predicted that within a few years it would be a hotbed of crime.

Newman's concept of defensible space had much in common with a new form of criminology that emerged in the 1970s and become known as "situational crime prevention." Criminologists in this vein argued that crime was about opportunity.[53] It was an approach that focused less on measures that would ameliorate poverty or treat mental illness and more on unlocked doors and poorly overlooked streets.[54] Let us say, for example, that a bike has been stolen. Traditional mid-twentieth-century criminologists would likely have begun their inquiries with a set of questions about the possible criminal: Were they immoral? Were they poor? What was their race, gender, or social class? Situational criminologists, however, would likely ask questions about the bike: How strong was its lock? How expensive was it? Was it chained up on a well-lit street? Rather than making the kinds of anthropological claims associated with earlier generations of criminologists, academics such as C. Ray Jeffery in the United States and Ron Clarke in Britain argued that criminals were rational individuals who were maximizing the opportunities afforded to them. While Jeffery spent his career seeking a neuroscientific basis for the link between crime rates and certain kinds of environments, Clarke became interested in "rational actor" behavioral models, in which crime could be controlled by carefully calibrated incentives.[55] Before going into academia, Clarke had been the director of the Home Office Research and Planning Unit, where he pioneered situation-based crime prevention techniques. Clarke's use of rational actor models as a basis for understanding criminality had its roots in the ideas of early neoliberal economists such as Gary Becker, who had attempted to calculate the relative economic externalities of different types of crime.[56] For Michel Foucault, who read Becker's writings on crime, this way of thinking produced the "anthropological erasure of the criminal."[57] With situational criminology proving compatible with the intensive policing of black communities in Britain and the United States, however, we must be careful not to overstate the absence of anthropological claims when these ideas were put into practice.[58]

For this new breed of criminologist, therefore, control over space became more significant than control over people. These were the intellectual conditions in which the built environment would come to play a key role in controlling crime in the 1970s and 1980s on both sides of the Atlantic. Newman was among a generation of planners and architects who maintained that minor environmental interventions would dramatically reduce urban crime rates. It is no coincidence that Coleman, one of the biggest supporters and practitioners of Newman's ideas in Britain, was perhaps the most vociferous critic of the council estate in postwar Britain.[59] Coleman was a geography professor at

King's College London who toward the end of her career led an in-depth investigation into the conditions of life on various estates in Britain. The resulting book, *Utopia on Trial*, was published in 1985 and featured a vitriolic attack on almost every aspect of high-density council housing. Declaring postwar estates to be "human disasters that smear many lives with traumatic experiences," Coleman advocated for the superiority of the low-rise cottage homes of the prewar era:

> The twentieth century has been split in two by a great revolution in housing. The first half of the century was dominated by the age-old system of natural selection, which left people free to secure the best accommodation they could. The second half has embraced the Utopian ideal of housing planned by a paternalistic authority, which offered hopes of improved standards but also ran the risk of trapping people in dwellings not of their choosing ... many of whom have been ruthlessly evicted from their little terrace houses, and sometimes mentally scarred by this process as severely as by the loss of a spouse or the loss of a limb.[60]

Coleman deployed an array of pseudopsychological evidence to claim that council estates were opposed to what she deemed to be unalterable aspects of nature:

> A limpet manufactures a protective shell. A snail creates a mobile home. A shrimp burrows into the sea-floor. . . . Throughout most of human history our inbuilt guidance system has led us to produce a shelter with an adjoining piece of territory, and to impress it with distinctive marks of identity. The decoration, the garden layout, the boundary fence, the name plate or other signals proclaim the residence of a unique family rather than a faceless unit among the masses. . . . Designs that incorporated defensible territory and scope for the occupants to make their mark proved popular and were repeated, while those that denied these needs proved hard to sell and were discontinued. Natural selection was still in command.[61]

Coleman claimed to have discovered an eternal, unchanging fact about the relationship between living beings and space—one that transcended time, place, and even species. She cited research supposedly showing that when a rat colony becomes too large, normal behavior among its residents gave way to "aggressiveness, homosexuality and other deviations."[62] Like Newman (whom she cited), Coleman believed that while detached suburban homes were the long-term ideal, a set of ameliorative environmental interventions could be made to improve many high-density estates.

After the publication of *Utopia on Trial*, Coleman visited estates in Toronto, Amsterdam, and across Australia, and was given an audience with Prince

Charles. Her book was a publishing success and received a second edition in 1990. Most important, though, *Utopia on Trial* was read and admired by Thatcher. Coleman's arguments resonated with critiques of state planning that were in the ascendancy in Thatcher's administration in the 1980s. While government policy was attempting to turn communities of tenants into private homeowners, here was evidence that privately owned and defensible space was something deeply ingrained in the human condition. Not only did Coleman provide a rationale linking a key element of Britain's midcentury developmental state with criminal violence, but she did so within an analysis of the social body that saw crime as the result of opportunity and urban design, as opposed to poverty or unemployment. She emphasized that her interventions would have a broad, ameliorative effect on a wide variety of different social problems at a low cost.[63] Here, then, was a vision of society that suited perfectly a government hell-bent on fiscal retrenchment, public order, and the phasing out of wealth redistribution as a means of poverty reduction.

In 1988, Coleman was invited to Downing Street to meet personally with Thatcher. While there, Coleman complained that her findings had been ignored by research bodies and local authorities, and appealed for help. Thatcher was reportedly "much taken" with Coleman, while a junior official in the Home Office noted that his department "entirely accepts" her arguments.[64] Following this meeting, Coleman was awarded forty million pounds from the Department of the Environment to implement a series of reforms to British housing estates. The department also promised a 100 percent subsidy for cooperative local authorities who were willing to implement her proposals. Coleman undertook this project as head of the Design Improvement Controlled Experiment (DICE). DICE was notable for its attempts to devise a rigorous and quantitative methodology. When working on the Ledbury Estate in South East London in 1989, Coleman's team drew up a list of sixteen factors that it believed to be harmful. Some of these, such as the number of stories and dwellings per unit, related to size and density, while others, such as the number and type of entrances along with the presence of overhead walkways, related to specific design features. Depending on the prevalence of these faults, the estate was assigned an overall "disadvantagement score," calculated by averaging the number of design infringements recorded on each block. The twenty tower blocks and low-rise structures that made up the Ledbury Estate, for example, received an overall disadvantagement score of 10.7, seen by DICE as dangerously high.[65]

Once the problems of a given estate had been identified and their relative severity calculated, DICE employed Department of the Environment funding to solve the problem as best it could. On the Ledbury Estate, various changes were made to increase the amounts of private, defensible territory. The ground-floor units of many of the blocks were converted into a "house," with "its own walled and gated front garden facing the road, and its own back garden without an exit."[66] The provision of walled gardens was a particularly important point for Coleman. She described how on one estate, the installation of ground-floor gardens had transformed the children who lived there "from anonymous menacing gangs to polite individuals."[67] Meanwhile, a sense of demarcated private ownership over common space was to be induced on the Ledbury Estate by reducing the number of entrances and removing communal walkways. The medium-size blocks would be ringed with fences to create "semi public areas . . . with a single access gate."[68]

The changes introduced on the Ledbury Estate were typical of the kinds of interventions made by Coleman to housing estates across the country. Across London as well as in Nottingham, Birmingham, Preston, and Manchester, ground-floor apartments were fitted with fenced gardens, collective walkways were demolished or bricked up, and tower blocks were segmented into different access zones.[69] Almost every intervention undertaken by the DICE team was designed to increase the amount of private or semiprivate space at the expense of accessible common areas while developing mechanisms for the increased surveillance of the common areas that remained. These subtle means of privatizing or fortifying space changed the appearance of many estates in Britain. The communal fantasies of many modernist architects were being dismantled in pursuit of defensible space. In the early 1990s, the Hyde Park Estate in Sheffield was remodeled using many of the techniques pioneered by DICE after a council report deemed elements of the building to be "unattractive and hostile."[70] The estate was entirely demolished and rebuilt, without almost all the communal features (such as the walkway and courtyards) of the previous development, and rebranded as a low-rise "village" complete with a village green.[71] Although DICE had no official role to play in the redevelopment of Hyde Park, the influence of Coleman was evident to the disgruntled former modernist architect Cedric Price, who referred to the development as a "pathetic Colemanville."[72]

Coleman's DICE project came to a sudden halt in 1990 after a change of government. In 1997, an independent audit concluded that the project's attempts to solve some of the social and economic problems faced by those living on housing estates had been limited. It noted that "none of the DICE schemes can be judged to have been effective in meeting the (admittedly ambitious) objectives set for it by Professor Coleman."[73] For the most part, Coleman's interventions had little effect on crime rates and poverty on the estates that she had worked on. The warren of waist-high fences, absence of overhead walkways, and segmentation of access routes remain on the Mozart Estate

FIGURES 4.2 (above), 4.3, AND 4.4 (pages 124–25). The Mozart Estate after it was redesigned by Alice Coleman's team. Note how access to each floor of the building is gated off and available only to the residents of that floor. Note also the low walls built to separate ground-floor apartments. A public courtyard is fenced off too. Photographs by author.

FIGURE 4.3.

today, thirty years after Coleman first arrived there. Despite her alterations, however, the estate has witnessed a number of high-profile instances of gang violence, including kidnappings and drive-by shootings.

While DICE itself was cut short, the situation-based criminological paradigm from which it emerged retained its dominance into the twenty-first century. Rebranded by the Association of Chief of Police Officers as "Secured by Design" in 1989, the reduction of crime through surveillance, "target hardening," and reducing the extent and accessibility of common spaces has been

FIGURE 4.4.

a dominant feature of the architecture of both public and private buildings over the last twenty years.[74] The 2014 Secured by Design handbook for housing developers, for instance, recommends changing the color of road surfaces within estates, "psychologically giving the impression that the area beyond is private." Benches, according to the handbook, "can be a valuable amenity or a focus for anti-social behavior." Meanwhile, "communal areas such as playgrounds . . . have the potential to generate crime, the fear of crime and anti-social behaviour."[75] One of the biggest legislative successes of this new approach to criminology came with the passage of the 1998 Crime and Disorder Act in the first full year of Tony Blair's premiership. Section 17 of the act threatened to put the burden of crime prevention on those seeking planning permission, forcing local authorities to assess any new structure for its potential to incentivize criminal behavior.[76] Much to the disappointment of many advocates for Secured by Design, this clause was never fully enforced by the justice system.

The end of the era of mass public housing in Britain was accompanied by new ideas about the ways that human beings related to built space. For planners like Coleman and Newman, it was a scientific fact that high-density council estates were doomed to end in misery and criminal activity for their residents—one that rested on essential truths about the human condition. This argument was used to undermine the collective nature of earlier developments, replacing the walkways and courtyards that were once seen as the necessary material bedrock for future social cohesion with fortified entrances, defensible spaces, and clearly demarcated private gardens. At the same time that estates were being privatized, first on a flat-by-flat basis and later en masse, residents were being encouraged to treat public and unsurveilled spaces as suspicious. While the emergence of a new type of criminology cannot alone explain why and how Britain's experiment with public housing came to an end in the 1980s, this story can help us understand an important shift in how the residents of council housing were perceived by architects, planners, and politicians. While architecture and urban planning had once been vested with a broad social mission—a belief that in the right hands it could mold new subjects or communities—by the late 1980s much of what remained of this optimism was a conviction that the right building design could reduce crime statistics. Yet the various modifications meant to create a defensible space, when tacked onto council estates, were only ever an awkward retrofit. As with attempts to sell individual flats within estates, attempts at privatization were stymied by the tricky persistence of the open-plan courtyards and walkways built by a previous generation of architects. As the remainder of this chapter will show, these perceived problems were only fully solved on the brand-new private developments that spread through British cities in the last two decades of the century.

The Private Housing Estate

In 1986, George Young, a junior Conservative minister in the Department of the Environment, ceremonially opened a twenty-two-story tower block in East London. Unlike Ronan Point, or the towers of Park Hill or Churchill Gardens, the Cascades was an entirely private development, purpose-built for

the elite employees of the businesses that were moving into the newly gentrifying London Docklands. While the planners and architects of midcentury
modernist estates had looked east to France, central Europe, and Scandinavia,
the Cascades was a US affair. Its developers had toured the United States,
gathering information about luxury high-rise developments.[77] An article in
the property supplement of the *Sunday Times* highlighted the building's novelty: "If you thought that tower blocks had been permanently discredited as
civilized places to live—think again. . . . [T]oday's yuppie buyer will be en-
chanted by the style of luxury high-rise life."[78]

In the 1980s and 1990s, a new breed of high-density housing development
appeared, built by private property developers. While these buildings were at
first mostly limited to parts of London, by the early 2000s they had become a
common feature of British cities. The emergence of such developments was
partly stimulated by a renewed political focus on the private rental sector. Private landlords had been scarce in the mid-twentieth century, a time when most
people either rented from councils or owned their own home. The Conservative government of the 1980s, however, had dreams of bringing back the rental
class. The 1979 Conservative manifesto talked about "reviving the rental sector," and the urban boom in private rented housing in the late 1980s and 1990s
was made easier by the 1988 Housing Act, which introduced more flexible
systems of short- and long-term rental contracts as well as abolished rent control.[79] This chapter will conclude by looking at the housing estate in its private,
end-of-the-century form. After the difficulties faced by councils attempting to
partly privatize their stock of high-density estates, these new structures granted
free rein to the auditing and segmentation of services along with intense forms
of security and surveillance.

Sometimes called "gated communities," private, fortified estates were a
common feature of late twentieth-century cities across the world. In the
United States, Brazil, and South Africa, such developments tended to follow
in the wake of national moments of democratization or civil rights victories,
in which the task of segregation, now de facto rather than de jure, fell increasingly onto the private residential sector.[80] The rise of gated communities in
Britain, although significant after the 1980s, has been slower. When Thatcher
bought a home in Hambledon Place, a gated community in Dulwich in South
London, such developments stimulated a brief flurry of interest. A local history society for residents of this part of London lamented that due to the
community's gates, a blue plaque commemorating her former house would
not be seen by the wider public.[81] By 2003, it was estimated that there were
more than a thousand gated communities in England.[82] This figure nevertheless overlooks a substantial number of private apartment buildings, many of
which followed the same logic.

FIGURE 4.5. Two Labour members of Parliament, Michael Meacher and Frank Cook, attempt to deliver a notice to Margaret Thatcher's home in her gated community in Dulwich with a family of unemployed homeowners from Middlesbrough, 1987.

The publicity materials for hundreds of developments in the London Dock-lands and the South London borough of Southwark, constructed during the 1980s and early 1990s, show a striking set of similarities among structures built by a wide variety of private developers. In their density, the serial nature of their production, their relative isolation from preexisting urban networks, and their provision of various services for residents, these structures resembled council estates. Many of the new developments that emerged in East London, for example, were complex high-density ones, comprising multiple structures linked together by courtyards and sculpted common spaces. A low-rise development of forty-seven private flats built by Bennett Homes in East London in 1988 offered residents a total planned environment, organized around a large cobbled quadrangle and two large gatehouses designed to evoke the homes of the nineteenth-century merchant class that lived by the docks.[83] Another development on the Isle of Dogs was described by developers as a "total concept."[84] Meanwhile, Heron Homes marketed a new development near St. Katherine's Dock that offered "total communities" for its residents.[85] The

FIGURE 4.6. The entrance to a private housing estate in Leeds. Photograph by David Ellis.

similarity between these large, comprehensive developments and their mid-century modernist equivalents did not go unnoticed by contemporary architects and journalists. The property section in the *Sunday Times* noted that developers were dissuading "the public from associating tower blocks with the monstrosities of the 1960s," while *Architects' Journal*, reviewing one luxury development, claimed "the visions of Le Corbusier . . . had finally been realised."[86] As with the shops, launderettes, and workplaces that were included at Park Hill and Hyde Park, many of these developments offered a diverse and sometimes obscure range of services beyond their lobby entrances. A late 1980s development built on the Isle of Dogs, for instance, promised a small shopping center, swimming pool, solarium, sauna, and gym.[87] Finally, needless to say, almost all these developments advertised heating systems that were under the control of each tenant.[88]

Those buying flats in new developments also had no trouble obtaining mortgages. Many developments offered flats for purchase as well as (or instead of) to rent. In 1987, for example, a four-story flat in Bermondsey with five bedrooms reportedly became the most expensive ever listed south of the

Thames in London, with an asking price of £2.5 million.[89] Indeed, many developers in East London offered potential buyers elaborate mortgages and plans to defer eventual payment, particularly in the wake of the early 1990s property crash that saw a drop in sales. Three property developers specializing in private flats in the gentrifying parts of East London, for instance, launched a scheme whereby buyers could defer half their mortgage for up to five years.[90] While mortgage lenders expressed concerns about offering capital to those in council flats because these flats were embedded in communal fabrics of corridors and courtyards, this did not seem to be a problem in new private developments in London.

Such developments were also able to distill and perfect many of the architectural practices developed by environmental criminologists in the 1980s. While planners such as Coleman had to retrofit these features into preexisting buildings, many of the new private developments built in the 1980s and 1990s were "secured by design" from the outset. In the publicity materials for these developments, descriptions of their sophisticated security arrangements take center stage. An advertisement for Free Trade Wharf, an enormous riverside development, is worth reproducing at length:

> Security has been recognised as of prime importance to residents. The main entrance is surveyed 24 hours a day by video cameras as are all external parking areas. Residents are provided with electronic passes which they can gain entry. The video and audio entry systems installed in each apartment allow the residents to view visitors at the security desk and to communicate with the porter. . . . Entry via the car park can only be gained with a special transmitter which automatically opens the gates.[91]

The emphasis on security is almost ubiquitous in such advertisements. Private developers boasted about their many innovative security technologies. The most common were video entry phone systems and closed-circuit television (CCTV) cameras. Many of these systems mirrored developments taking place on high-density council estates. Although intercom systems had been in use on some estates since the 1950s, they became increasingly prevalent from the 1970s and 1980s onward, being installed as part of upgrading and modernization programs.[92] In 1989, meanwhile, proposals for the redevelopment of the Hyde Park Estate in Sheffield underscored a security apparatus that was similar in complexity to those advertised in private developments. The estate was fitted with permanently staffed reception desks fitted with video surveillance of its public places. Visitors were only able to gain access after calling a resident's entry phone system.[93]

CCTV cameras, likewise, had become routine on council estates from the 1990s onward. Before that decade, the technology, perfected in the late

1960s, had been mostly used in stores to deter shoplifters.[94] By the millennium, the London boroughs of Islington, Hackney, Newham, and Wandsworth, along with cities such as Birmingham, Newcastle, Nottingham, Hull, and Bristol, were installing CCTV as standard on housing estates. In one housing estate in Doncaster, it was reported that CCTV cameras monitoring the public areas were connected to residents' television sets so that they could watch the live feed from home.[95] On council estates, the introduction of CCTV and entry phone systems were post hoc retrofits. In private, mass housing developments, however, these measures could be implemented from the outset.

As well as the inclusion of gates, cameras, and security guards, private housing developers included many of the subtler aspects of defensible space. It was common practice for ground-floor apartments, for example, to be provided with fenced gardens—a familiar device of Coleman's DICE project. The ground-floor flats of Horseshoe Court and Russia Court, two luxury apartment units built by different developers, were separated by high walls and fences from both the common areas of the development and the public riverside walkways that passed by outside.[96] The large walkways connecting separate blocks so despised by Coleman and Newman were largely absent in such private developments, which for the most part advertised separate entrances for each major structure. Each "wing" of Prospect Wharf, for example, had its own staircase, foyer, and elevator.[97] One promotional article even alluded to Newman by citing approvingly a Dockland development's use of defensible space.[98] These luxury units were the logical outcome of an increasingly institutionalized theory about the relationship between architecture and crime. Set apart from the street by high walls and fences, monitored by CCTV cameras, and secured by video entry phones, these new developments offered residents a powerful sense of enclosure.

The new, private developments were often governed by residents' associations that managed the day-to-day tasks of mediating disputes, making decisions over common spaces, and collectively bargaining with contractors. Although these organizations were, by definition, collective endeavors, they were frequently seen as necessary instances of cooperation in order to preserve a common investment. A commentator's advice for those considering forming such an association shows the difficulty in navigating the contradictions between public space and private ownership:

> Flat owners are a diverse group of people whose one common feature is that they share a building which is separated into individually owned and occupied units. Each unit relies on all the others for support and protection. They are interdependent, and without being enveloped in an integrated

structure each unit would soon become impossible to manage and possibly unsaleable. Each flat-owner will want to ensure that a proper structure is in place which provides rules for enforcing obligations between flat-owners and for how the building as a whole is maintained and how it is insured.[99]

Private residents' associations usually had their own constitutions, specifying a quorum for decision making and meeting frequency.[100] Often legal advice and draft constitutions were dispensed by the Federation of Private Residents' Associations (FPRA), an organization founded in 1971 to advance the interests of private tenants in the rental sector. Thanks in part to the FPRA's lobbying efforts, private residents' associations were deemed by the 1980 Housing Act to be the legal official representatives of private housing developments.[101]

Much of the FPRA's energies were spent mediating legal battles over the maintenance of common spaces in private housing developments. Many of the legal challenges involving the FPRA were disputes over the financial responsibility for various alterations. Legally, landlords were allowed to charge residents for maintenance and repairs but not for "improvements" that resulted in long-term substantive changes to the building. The large number of such disputes is testament to the complete disaggregation of forms of provision in private housing units. In 1990, for example, a legal challenge following the sale of a previously communal roof terrace to a third party resulted in a reduction of rents and service charges for the residents.[102] In South London in 1986, a judge ruled that a landlord was allowed to charge residents for painting the exterior wooden frames of windows, but not their replacement with double glazing.[103] In 1993, elsewhere in London, a tenant successfully claimed that the disrepair of common spaces breached a covenant that he had signed guaranteeing "quiet enjoyment" of the premises.[104] These disputes show that private tenants were highly organized, both on a building-by-building basis and as part of a nationwide structure of support, when it came to consuming as well as contesting the services provided in private housing developments.

The role of these organizations in contesting services, managing common spaces, and taking an active interest in the security of their buildings can be seen in the materials produced by a small residents' association in a large market town in England.[105] The residents' association was created to organize the tenants of Parker Grange, a private housing development comprising twenty-one flats spread between two multistory buildings, built in 1982. The association was organized as a limited company, with each tenant receiving a single share. With a quorum of just three residents, the members of the association would meet annually to discuss various issues relating to the management of the common resources they shared. Such issues ranged from the installation of lights in the development's parking lot to conversations about sending a delegation to the local vicar to complain about the loudness of the nearby church bells.[106]

The residents of Parker Grange were scrupulous in their monitoring of the services provided and their costs. When a minority of residents complained about poor TV reception in 1983, for example, it was decided that repairing the television antennae of each building would be too expensive and "those experiencing poor reception would have to make their own arrangements."[107] In 1987, the residents decided against the creation of a collective "sinking fund" for repairs, arguing that "such expenditure should continue to be met as it arises by extra individual contribution at time of need."[108] Perhaps the bitterest debate over provision occurred in 1984, when a resident, Fairclough, sent a series of detailed requests to the management seeking more information about the service charge. He claimed that charging each household the same amount for different services was unreasonable, and the security system as well as the floor- and window-cleaning costs should be differentially charged, as "it would reasonably be expected that wear and tear would be higher in the downstairs block." Fairclough was particularly concerned about the distribution of costs between residents of the two buildings, demanding to see maintenance costs for each. He even challenged the costs of the lighting for common areas after conducting his own test of the electricity supply.[109] The denial of his requests to further segment the service charges paid by residents to the management sent him into a rage. One letter to management, following a meeting about the issue, revealed the animus that these debates could engender: "You deliberately and with some malice prevented me from stating my case. In fact, you prostituted your office to argue against me. . . . You openly encouraged a hostile reaction from the meeting, and, did nothing to restrain the unseemly verbal abuse of Mr. Childs and myself. . . . All in all, I regret to say your competency in chairmanship is abysmal."[110]

At almost every opportunity, some or all of the residents of Parker Grange opposed collective forms of provision. Service charges were closely audited, frequently contested, and, if possible, charged on a household-by-household basis.

More than anything else, however, the residents of Parker Grange debated security. The fortification of their homes recurred with an obsessive frequency at association meetings. Many early discussions about safety betrayed a paternalistic conservatism. The minutes for a 1985 meeting noted that "in view of the many ladies residing in the blocks, Messers Smith and Stevens suggested that there should be permanent internal safety lights illuminated on the same basis as the outside lighting. It was pointed out that the majority of flats had spyholes and door telephones. Leaseholders were advised to use the safety chains provided."[111]

Meanwhile, the positioning of a plaque detailing the industrial history of the site on one of the development's walls came under fire during the same meeting out of concern that it might attract "trespassers."[112] At the 1987 meeting, the storage of fire extinguishers in the landings and corridors of the buildings came under scrutiny as the equipment was "too easily stolen."[113] The residents at different times railed against "trespassers apparently under the influence of drink," the noise from the local youth club, and even roosting pigeons, responsible for "droppings cascading out of the West door."[114] Anything that intruded onto the heavily fortified and sanitized environment of Parker Grange was cause for concern. In 1991, a reminder to residents to double lock their doors was marked with the heading "URGENT!!! SECURITY WARNING!!!"[115]

It is clear from the records of Parker Grange that any form of common space or any collectively managed service was a source of tremendous anxiety for its residents. Corridors, parking lots, and landings were imagined to be sites of criminal and sometimes even sexual danger. The spending of funds on a collective rather than individuated basis, meanwhile, was fraught with concerns about value for money and led to tempestuous arguments between residents. Despite the ostensibly massified and communal nature of the built environment as well as the stairwells, corridors, gardens, and courtyards that the residents had common rights to, Parker Grange was a site for fiscal and spatial retrenchment.

At the beginning of the last chapter, I asked you to imagine that you were on a train leaving Victoria Station in London, heading south. As the train crosses the river, looking west, passengers can see the sprawling council estates of Wandsworth. Passengers looking east, however, are confronted with a vertiginous wall of luxury housing developments, each containing thousands of units that press up against the side of the railway tracks immediately south of the Thames. Battersea Power Station, whose excess heat had once been piped under the Thames to service thousands of working-class council tenants living on the Churchill Gardens Estate, is now almost entirely obscured by this shield of luxury apartment buildings, all constructed since 2015. One of these developments, Embassy Gardens, boasts a swimming pool suspended in the air connecting two of its blocks, where residents can look down through glass at the pedestrians below. Behind its gates, the development offers residents a "complete London experience": a café, private cinema, sprawling rooftop garden, "art trail," and its own private members' club in which every resident is automatically enrolled. Each home, though, is billed as an "individual experience." The complex is wildly abstracted, not just from its surrounding neighborhood, but from the entire city. Its promotional material notes that "often our residents live between continents and feel they belong to many cities." An accompanying video outlining a typical weekend for the residents of Embassy Gardens starts with "international friends" flying in "for the weekend," illustrated by a single stiletto descending the staircase of a private jet.[116]

The first round of flats in Embassy Gardens was released for sale in June 2017, each for more than one million pounds. The same month, seventy-one people were killed in a fire in Grenfell Tower, a twenty-four-story block on the Lancaster West Estate, five miles north of Embassy Gardens. The recent history of Grenfell Tower is a familiar one. Built in 1974, it was owned and managed by Kensington and Chelsea Council until 1996. That year, the council transferred all its stock to a tenant management organization, an indeterminate body run by a mixture of residents and council appointees. Grenfell was split between tenant management organization residents and private renters, some paying as much as two thousand pounds a month for a two-bedroom flat. Its 2016 refurbishment had been outsourced to a private developer, Rydon Limited, and Rydon in turn had outsourced the tower's external cladding, which was likely responsible for the rapid spread of the fire, to another private company, Harley Facades. Seven other companies were listed as playing a role in the management and refurbishment of the tower.[117] The year before the fire, it was reported that residents of the tower had repeatedly complained about the tenant management organization's lax attitude to fire safety.[118] What's more, like most other blocks of its size, Grenfell had been retrofitted with electronic security doors that restricted the access of residents to different parts of the block in the name of crime reduction. In an interview conducted shortly after the fire, one resident said that he was able to help people escape from the back of the tower block only because he had happened to bring his electronic key fob with him when he left his flat.[119] Many of the working-class victims of the Grenfell fire were first- or second-generation migrants to Britain.[120] Like the residents of Embassy Gardens, they probably felt that they belonged to multiple cities, although here the comparison ends. Perhaps not since Engels traipsed through the shattered courtyards that cluttered the banks of the Irk in Manchester or since the Glasgow police conducted midnight raids to monitor the overcrowding of tenements have the conditions of British housing been so unequal, with devastating, fatal consequences.

The last two chapters have traced the evolution of high-density, comprehensively planned housing estates in their multiple, different twentieth-century guises, looking at ramshackle slums, philanthropic tenements, modernist public housing estates, and luxury gated communities. Regardless of their architecture or conditions of ownership, these spaces raise a similar set of questions. What is the relationship between an individual household and its surroundings? Who has access to and feels ownership over public space?

How does the development as a whole relate to the surrounding urban fabric? The answers to these questions changed during the course of the twentieth century. For a few decades, it was hoped that council estates would not only solve Britain's housing shortage but would do other kinds of work too, modernizing the domestic lives of British citizens and forging new communities among erstwhile strangers. From the 1980s on, a different set of answers emerged. A new generation of owner-occupiers tried, and in many instances failed, to unplug their council flats from the surrounding communal infrastructure through disconnecting heating systems, securing individual mortgages, and auditing their service charges. At the same time, public space became suspect. The coherent social body imagined to be the consumers of the shared amenities and spaces that characterized high density council estates atomized. The courtyards and corridors—once seen as streets in the sky that were supposed to re-create the vibrant associative world of inner-city slums— were demolished or fenced off in the name of defensible space. The denigration of council estates was heralded by politicians, but it was also underwritten by mortgage lenders and essentialist social scientists working on both sides of the Atlantic. By the end of the century, a new kind of mass housing had emerged, fortified, individuated, commoditized, and for the most part, available only for the rich.

What's more, the fate of the council estate lets us glimpse what is distinctive about Britain's neoliberal built environment, a theme that will continue to be developed over the next two chapters. First, we can see the emergence of a political formation characterized by the termination of any hope that the social body could be remade as an aggregate—in this instance, the possibility that strangers could be formed into communities by the qualities of urban space. Second, in the absence of a social that could be reformed, the design and management of residential environments became geared toward the individual ownership of space (and the subsequent thwarting of criminals that this necessarily entailed). Yet the vision of state and society promoted in the mid-twentieth century cast a long shadow, inhering in the collective heating systems and communal spaces of council estates that continued to exist for decades after the election of Thatcher in 1979, shaping, limiting, and recasting attempts to reimagine the British city. We are beginning to see how the British neoliberal city was characterized by the remaking of urban forms that were reluctantly inherited from a previous era, one in which they were intended to do different kinds of work.

5

The Shopping Mall

IN SPRING 1990, a team of expert seismologists from California flew halfway around the world to advise on the construction of what was to be the world's tallest building.[1] Their destination was not Dubai, Tokyo, or London but rather an enormous shopping mall on the outskirts of Birmingham named Merry Hill. Even without the proposed 2,000-foot tower, Merry Hill dominated the landscape. The mall boasted 2.5 miles of indoor pedestrianized concourses, with more than 250 individual shops divided between five discrete zones. Inside, there was a ten-screen cinema and full amphitheater that hosted fashion shows, carnivals, home exhibitions, live music events, and even a "Miss Merry Hill" pageant.[2] Visitors could eat at an "international" food court with an immense prosthetic hot air balloon at its center, designed to evoke Phileas Fogg's journey around the world in eighty days. The mall had its own quarterly magazine, a fleet of more than forty minibuses, and, perhaps most impressively, a state-of-the-art monorail that linked the parking lot, the shopping mall, and a nearby cluster of offices. One hundred and fifty CCTV cameras monitored by a central control room watched over the mall's 23 million annual visitors.[3] In addition to the fifty private security officers working in the mall, there were seven permanently stationed members of the West Midlands Police. To cap it all, the Merry Hill Tower, the construction of which was eventually shelved, was set to be more than twice the height of the Eiffel Tower.[4]

The feeling of stepping from a windy sidewalk or exposed parking lot through the double doors of a shopping mall into a brightly lit cocoon of soft music and boxed storefronts is a familiar part of urban and suburban life across the world. Perhaps for this reason, there is a surprisingly advanced academic literature on shopping malls—mostly appearing in three different contexts. First, geographers and critical theorists have looked to the shopping mall as the pinnacle of postmodern unreality—places where time and space have collapsed into a series of disembedded images.[5] These thinkers have been fascinated by the way that malls cultivate a feeling of artificiality, juxtaposing a slew of cultural signifiers that are never coherently processed or ordered. Writing on the West Edmonton Mall in Alberta, Canada, for instance, which boasts its own Chinatown, a Bourbon Street, and a replica of Christopher Columbus's ship, the *Santa Maria*, Margaret Crawford observed how "barriers between real and fake, near and far, dissolve as history, nature, technology, are indifferently processed by the mall's fantasy machine."[6] A second body of research on shopping malls comes from historians of the United States who have turned to urban history to explain the contradictions and collapse of the post–New Deal settlement. These scholars have shown how shopping malls were implicated in the decline of downtowns along with the ghettoization and retrenchment of US cities.[7] Lizabeth Cohen in particular has argued that the shopping mall effectively resegregated US cities at the same time that important civil rights battles were being fought over access to public space in downtowns.[8] Finally, academics working in various fields have shown how the proliferation of shopping malls has been a significant feature of the rapidly urbanizing Global South.[9] Anthropologist Arlene Dávila, for example, writing primarily about Colombia, has demonstrated how a wave of shopping malls built in the last twenty years satisfies a desire for intensive policing, real estate speculation, and "lingering and being seen" on behalf of an emerging middle class.[10]

What, then, does any of this have to do with the West Midlands of England? This chapter concerns the history of the shopping mall in Britain. My argument is that unlike shopping malls in the United States or nations that were urbanizing for the first time, shopping malls in Britain emerged in tense negotiation with a state-directed and developmental retail infrastructure established a generation earlier. In other words, before there was the shopping mall, there was the shopping precinct. I asserted in chapter 2 that the shopping mall and shopping precinct are two distinct types of space. I maintain this distinction in order to show how a qualitatively new urban form arose in Britain in the last third of the twentieth century. The history of the shopping mall allows us to see how during this period a new relationship between the consumer, state, and economy emerged in Britain. The wave of shopping malls built in the 1970s, 1980s, and 1990s promoted a different vision of the British city, one that was engineered for consumer spending instead of civic public space, was imported from the United States yet became identical the world over, and had a different vision of development and modernity than its midcentury ancestors.

I will explore the shopping mall's distinctive contribution to late twentieth-century British life by historicizing three of its most important features. First, while shopping precincts were embedded in the preexisting urban fabric, with footpaths opening directly onto bustling city streets, shopping malls are altogether more isolated, ringed by moats of asphalt and banished to the fringes of towns and cities. This spatial isolation mirrors the uncoupling of shopping malls from the social and developmental aims of their forebears. As opposed to being functional nodes for the distribution of goods or reordering of town centers, shopping malls became destinations in themselves, spaces for leisure and recreation that would transcend the daily routines of household reproduction. To put it another way, they became spaces for families versus housewives. Rather than being *of* the city, they were apart from it, which enabled it to be reimagined as something fantastic and otherworldly.

Second, shopping malls may seem otherworldly, but they were also becoming familiar the world over. Retail space in Britain has been global for a long time of course, and we saw in chapter 2 how Smithfield Market in the nineteenth century controlled imperial supply chains that spanned hemispheres. What was new in the late twentieth century was that the appearance, management practices, and ownership of large parts of Britain's shopping infrastructure came to closely resemble that of the rest of the world. The shopping mall is a globally standardized type of urban space—an environment that is confusingly similar, whether you are in Nairobi, Florida, or Sheffield. Indeed, as we have seen, shopping malls first appeared in the United States in the 1950s, the brainchild of a Viennese refugee. The earliest malls in Britain consciously followed North American examples and thus should be seen as foot soldiers in what Victoria de Grazia has called "America's advance through twentieth-century Europe."[11] As they spread to every continent, a sophisticated body of shared technical expertise began to emerge. Mall managers sought to perfect their development's heating, lighting, pedestrian flow, security, and even music through sharing expertise in manuals, conferences, and international organizations. As malls became standardized in feel and appearance, they also became increasingly international in ownership. Their similarity allowed them to be traded, like financial instruments, between different individuals or companies that had never set foot inside their property.[12]

Third, the shopping mall entailed the privatization of the shopping precincts that were built in the first three decades after the war. As in the case of housing, I take "privatization" to mean more than merely a change in ownership. Just as flatted council houses had to be uncoupled from their immediate environment in order to become salable assets, many of the shopping precincts built in the 1950s, 1960s, and 1970s had to be similarly isolated from their context. The 1980s and 1990s saw doors between streets and central shopping precincts locked, or sometimes even installed, for the first time. Private security came to replace city police. In many of Britain's postwar new towns, the shopping precincts built by publicly funded development corporations were the only entity resembling town centers. When most of these spaces were sold to property developers in the 1980s and 1990s, there were important implications for public space, entailing battles, as we will see, that went all the way to the European Court of Human Rights. As with housing, Britain's neoliberal built environment was characterized by its relationship with a prior developmental infrastructure.

The Arrival of the Shopping Mall in Britain

The first developments in Britain to be consciously inspired by US suburban malls, Elephant and Castle Shopping Centre in south London and the Bullring Centre in Birmingham, were judged to have been unmitigated disasters. The former was designed by Paul Boissevain and his wife, Barbara Joan Osmond, while the latter was designed by Sydney Greenwood. Both Boissevain and Greenwood had each spent time traveling in the United States in the 1950s. They would have visited cities that were losing their center of gravity. Dense downtowns and inner-city neighborhoods were being hollowed out, as white middle-class people moved in the tens of millions into sprawling suburbs.[13] By 1980, more than a hundred million people in the US were living in suburbs, more than were living in explicitly urban or rural environments.[14] This transition was enabled by rising car ownership and a massive, federally funded highway construction program, initiated in 1956. It was also enabled by hundreds and hundreds of shopping malls, anchoring new suburban communities in place and allowing their residents to bypass downtowns. Writing in 1985, one journalist calculated that there were more shopping malls in the United States than colleges, television stations, school districts, cinemas, or hospitals.[15] As we have seen in chapter 2, Gruen, the refugee who invented the shopping mall, failed in his aim to create an urban form that would counteract the disintegration of the US city. When Boissevain and Greenwood traveled to the United States, they saw this process in its infancy. Along with the self-service supermarket, the shopping mall migrated to Europe from the United States in the postwar decades, arriving with the sheen of affluence and the promise of a new kind of suburban modernity.[16]

Meanwhile, Britain in the mid-1960s was in the midst of a feverish commercial property boom.[17] Britain's commercial property market had arisen in the mid-nineteenth century as investors, most often insurance companies, began to see commercial buildings as means of securing stable rates of return through rents.[18] The interwar period had seen the emergence of specialist real estate agencies targeting retailers and businesses in need of urban office space. Firms such as Healy and Baker started to map the shopping districts of British towns, compiling data on every business along with the size and quality of their buildings.[19] In the immediate years after the Second World War, however, development controls and material shortages had restricted the construction of new shops and offices. This fact, coupled with the destruction of parts of British towns and cities by German bombers, meant that the prices of existing commercial real estate skyrocketed. A Conservative government, elected in 1951, rolled back the restrictions on property development and removed the 100 percent tax on development profits introduced by the 1947 Town and Country Planning Act. The result was a boom in commercial property building that produced a generation of millionaires while flooding British towns and cities with new shops and offices.

The shopping mall arrived from the United States in the final wild years of this boom, and some of its most conspicuous failures were the consequence. The Elephant and Castle Shopping Centre was perhaps the most notorious. As early as 1930, the Elephant and Castle neighborhood of London had been a source of despair for the LCC. The neighborhood, whose unusual name came from an early modern coaching inn, had become a snarled and decaying bottleneck, a problem for motorists trying to drive through the city. Ugliness and congestion were compounded by repeated bombings during the war, which left more than half the area's building stock damaged beyond repair.[20] Abercrombie's postwar plan for London called for the area to be transformed into a major traffic gateway to the south of England.[21] By the late 1950s, the LCC had a bolder vision. The intersection would be turned into a giant traffic roundabout, undercut by pedestrian subways and encircled by private and government offices. At the heart of this development, the LCC proposed a vast indoor shopping mall—a development, it was claimed, that would be unlike any other in Europe.[22] The LCC decided to outsource this project to a private developer and received thirty-six different applications.[23] Eventually it settled on the ambitious proposal put forward by Boissevain and Osmond on behalf of the property group Willet Limited. Neither the architects nor Willet had any prior experience in designing retail space, and there was no precedent in Britain for what they wanted to build.

The finished development spanned three floors and offered space for more than one hundred shops along a series of pedestrian concourses. In Coventry's shopping precinct, each individual store was responsible for its own heating, lighting, and music, with the courtyards and walkways outside subject to the same standards of cleaning, policing, and planning controls as other city streets. In Elephant and Castle, these powers were transferred to management. For the mall's first tenants, ceding this kind of control was a Faustian pact, and one that many would end up regretting. Store owners were given a document that explained in detail the respective responsibilities of the tenant and development company. First to be emphasized was the total control of the company over all the common spaces, consisting of the mall's service bays, toilets, concourses, stairways, and escalators.[24] Tenants paid a service charge to cover the cleaning, maintenance, and policing of these areas. The strictest regulations concerned the aesthetic presentation of the interior stores. Guidelines were set out concerning the exact size, height, and illumination of shop signs and ventilation methods.[25] Early observers were fascinated by the novelty of these acts of cooperation between different enterprises. The commercial editor of the *Financial Times* noted that although the shops were "competing against one another for custom," they would have to develop a "strong sense of Team Spirit."[26]

The delicate compact between the stores and the mall's management quickly fell apart. When Elephant and Castle opened in 1965, just 29 of a possible 120 stores were trading, and less than a year later one desperate tenant offered to sell his lease for four hundred pounds.[27] The development proved unable to attract shoppers from other parts of London, as it had little to offer that could not be found on regional high streets around the city. Throughout its history, much of the space of the upper floors remained entirely empty, save for a handful of isolated shops trading far out of sight. In a survey conducted a few years after the building opened, many shoppers "expressed surprise that there were any upper floors at all."[28] Unrest among tenants continued for more than a generation. In 1991, after a fourfold increase in service charges, 34 stores went on rent strike, requiring the intervention of the local member of Parliament.[29] Although Birmingham's Bullring Centre, built the year before Elephant and Castle, fared slightly better than its London counterpart, it was still widely regarded as a shabby and confusing space. With its black rubber tiling and total absence of daylight, the Bullring was eerie and claustrophobic.[30] Like Elephant and Castle, it was a US import, hastily transplanted into the middle of a British city at the height of an unsustainable property boom.

As we saw in chapter 2, mid-twentieth-century shopping precincts were built as an infrastructure for underpinning postwar consumer affluence and for preparing towns and cities for the coming age of the automobile. At a time when rates of car ownership remained relatively low and few families owned fridges, these spaces existed as a means of modernizing the experience of female domestic labor.[31] Despite their apparent novelty, Elephant and Castle and the Bullring Centre did not depart in any significant way from these aims. Elephant and Castle was marketed as a functional and explicitly feminized space—somewhere for South London housewives to make weekly or even daily visits.[32] Convenience was emphasized over leisure. A 1967 advertisement for the mall boasted, "No rushing to and fro to try and get everything you need for the weekly shopping—just make up one shopping list and you're finished."[33] Another enthusiastic advertisement claimed that the mall would liberate "the heavily laden housewife . . . particularly when the weather was unkind."[34] For the mall's second anniversary, its management organized a two-week festival for new housewives, featuring talks on the history of cooking, exhibitions of room settings, sales on cosmetics, and a competition to win a washing machine.[35] What's more, like shopping precincts, these early malls were woven into the urban fabric of their respective cities. While the Coventry shopping precinct was arguably Gibson's biggest achievement, it remained one element in a holistic redevelopment plan, which included offices, municipal buildings, and even a new cathedral. Like Gibson's precinct, Elephant and Castle was designed to fuse seamlessly with its surrounding urban landscape. Its concourses opened directly onto the Northern Line branch of the London Underground, and the mall sat beneath a tall office block that was owned by the same developer.

Despite the widespread denigration of Elephant and Castle and the Bullring Centre, a number of other shopping malls were built in British towns in the 1960s and 1970s—places like Chester's Grosvenor Centre (1965), Croydon's Whitgift Center (1970), Nottingham's Victoria Centre (1972), Derby's Eagle Centre (1975), and the handful of malls built in northern England by the Arndale company.[36] Like the Elephant and Castle and Bullring centers, and unlike the malls that Boissevain and Greenwood would have seen in the United States, these were mostly built in central locations and were part of more ambitious redevelopment schemes. Nottingham's Victoria Centre, for example, was built on the site of a former train station and sat, almost invisible, beneath a tall block of flats. The suburbanization of shopping malls in Britain was delayed by local authorities, who used Britain's powerful postwar town planning machinery to preserve existing towns and cities along with the greenbelts that surrounded them. The private developers who succeeded in being awarded permission by local authorities to build central shopping centers did so in the knowledge that they would be granted an effective monopoly.[37] These private, central developments were therefore caught between typologies. They marked the twilight of the functional and developmental shopping precincts of the 1950s and 1960s as well as the dawn of the fantastical suburban shopping malls of the 1980s and 1990s.

Brent Cross

When the next step toward a US-style shopping mall in Britain was taken, it was oriented toward a new kind of consumer. Brent Cross, situated in the northern suburbs of London, was a long time coming. It opened in 1976 after almost twenty years of fraught negotiations. The Hammerson Company, the owners and builders of Brent Cross, began negotiations with Hendon Council as early as 1957, but in 1965 had its planning permission revoked by the Ministry of Transport, which expressed concerns about the effect of the proposed mall on traffic routes in North London. It took a working group made up of the Ministry of Transport, the Greater London Council, the London borough of Barnet, and a consortium of private traffic consultants to break the impasse and approve the plan.[38] During the delays, officials from the local council went on a tour of Canadian and US suburban shopping malls to discover what they were in for.[39] With Elephant and Castle, the local authority had taken the lead—agitating for a shopping mall and commissioning architects to build it. Brent Cross, however, was an insurgent enterprise led by developers.

Occupying more than fifty-one acres and orbited by thirty-five hundred parking spaces, Brent Cross was the first US-inspired out-of-town shopping mall to be built in Britain.[40] The mall was constructed according to the "dumbbell" model, a popular US design in which two large department stores (in this case, John Lewis and Fenwicks) acted as anchors for pedestrians at either side of the building, while the remaining stores attracted the foot traffic flowing from one department store to the next. This was a design, pioneered by Gruen, to guarantee an even flow of pedestrians. It prevented Brent Cross from succumbing to the same problems of vacancy affecting Elephant and Castle. Meanwhile, each store was given access to its own external service bay, thus isolating shoppers from the distribution of stock.[41] These features allowed Brent Cross to be completely autonomous from the rest of the urban landscape. A report on Brent Cross drawn up by the Greater London Council underscored the novelty of this autonomy, noting the lack of public offices and places of recreation.[42] Anyone who has attempted to make the awkward and meandering journey by foot to Brent Cross from Hendon Central Underground Station can confirm the mall's isolation from public transit routes. Brent Cross, in other words, was designed for the growing numbers of Britons who owned cars.[43] An early survey of shoppers found that 72 percent had arrived by car (with only 16 percent coming by bus).[44]

Unlike Elephant and Castle, which was marketed as a feminized space for routine household shopping, Brent Cross was seen as an exciting destination in itself. It sold itself on pleasure over function. The ideal subject was not the housewife but the "family." To this end, developers made a conscious decision to limit the number of food shops that were allowed to lease space in the mall. William Tindale, the head of the developing company, remarked in an interview that his firm had turned away several applications from butcher shops because "that wasn't the business we were trying to attract."[45] Meanwhile, commentators enthused about the thrilling otherworldliness of the development. One reporter wrote that "the building rising up . . . from a flat plain of empty car parks . . . looks very long and large—like a massive Odeon cinema tacked on to an ocean liner."[46] Writing forty years later, another journalist remembered his first visit, observing, "It was as if Kubla Khan himself had

FIGURE 5.1. Brent Cross shortly after opening. Reproduced with permission of
Brent Cross Shopping Centre.

descended upon Hendon. The fountain! The dome! The escalators! The air
conditioning! The space!"[47] Another commentator said that the mall "draws
the inevitable comparison with religious architecture," and yet another noted
that it resembled Disneyland.[48] With the addition of cinemas, restaurants, and
playgrounds, shopping malls in Britain, beginning with Brent Cross, became
outlandish and ethereal destinations, important yet underappreciated elements in the new infrastructure of family leisure time.[49]

One of the most important differences between the shopping mall and
shopping precinct was that precincts were the outcome of a set of processes
initiated by the state. Built to reorganize postwar towns and cities, they were
inextricable from the towns and cities in which they were embedded, and for
which they were the focal point. They were built to precise specifications, determined by the size and needs of their catchment areas. Although Elephant
and Castle and the Bullring Centre were inspired by the kinds of shopping
malls that Gruen had spent the 1950s and 1960s perfecting in the United States,
they failed as adequate functional centerpieces for their respective locations. It
was when property developers were able to escape the baggage of developmental

politics and migrate to the open flatlands of suburbia that a new, postdevelopmental type of retail space could take root in Britain, beginning with Brent Cross. Although the government and local authorities still built the roads and infrastructure networks on which suburban malls were dependent, granted planning permission to developers, and in some instances incorporated out-of-town malls in regional development plans, the initiative now lay with private capital. If the shape, feel, and purpose of British retail space were no longer to be decided by council town planners or government economic committees, what, then, would determine the nature of these spaces? To answer that, we need to look beyond Britain.

Global Standardization

There is a case to be made that the rapid spread of shopping malls to different corners of the earth has resulted in one of the most significant standardizations of urban space that has ever occurred. Hundreds of thousands of acres of urban land, on every inhabited continent, are enclosed, heated, and lit to international standards. There are approximately 1,100 shopping malls in the United States, for example—a figure that increases dramatically if strip malls and urban gallerias are included.[50] There are 558 shopping malls in Brazil, and 600 in India.[51] Perhaps the biggest growth in recent decades has been in China, where there are more than 4,000 shopping malls.[52] Malls are organized on a global scale by the International Council of Shopping Centers, a body founded in the United States in 1957. The council currently has 70,000 members among almost 30 national or regional branches. Britain's own branch, the British Council of Shopping Centres, was founded in 1983.[53] Shopping malls are therefore a cellular, minimalist, and infinitely repeatable spatial type. This is not to say, of course, that they are not used differently in different contexts. Indeed, many have observed how shopping malls in the Global South have housed informal as well as formal economic activity.[54] But their primary features are standardization and interchangeability.

In Britain, Brent Cross was followed by a wave of suburban shopping malls in the 1980s and 1990s. This period saw the building of Merry Hill (Greater Birmingham, 1986), Gateshead MetroCentre (Greater Newcastle, 1986), Cascades (Portsmouth, 1989), Meadowhall (Sheffield, 1990), Lakeside (Essex, 1990), White Rose Centre (Leeds, 1997), Cribbs Causeway (Bristol, 1998), Trafford Centre (Greater Manchester, 1998), Bluewater (1999, Kent), Oracle (Reading, 1999), Braehead (Glasgow, 1999), and Festival Place (Basingstoke, 2002).[55] As a result of these developments, large tracts of British retail space became subject to architectural techniques and management practices that were developed and honed elsewhere.

The 1970s and 1980s saw a proliferation of technical manuals and advice literature on the best ways to build and run a shopping mall, a body of practice that was reinforced by conferences and seminars hosted across the world by the National Council of Shopping Centers and disseminated in US publications such as *Shopping Center World* and *National Mall Monitor*. In setting forth precise recommendations for the ideal layout, temperature, lighting, and acoustics of shopping malls, these manuals were conducting something close to an anthropology of the ideal consuming subject.[56] Writing about the commercial street life of early twentieth-century Britain, literary theorist Rachel Bowlby has described the emergence of the "passerby," referring to someone who moved half distractedly through urban space, subconsciously processing their immediate environment. Unlike the aimless flaneur, the passerby moved through cities on a definite journey but was still capable of being captivated by signs or window displays, making them the ideal target for advertisements.[57] In shopping malls, customers were ordered and channeled with a fixed purpose: they were neither the aimless flaneur nor the passerby moving through. Instead, they had already arrived. The job of developers was to keep their subjects circulating safely and comfortably while persuading them to spend their money.

The temperature and lighting of malls was a particular preoccupation for developers. A US manual from 1973 suggests that "the illumination level for mall areas should be subdued and yet adequate to stimulate people and to create a restful and inviting atmosphere." Elsewhere it was recommended that malls be heated at exactly seventy-five degrees Fahrenheit with 50 percent relative humidity in summer, dropping to seventy degrees in winter.[58]

Another important element was layout. As we saw, the lack of incentives for visitors to use the entire space of the mall was the undoing of Elephant and Castle. One manual recommended breaking long concourses into separate courtyards to sustain interest.[59] A British manual published in 1982 was more exact, calculating the precise width of pedestrianized concourses required to maximize profits. The author specifies a minimum concourse width of fifteen to twenty feet, with "room for window shoppers to pause, while allowing circulation past them," but not so wide that it will "deter them from crossing from shops on one side to those on the other side."[60] A 1985 manual took this even further, providing tens of different abstract layouts that designers could replicate. The frequency with which each concourse was broken up by courtyards, fountains, or other features was described by this text as a mall's "signature or score" or "linear node string," conferring a relative distinctiveness to any given development.[61]

Another technique for regulating space was the presence of piped background music. Although the playing of background music in shops goes back to the early twentieth century, when live bands would perform in large urban department stores, the development of ambient, almost inaudible music is a technology that has been honed by shopping mall developers.[62] The integration of music with systems of lighting, heating, and electricity, usually under the oversight of a single "facilities manager," allows the music to become part of the mall's architecture, a technology for creating consistency within its space. Music was supposed to fill the spaces of a mall evenly yet imperceptibly, like light and heat. This music often consisted of orchestral arrangements of well-known songs with little voice or percussion. Customers would subconsciously recognize the texture or rhythm of particular songs without having their attention drawn away from the important task of shopping.[63]

Security was also a pressing issue. A manual from the 1970s is a window into the coercive violence that the privatization of retail spaces makes possible—a reminder that their development in the United States went hand in hand with the growth of urban riots and political unrest in increasingly segregated cities. This handbook notes that if "it appears that a group may become violent, then the center should take immediate steps to protect certain key areas," and "fire protection is especially important in this decade with the frequent threat of fire bombs."[64] Meanwhile, large groups of young people were a regular cause for concern:

> Teenagers and youths, [are] firstly, potential customers and, secondly, a potential threat to security. The change from former to the latter usually occurs when the individuals coalesce into a recognisable group whether by their all wearing football scarves, adopting a particular mode of dress or moving through the centre in unison. Then the task is to remove the source of anxiety as quickly as possible by persuasion or force of law if necessary.[65]

The owners of the Sunshine Mall in Clearwater, Florida, complained of "restless teenagers . . . idly roaming through the nation's malls . . . smoking marijuana in the parking lot." The mall's solution was to form a vigilante group of teenagers, named "Pig Patrol," which was paid a small amount of money to police the mall's public spaces.[66] A 1984 article in *Shopping Center World* dripped with anxiety about the dangers of public space, claiming that the nature of shopping mall crime was changing, "becoming more violent" as "ever-present shop-lifters and occasional muggers are being supplanted by killers, rapists and child molesters." Just as some planners believed that council estates could be redesigned in ways that minimized crime, mall developers incorporated security measures into the fabric of their structures. The same article highlighted a series of security measures undertaken by recently developed malls, including centrally monitored CCTV cameras, noise detectors that automatically bathe potential criminals in bright spotlights, and the press-ganging of gardeners, cleaners, and maintenance workers to serve as informal security advisers.[67]

Unlike the planners of shopping precincts who attempted to anticipate levels of consumer demand by prescribing the number of hairdressers or butchers in any given development, shopping mall developers sought only to create the environmental conditions that would cause people to spend the most money. Again, we can see in these manuals a new pessimism about the ability of urban space to remake society. Just as the environmental criminologists who remade council estates believed that the job of architecture was to police rather than reform working-class Britons, shopping mall developers were in the business of enabling rather than prescribing desire. By the end of the 1980s, the modular and globally standardized shopping mall was becoming a commonplace feature of British towns and cities. Urban spaces of consumerism were being reimagined to suit a new kind of consuming subject. Merry Hill, the example that introduced this chapter, marked the apotheosis of this new urban form.

Merry Hill

Before Merry Hill, there was the Round Oak steelworks. Round Oak was one of the largest steelmaking complexes in Britain. Founded in 1857, by the mid-twentieth century the works boasted five blast furnaces and employed three thousand people, a significant proportion of the male population of the small town of Brierley Hill. The works were a defining feature of the Black Country, a scattered and sooty industrial corridor running to the west of Birmingham. In the 1950s, journalist Collie Knox visited Round Oak and described what he saw:

> The town of Brierley Hill, towered over by the skyscraper chimney stacks of Round Oak, and lit at night by the glow from its furnaces, teems with industry: steel, iron, fire-brick and glass. Nearby stands Dudley, historically the centre of the Black Country where the iron industry goes back to the Middle Ages. . . . The Black Country is the centre of a thousand trades, and in the grey skies and the belching factory chimneys there is a certain grim beauty.[68]

Along with many other British steel foundries, Round Oak was nationalized in 1951 by the postwar Labour government and then, also like steel foundries across the country, closed in the early 1980s after being hit by falling global demand. The closure of Round Oak in 1982 plunged an area that was already stricken by deindustrialization into deep crisis.

As the Black Country's industrial economy was disintegrating, the small town became the object of a radical and highly experimental urban policy drawn up by Thatcher's recently elected government. In the 1960s and 1970s, successive governments had tried to solve the problem of urban poverty with injections of public funds and the selective granting of Industrial Development Certificates.[69] Beginning in the late 1970s, there emerged a new sense that inner cities were facing a collapse of their economic infrastructure—a collapse that would supersede and outlast any short-term ameliorative attempts to improve the material conditions of their residents. This was the headline of a 1977 white paper on inner cities, which formed the intellectual basis for a radical transformation of British urban policy under Thatcher in the 1980s.[70] In short, the problem of deindustrialization and structural unemployment in places like Brierley Hill was to be solved by enticing private capital through targeted acts of deregulation. The first few years of Thatcher's government saw a variety of experiments on this theme. Urban development grants, introduced in 1982, provided local authorities with small amounts of money with the condition that they were spent on projects for which private capital would put up most of the money. National garden festivals, held every two years from 1984, were large garden shows designed to incentivize the clearing of derelict land and prepare parts of inner cities for private development.

By far the most radical of these policies, however, was the enterprise zone.[71] Enterprise zones had a long gestation period prior to their arrival in 1981. They were the brainchild of the Labour Party–affiliated urban planner Peter Hall, who in the late 1960s had fantasized about the removal of all planning restrictions from large regions of Britain in order to create fantastic landscapes of houseboats, weed shops, and Vegas-style strips.[72] In 1977, in a high-profile speech to the Royal Town Planning Institute, Hall called for declining inner-city areas to be freed from all state regulation and taxation. He imagined that places like the Isle of Dogs in East London would secede from Britain's customs regime and the European Economic Community, becoming "crown colonies" or protectorates similar to colonial Hong Kong.[73] The idea was picked up by Geoffrey Howe, then chancellor of the exchequer under Thatcher. Howe watered down Hall's scheme and turned it into a policy, creating eleven enterprise zones in economically depressed areas, each a few hundred acres in size. Businesses in these areas could expect exemption from certain land taxes, a streamlining of the planning process, exemption from industrial training boards, and minimal requests from the government for statistical information for a ten-year period. The removal of all fire and building regulations as well as bus and taxi licensing, and the suspension of laws forbidding discrimination on the basis of sex or race, were discussed but never implemented.[74]

The land adjacent to the Round Oak steel plant, which at that point was entering its final year of operation, became one of the first enterprise zones in 1981. After Round Oak closed, the zone was expanded to include its former buildings. One of the unforeseen consequences of the Thatcher government's enterprise zone policy was the construction of the two largest shopping malls built in Britain in the 1980s—the Metrocentre, which opened in the Gateshead enterprise zone near Newcastle in 1986, and Merry Hill. Merry Hill was the creation of Don and Roy Richardson, twins who left school at fourteen to work for their father selling surplus wartime army trucks. Their father's company branched out into logistics more generally and then, from the 1960s on, began to trade in property—mostly buying up disused industrial sites in the West Midlands.[75] The self-styled "shopping city" that the Richardson brothers created in Brierley Hill boasted 250 shops arrayed along 2.5 miles of concourses. It was unlike anything that had been seen in Britain. In chapter 2, we saw how Gibson had only been able to build his Coventry precinct with the help of a government declaratory order that gave exceptional powers to the local authority. Although similar in size, the enterprise zone was an inversion of the same exceptional logic. While one instrument centralized control in the hands of the state, the other functioned as a tiny tax haven—a power vacuum for the unimpeded play of free market forces.

Like Brent Cross and other suburban malls, Merry Hill existed in isolation from its nearest urban center—in this instance, Birmingham. There were no offices or housing on the main shopping site, and the mall was cut off from public transportation routes. Those without cars were dependent on the mall's scheduled minibuses to take them to and from Birmingham and elsewhere. Meanwhile, Merry Hill's monorail, which only connected the different parts of the mall, was a grim reminder of the fate of some of the more ambitious public transit schemes drawn up by a previous generation of planners. The 1960s had seen proposals for glamorous, high-tech municipal monorails in various British cities including Milton Keynes, Washington, Tyne and Wear, and Leicester, although none of them were ever built. These monorails were posed as solutions to the social and environmental problems of mass car ownership.[76] Fully private and intended only as a curiosity to delight those who had arrived by car, Merry Hill's monorail served as a ghostly pastiche of an alternative vision of urban mobility that never came to pass.

Meanwhile, the mall was advertised as a place for family leisure rather than household reproduction. One advertisement urged visitors to remember to take their camera for "happy family snaps."[77] Merry Hill's monthly "magazine" offered a vision of shopping that was about self-creation and pleasure versus necessity. One extraordinary "editorial" written by a local journalist read,

> I think therefore I shop. From the moment I could speak I was gurgling Gucci Gucci goo. . . . I offer no apologies. . . . [S]hopping is the most fun you can have vertically and clothed. . . . How else will you be able to share

with us connoisseurs of consumerism, the thrill of walking into a shopping mall and feeling the synapses in the brain snap, crackle and pop at all that life enhancing merchandise just waiting to take up residence in your home? . . . It's warm, it is glamorous, it's where aspiration flourishes.[78]

It is worth pausing to reflect on how far this language had come from the mathematical formulas developed in the 1950s and 1960s to calculate the character and scope of consumer demand. The Merry Hill magazine was addressing a consumer motivated by desire rather than necessity, a subject whose whims could not be precisely planned for. The difference between the consuming subject imagined by local authorities in the first two decades after the war and the author of this editorial is analogous to the difference between mercantilist and free trade political economies. In the former, demand was placed in a fixed, zero-sum relationship to supply. The latter, meanwhile, constructed consumers who didn't yet know what they wanted, but whose synapses fizzed as they strolled through Merry Hill's concourses.

The mall also marked the total erasure of the Round Oak factory and industrial world to which it belonged. The mall's main cultural signifiers, from the Swiss-built monorail to the Jules Verne–like food court, were global rather than local in scope. Indeed, as if to illustrate the mall's modularity, when the monorail was closed in 1996 for safety reasons, its carriages and tracks were shipped to an almost-identical mall in Queensland, Australia, where they operated until 2017.[79] While the large numbers of indoor fountains and pools were supposedly a reference to the canals of the Black Country, this was an illusion that was described by one observer as "distant and doubtless lost on visitors—no industrial canal was ever so blue or clean."[80] Instead, Merry Hill embraced its postindustrial vision, with a "finance court" that offered a particularly conspicuous example of what Amy Edwards has called "financial consumerism": the popularization of share ownership and complex forms of banking in the 1980s.[81] The finance court hosted all of the mall's banks and also broadcast live financial news on a series of TV screens.[82]

Although the mall was conceived of and initially built by two local property developers, it quickly became ensnared in a circuit of capital that went far beyond the West Midlands. In 1990, the Richardson brothers sold Merry Hill to a British property development company called Mountleigh, owned at that point by two US businesspeople, Nelson Peltz and Peter May. Mountleigh arrived relatively late to the game of property speculation. The company had been incorporated in 1863, and for the first hundred years of its life it manufactured textiles. Originally called the North Warwickshire Worsted and Woollen Spinning and Weaving Company, Mountleigh owned a handful of textile mills around Coventry; by the 1960s and 1970s these were in decline, along with the

FIGURE 5.2. Round Oak steelworks in Brierley Hill, photographed in 1941. Reproduced with kind permission of Dudley Archives and Local History Centre.

FIGURE 5.3. The interior of Merry Hill shopping center. Reproduced with kind permission of Dudley Archives and Local History Centre.

FIGURE 5.4. Merry Hill's monorail. Photograph by Lewis Bevan.

rest of Britain's textile industry. In 1976, Mountleigh's owner, at that point Tony Clegg, devoted one day a week to property speculation, making use of the large landholdings that his company had acquired over the last century. It quickly transpired that Mountleigh's landholdings, most of which were unused, were worth far more than its declining textile mills. Within eight years, Clegg had increased Mountleigh's annual turnover from 5.24 to 529.5 million pounds. Clegg became one of the richest and most notorious property speculators in Britain. By 1989, with his health failing and the overheated 1980s property boom collapsing into recession, Clegg sold his shares in Mountleigh to Peltz and May.[83]

Peltz and May had spent the 1980s making millions buying and selling junk bonds in the United States. The two men had owned a vending machine company, Triangle Industries, which they used as a vehicle to buy shares in other companies. Peltz and May bought Clegg's holdings in the ailing Mountleigh as a means of forcing their way into the European market.[84] In the late 1980s, this was a common practice, as a glut of overseas capital flooded Britain's commercial property market. During this period, similar raids on British companies or specific developments were made by the South African–controlled Trans Atlantic Insurance and the Swedish developer Skanska as well as a variety of different Japanese pensions firms, which, looking for stable rates of return, invested in projects such as the shopping mall in the middle of the new town of Milton Keynes.[85] The new owners of Mountleigh, Peltz and May, had close ties with notorious speculator Michael Milken, who had been arrested the previous year for insider trading, an event that had become symbolic of Wall Street's feverish volatility in the 1980s. The pair's ties to Milken were picked up on in the West Midlands by a suspicious local press.[86]

Having purchased Merry Hill for Mountleigh, Peltz and May departed after two years, leaving the company in the hands of Gordon Getty, another US venture capitalist. By 1992, the company's shares were distributed among an increasingly bizarre and international group of speculators. As well as Getty, parts of Mountleigh were owned by the Pritzker family, which also owned the Hyatt hotel chain, and a Dutch property consortium called Accumulator.[87] That year, Mountleigh finally went into receivership, unable to pay off its loans due in no small part to the fact that the company had been unable to sell Merry Hill, even at a reduced cost of £125 million (£35 million below its estimated value).[88] Mountleigh came close to off-loading the mall to another US property company, but the deal fell through when rumors circulated that Merry Hill's foundations were saturated with toxic residues from the Round Oak steel plant and the mall was about to be condemned by the government.[89] This never happened, but its lingering threat was a poignant reminder of Merry Hill's repressed industrial prehistory.

Built thirty years apart, Merry Hill and the Coventry shopping precinct described in chapter 2 served fundamentally different visions of town planning, financing, and society. Gibson's precinct was modernist and pragmatic; it was a space for rationalizing and reordering the narrow medieval core of a midsize town. Coventry was commissioned, planned, and owned by the local authority, and was the singular vision of one of its employees. It reflected a moment of enthusiasm for state-directed urban development and the optimistic view that consumer desire was finite and calculable. Conversely, Merry Hill was banished to the suburbs and abstracted from time and place. It was enabled by a right-wing turn in urban policy, which set out to solve the problem of deindustrialization through supply-side incentives to court private capital rather than direct state investment. As much as it was a physical space, it was also one of many assets on the books of a constantly changing global holding company whose owners had perhaps never been to the West Midlands of England. It was a product of a world where consumerism was pleasurable in itself over and above the necessity of household reproduction and could be augmented by the right environmental controls. Merry Hill also marked something of a limit case. Spaces as outlandish as Merry Hill remain unfamiliar to many Britons and make up a minority of the country's approximately 750 shopping centers.[90] It should be seen as the ideal realization of an urban type that in a more diluted form is ubiquitous across the country. This chapter will end by looking at this dilution.

The New Town Center

In the 1980s and 1990s, many of the shopping precincts that were built in new towns, blitzed cities, or former comprehensive redevelopment areas in the preceding three decades became gradually subject to the historical processes outlined in this chapter. These spaces no longer had to shoulder the burden of daily household reproduction, and their developmental goals had since been either achieved or abandoned. And yet, like high-density housing estates, these spaces continued and continue to exist. Many became shabby, zombified remains that feel peculiar and retrograde when compared to their shinier, more recently built cousins. Many have been rebuilt and reimagined, while some have been entirely erased. Sheffield Castle Market, a precinct built by Womersley, the same architect who designed the Park Hill Estate, was demolished in 2015. More famously perhaps, Portsmouth's brutalist Tricorn Centre, once voted one of the ugliest buildings in Britain, was demolished to make way for a large parking lot in 2004. Many of those that remained were severed from the cities in which they were embedded and elevated into global circuits of capital, ownership, and expertise. In other words, they were privatized. As we saw in the last chapter, "privatization" is about more than the transition from state to private ownership. It is as much about access, policing, appearance, and the way that an urban form is imagined to relate to its surroundings as it is about ownership.[91]

The refurbishment and subsequent sale of the Westgate Shopping Centre in Oxford, a multistory shopping precinct built and owned by Oxford City Council, typified the way that a change in ownership entailed an intensification of the management and policing of urban space. When it opened in 1972, Westgate connected seamlessly with Oxford's High Street, with the shopping precinct's concourses acting as routes beyond to another neighborhood. By the mid-1980s, the development had become the object of an intense moral panic after increasing numbers of unemployed young men had taken to congregating in its concourses. In the early 1980s, business owners and customers began to complain to the council about the large numbers of "drunks, punks and skinheads" who reportedly spent days at a time living in the mall. The local newspaper, the *Oxford Mail*, launched a campaign to expel these people, who at different times were labeled "dossers," "rockers," "tramps," and "undesirables."[92] The newspaper called the Westgate a "showpiece of squalor," describing pavements that were "lined with urine, vomit and rubbish."[93] One Oxford

FIGURE 5.5. Cartoon printed in the *Oxford Mail* showing the police evicting a family
from a bench in order to make way for homeless people. Reproduced with kind permission
of the *Oxford Mail*.

resident wrote to the *Oxford Mail* asking what inoculations he and his wife
would require before visiting the Westgate that weekend.[94]

The unemployed and economically unproductive men that congregated in
the Westgate were compared unfavorably to families with children, the precinct's
ideal constituency. A sarcastic letter written to the *Oxford Mail* pointed out
that "yet another minority group is starting to make its presence felt . . . that
radical group is known as families. If something is not done soon they will be
sitting on the seats provided for drunks." An accompanying cartoon published
in 1982 showed a group of drunk young men with Mohawk haircuts, piercings,
and tattered clothes successfully complaining to a police officer about a well-
dressed family sitting on a bench in the mall.[95] A major obstacle faced by those
trying to police the Westgate Centre was the fact that the shopping precinct was
never locked, even at night, and its concourses were legally inseparable from
the streets outside. In 1982, the council tried to install new, "drunk-proof"
benches that were impossible to sleep on, but this had little success. It was clear
by the mid-1980s that the Westgate Centre would have to be spatially reordered
in ways that excluded these young men and welcomed housewives and families
with open arms. While homeless or economically unproductive people had
been excluded from the Brent Cross and Merry Hill malls by their location on
the periphery of towns and cities, isolated from public transit routes, places like
the Westgate Centre required more intrusive interventions.

By 1986, Westgate's businesses were demanding rent reductions, claiming that their customers were now too terrified to shop there. That year, Oxford City Council gave up and cashed in, selling the development to a private consortium. Under the terms of the sale, the municipal functions of the building—its public toilets, external staircases, and parking lots—were uncoupled from its commercial core. While these facilities continued to be owned by the council, the private consortium acquired the internal concourses of the center and the right to lease its stores.[96] Immediately prior to the sale, the council had initiated a comprehensive upgrade of the Westgate's security, effectively sealing it off from the rest of the city. While the structure had previously lacked doors on its entrances and was open at all hours, it was now to be closed off at certain times. Doors were designed that were visually unwelcoming and slammed shut of their own accord.[97]

The new Westgate Centre required a change in the legal designation of the building's concourses. The concourses had originally been "highways," routes where all pedestrians have customary rights, not just to pass along but to conduct any behavior not deemed to be a nuisance or obstruction.[98] In other words, they were subject to the same laws as any other city street. The fitting of doors and the introduction of closing hours, however, required that the concourses be legally redefined as walkways.[99] Set out by the 1980 Highways Act, a "walkway" referred to a pedestrian route that was under the ownership of a body that had the power to close the route at certain hours and enforce specific bylaws regulating the behavior of its users. This change in the legal status of Westgate's internal space made it more difficult for homeless visitors to congregate under its roof and meant that these people could be forcefully evicted every night after the shops closed. The change in designation from highway to walkway also had implications for the policing of the Westgate Centre. At night, it would no longer be patrolled by city police, who did not have keys to the building.[100] Authority became split between the police and new private security staff who were hired by Westgate. These security guards were expected to perform a double function. On the one hand, they were employed to exert a controlling influence on the space, preventing large groups from congregating for too long in its concourses. On the other hand, they were expected to act as information guides to customers.[101] Just as large council estates, built as collective entities, had to be fundamentally changed to accommodate a new logic of private ownership, Westgate Shopping Centre was securitized and sealed off from the rest of the city before being sold by the council.

The redevelopment of municipal space in ways that effectively excluded certain categories of people in Oxford was repeated across the country in the 1980s. By the 1990s, the right to access the once-municipal, now-private space in town centers was becoming a contentious legal issue. In 1995, questions about who was and was not allowed to spend time in shopping centers came to a head in the small market town of Wellingborough in Northamptonshire. Like many other towns of its size, Wellingborough contained a shopping precinct that was built in the early 1970s and leased by the local authority to a private developer called CIN Properties. The twelve-acre center comprised a handful of medieval and once-public highways that ran through the town, and as in Oxford, the former streets had become walkways, closed between 11:00 p.m. and 7:00 a.m. In 1995, the center's private security team issued a lifetime ban to a small group of mostly black, unemployed young men who had been congregating in its concourses.[102] The injunctions against the youths were appealed but then upheld in a landmark case, *CIN Properties Ltd. v. Rawlins*. The case reaffirmed the absolute right of landowners (or renters) to exclude people from their property. The conceptions of "trespass" and "property" around which the case was fought had their origins in the protection of residential property from incursion, a precedent established by centuries of customary law. In other words, the slow accretion of customary law regulating the absolute right of private property in land—a right that had emerged in the context of domestic curtilage and feudal landholdings—had been given new legal life by shopping malls in British towns.[103] With the shopping precinct providing one of the main places of congregation, socialization, and employment in Wellingborough, the lifetime bans handed to these young people had consequences that went well beyond their ability to access a certain space.

While *CIN Properties Ltd. v Rawlins* set a precedent for the permanent exclusion of specific individuals from private shopping centers, a subsequent legal battle also emerged about how such spaces could be *used*. These questions had been foreshadowed on the other side of the Atlantic. With shopping malls becoming part of the infrastructure of US suburbia in the 1950s and 1960s, the question of whether or not these spaces could be used for protest or democratic assembly began to be discussed. In 1968, following the expulsion of union workers picketing in a private retail plaza in Pennsylvania, the US Supreme Court ruled in favor of the union, arguing that the mall was the "community business block," and its concourses were the "functional equivalents of the streets and sidewalks of a normal business district."[104] In that case, the court had ruled that rights to free speech obtained on private property, as long as that property was open to the public. The 1968 ruling did not last long, however. In 1980, the private security team of the PruneYard Shopping Mall in Campbell, California, evicted a group of high schoolers who had set up a card table in a corner of the mall's central courtyard to distribute flyers and gather signatures against a recent UN resolution concerning Israel. The students were told to move to the public sidewalk at the mall's perimeter, but instead they filed a lawsuit, which ended up in the Supreme Court. This more conservative

Court ruled against the students, setting a precedent that rights to free speech and assembly did not automatically apply to shopping malls.[105] It was left up to each state to decide whether the owners of shopping malls would have the final say in the arbitrary expulsion of individuals. By 2003, only six states— California, Colorado, Massachusetts, New Jersey, Oregon, and Washington— supported people's rights to protest and assemble in shopping malls.[106] A similar precedent was established in Canada in 1976 after the country's Supreme Court upheld the expulsion of a striking worker from a shopping mall in Winnipeg for picketing her workplace.[107]

It was perhaps inevitable that when an equivalent court case emerged in Britain, it would concern a once-municipal-owned shopping precinct in a new town. The malling of shopping precincts was felt particularly acutely in new towns. In most cases, shopping precincts were the effective town centers of these settlements—places that also housed municipal libraries, police stations, and other public services. As we have seen, shopping precincts in new towns were planned, commissioned, and for the most part owned by state-appointed development corporations. New town development corporations were always intended to be temporary bodies, but Thatcher's government accelerated the process by which these bodies were to be wound down, meaning that in the early 1980s many new towns hastily sold their assets to private developers.[108] When the Milton Keynes shopping precinct opened in 1979, for example, it was still owned by the state-run development corporation that had built it, and its concourses were open twenty-four hours a day.[109] In the mid-1980s, its concourses began to be locked at night, and shortly afterward the mall was sold to a private development company. A similar story can be told about the holistically planned shopping precincts of new towns such as Cumbernauld (purchased by a property developer in 1996), Telford (purchased by a pension fund in 1990), and Basildon (whose central shopping precinct was demolished in 1980 and turned into the Eastgate International Shopping Centre).

In 1998, a group of protesters set up two stands at the entrance to the Galleries Shopping Centre in the new town of Washington, Tyne and Wear, on the outskirts of Sunderland, to contest the redevelopment of a nearby playing field. Private security guards soon asked them to leave. In a letter justifying the decision, the Galleries' manager wrote that "the owner's stance on all political and religious issues, is one of strict neutrality and I am charged with applying this philosophy."[110] Like other new towns, when Washington was planned and built in the mid-1960s the central shopping precinct was owned and managed by the state-run Washington Development Corporation. In 1987, the center was sold to a private property developer called Postel Properties Limited. Also like many new towns, the shopping precinct was the town's focal point, even marked on maps as the "town centre," and housed many social services including a housing office, careers office, library, police station, and health center. The protesters took their complaints to the European Court of Human Rights in Strasbourg, claiming that Articles 10 and 11 of the European Convention for the Protection of Human Rights, guaranteeing the rights to free speech and free assembly, were violated. In 2003, the court ruled against the protesters. As a result of this ruling and *CIN Properties Ltd. v Rawlins*, the effective town centers of many British new towns, or towns that were heavily replanned after the war, are now subject to the same legal regimes as out-of-town shopping malls such as Brent Cross or Merry Hill.

The introduction of mall-like spatial practices into town centers in Britain since 1980 has added complexity to any neat definition of either public or private space. New developments have opened in the last ten years that appear porous and indeterminate, yet are owned by developers and intensely policed.[111] These include spaces such as Granary Square near King's Cross or the Liverpool One shopping mall that opens onto the city's waterfront. The splintering of public space in the new millennium marks the end of this story. The shopping mall's coherence as an urban form seems to be collapsing, but its technologies for policing and regulating public space have seeped into urban space—invisible yet heavy like dark matter. The increasingly unstable boundaries between public and private urban space in Britain have attracted interest from academics, journalists, and even developers.[112] It is not the purpose of this chapter to intervene in these debates, however, nor to develop a working and consistent theorization of public space. I hope instead to have described a set of historical processes that would underpin any definition and to have shown that such a definition would be historically contingent. To the extent that retail space in Britain was ever "public space," it was thanks to a mid-twentieth-century configuration of architecture, security tactics, and legal precedent that was reworked as the century came to a close.

This chapter has traced the history of the shopping mall in Britain, demonstrating how it emerged from the ashes of a developmental compact between urban planning and the management of consumer demand. I have shown how shopping mall developers in Britain replicated a globally standardized type of urban space, aligning parts of Britain's built environment with that of the United States and world. Their modularity allowed malls to be bought and sold as investments by an increasingly international group of property speculators. As with the reformed council estates of the 1980s and 1990s, shopping malls manifested a skepticism that the desires of an aggregate mass of people could be anticipated and remade. Rather, they brought with them a new kind of consumer subject, one who was motivated by a boundless desire and whose contours could not be precisely anticipated.

FIGURE 5.6. Empty mock Venetian gondolas in the deserted South China Mall in Dongguan. Photograph by Remko Tanis

Once again, however, we can see how the neoliberal city in Britain was characterized by the surprising and stubborn endurance of a midcentury built environment engineered by a developmental state. The shopping precincts, commissioned and built by local authorities in the immediate postwar decades to reorganize towns and cities as well as distribute the spoils of postwar growth, outlived their historical moment. As with the council estate, shopping precincts could not be sold to private developers without first being remade. The centrality and porousness of such developments, once seen as a key part of their developmental purpose, was a major obstacle to their privatization. Coercion was required, meaning the arbitrary expulsion of certain individuals and the restriction of rights to democratic public assembly. Just as individual flats were not easily separated from the council estates of which they formed a part, shopping precincts could not easily be severed from the town centers in which they were often the centerpiece. The awkwardness of these intermediary spaces for property developers, mortgage lenders, and neoliberal politicians accelerated the proliferation of entirely new urban forms by the millennium, whether it was gated residential communities or vast shopping malls in the suburbs.

As a discrete, autonomous urban form, the shopping mall is dying, withering away in a contagious global rot that appears, fittingly, to have begun in the United States, where malls were first conceived. In 2017, Credit Suisse estimated that almost a quarter of US malls could be abandoned by 2022.[113] A combination of the 2008 financial crisis, the growth of big-box stores such as Walmart, and the rise of online shopping are resulting in increasing numbers of flooded, empty, and shuttered malls. Even in China, which saw an eruption in the numbers of shopping malls in the last twenty years, the disease seems to be spreading. The biggest shopping mall in the world, the New South China Mall, was until recently a dead mall too. Built in Dongguan in southern China in 2005, it provides space for 2,350 stores, and its multiple, soaring atriums are themed after different parts of the world, including a mock Arc de Triomphe and Egyptian sphinx. There are reports that as of 2018 the mall is recovering, but for most of its life, it was almost entirely empty. One extraordinary photograph of the mall shows three ornate gondolas, sadly parked in a mock Venetian canal beneath tier after tier of empty storefronts.[114] Britain has no proliferation of dead malls yet, but the number of visitors to shopping malls appears to be declining.[115] Merry Hill could soon be as derelict as the steel foundry on which it was built.

6

The Business Park

ON A JANUARY day in 1982, the staff members of LKB Biochrom, a small company specializing in the production of niche scientific instruments, arrived at work to find a note from their employer. Addressed only to the company's male workforce, it contained a request from the next-door neighbors:

> A new company on the Science Park, Cambridge Life Sciences, uses human urine as the raw material for one of their products. Due to the current adverse weather conditions, their normal supplies of this unusual starting material have failed. We have been asked if employees of LKB Biochrom would donate their urine for experimental purposes.[1]

A plastic container was left in the company's male restrooms, and after enough urine had been gathered, the company was gifted a barrel of beer as thanks. This exchange took place on the leafy grounds of Cambridge Science Park, a mute scattering of offices and laboratories that had opened in 1973. Designed to forge links between Cambridge University and private business, the park was a quiet and cordial expression of avant-garde technofuturism nestled in the Fens, the first of its kind in Britain. Although bizarre, this exchange was not atypical in an environment intended to foster professional and social collaboration between different enterprises. Designed to be more than the sum of their parts, the businesses leasing this shiny complex of huts shared resources and ideas with their neighbors as well as with Cambridge scientists and students. Their employees ate, drank, dieted, and even prayed with one another.

The final chapter of this book concerns suburban, postindustrial, and holistically planned developments such as the Cambridge Science Park. These were initiated and managed by a single authority, usually a private developer, and hosted a mixture of offices, light industry, and private research centers. They were developed in relative isolation from the cities that surrounded them, providing their own roads, landscaping, and security. By the end of the 1980s, there were more than four hundred such developments in Britain, and cities and towns were ringed by necklaces of squat white buildings, silent parking lots, and glistening lawns.[2] Business parks were to corporate offices and small high-tech factories what shopping malls were to high street stores. I use the term "business park" to describe a host of different developments that at various times have been called "office parks," "science parks," "research parks," "industrial parks," or "technology parks."[3] These environments were planned for work in the abstract and were laid down in advance in order to attract a variety of different tenants that would rent preexisting buildings and share communal spaces. In this sense, the business parks of the 1980s and 1990s have their analogues in the industrial estates of the 1930s, 1940s, and 1950s that were the subject of chapter 1. Business parks emerged at a time when the geography and nature of work was changing in Britain, becoming more suburban and less industrial. The period between 1960 and 1980 saw a mass migration of jobs and capital out of British cities. Between these years, London alone lost seven hundred thousand manufacturing jobs, or more than half its 1960 total. During the same window of time, the number of manufacturing jobs in rural areas across the country increased by a hundred thousand, despite a large contraction in manufacturing generally during this period.[4]

There is a rich historiography concerning the changing nature of work in twentieth-century Britain. My purpose here is not to rehearse the history of deindustrialization, the increasing prevalence of women in the labor market, or the rise of flexible or casualized forms of work, although business parks were shaped by all these processes.[5] Instead, I will chart the history of a new late twentieth-century urban form, looking at the kinds of working subjects that this form hoped to produce and attract, and its relationship to the state and to the wider world.[6] I will describe the evolution of this form by investigating three different examples: the Stanford Industrial Park built in California's Silicon Valley in 1953; the Cambridge Science Park, planned and built by Trinity College Cambridge in 1973; and Stockley Park, a vast high-tech development constructed in stages on the western fringes of London throughout the 1980s. While most of the hundreds of business parks built in Britain are small and mundane, almost invisible to all but those who work there, I dwell on the most dramatic iterations of these urban forms—sites whose developers believed, rightly or wrongly, that they were creating landscapes that would shape the future of working life.

Government-financed industrial estates in Britain had emerged as part of a developmental project, animated by the belief that regional imbalances could be redressed by controlling the location of industrial development. In contrast, business parks had no such burden. The first university-owned science parks went against the grain of Britain's industrial policy, and the explosion of suburban business parks in the late 1980s occurred only after a change in planning law in 1987. While industrial estates, inspired by Trafford Park on the outskirts of Manchester, radiated outward through the British Empire and beyond, business and science parks were creatures of US suburbia, direct imports from places like Silicon Valley or the Research Triangle in North Carolina. Industrial estates were organized around a knowable and malleable working-class subject and were designed to maximize discipline and utilitarian efficiency. Business and science parks, however, with their curvilinear streets, abundant nature, public art, and opportunities for chance encounters, were spaces planned in order to foster more intangible qualities of inspiration and well-being. Their ideal subjects were elite, flexible, and, as we will see, mostly male workers. Receptionists, cleaners, gardeners, and security guards were employed in business parks, but they left little footprint on the imagination of planners and developers. This chapter will end where the first chapter began, at Trafford Park. Ruined by deindustrialization and choked by geography, Trafford Park was transformed by a state development corporation into a massive, if only partially realized, business park by the 1980s. As with the private housing estate and shopping mall, this new urban form required a reimagining of the old.

The Science Park

In 1960, a group of wealthy benefactors gathered at Stanford University to hear a speech from one of the university's senior officials. The audience, most of whom were alumni from across the country, were clearly concerned about how the university was managing its enormous 8,800-acre landholding, a sunlit, undulating strip of land south of San Francisco Bay. Over the previous seven years, land rich but cash poor, the university had earmarked a parcel of this land for industrial development, prompting an evident ripple of concern among its benefactors. In his speech, the official sought to reassure his audience that the Stanford Industrial Park was unlike anything they had ever seen before—a development that would force them to rethink the very idea of what industrial work could look like:

> Before taking a position on the question of industry in the hills, we must first ask ourselves, "What is industry?" Many of you have probably come from the east or Midwest, like myself, and industry means smoke stacks, heavy thumpings, coal cars, soot and many other things not associated with pleasant living. Industry, as we know it in the peninsula area, is something entirely different. It can mean broad lawns, employee patios, tree planting, walls of glass, recreation clubs, research and development, and a place for creative people to work. The buildings often resemble schools and colleges more than industrial plants.[7]

The Stanford Industrial Park was a new type of space—an attempt to combine academic research and for-profit production on a single, carefully landscaped patch of suburban land.[8] As the university official correctly observed, it emerged at a time when the look and feel of US industry was beginning to change.

In the early twentieth century, at the same time as Trafford Park was under development in Manchester, a handful of industrial estates were built in the United States, mostly under the ownership and management of large railroad companies.[9] By 1940, there were more than forty of these developments, and they tended to orbit large western or midwestern cities such as Chicago or Los Angeles. As we saw in chapter 1, these spaces, unlike those in Britain, mostly remained in private hands and never featured as part of a broader nationwide industrial strategy. After the Second World War, US industrial estates began to compete with a new and greener type of industrial space. Freeways rather than railroads started to determine the location of industrial development, and manufacturing companies began to petition local governments for the right to develop in suburban locations, where land was cheaper.[10] The 1940s, 1950s, and 1960s saw a rash of "industrial districts," comprehensively planned by developers and appearing in suburban locations like Boston's Route 128 corridor. These new industrial districts were usually subject to planning controls that limited the amount of noise and pollution that could be generated. They mostly eschewed the term "estate," with many opting instead for "park," hoping to identify with a different aesthetic. The Industrial Parks USA exhibit at the 1958 Brussels World's Fair, in which the Stanford Science Park was prominent, popularized the term and drew international attention to these new developments.[11] It was not just new factories and research plants that were suburbanizing in the first two decades after the war. Like millions of middle-class white people, large established businesses also fled to the US suburbs, moving their headquarters to planned and landscaped "campuses." These spaces, such as the General Motors Technical Center built on the fringes of Detroit in 1956, were often modeled on university campuses, with the intention of attracting academics for research and development. US architectural historian Louise Mozingo coined the term "pastoral capitalism" to describe the new look and feel of workplaces in the United States during this period.[12]

Stanford Industrial Park was an early pioneer of such developments. The area south of San Francisco Bay had been a hub for the manufacturing of small electrical products for generations before it became known as Silicon Valley in the 1970s. This was partly a result of Stanford University's well-funded electrical engineering department, whose graduates, from the 1920s onward, often started businesses nearby, sometimes with the support of the university. After the war, the electrical engineering labs and factories surrounding the university were increasingly servicing government aerospace and defense contracts.[13] Stanford Industrial Park was the brainchild of Frederick Terman, a Stanford scientist and pioneer in the field of radio engineering who was being promoted rapidly through the university's hierarchy, becoming provost in 1955. Terman advocated successfully for the park and courted its first tenant, Varian, an electromagnetics company founded by four graduates of Stanford's electrical engineering department and on whose board of directors he sat.[14]

In order to justify its bucolic, rural setting in the Santa Clara Valley, the park did everything it could to distance itself from heavy industry. Businesses renting space were prohibited by covenants from the "giving off of offensive gas, smoke fumes, dust, odors, waste products, noise or vibrations."[15] Although tenants were encouraged to design and construct their own buildings, they did so under the strictest aesthetic control. Park administrators were allowed to veto any building that was deemed ugly or inappropriate. All development plans by prospective tenants were submitted to a committee of Stanford faculty, chaired by the Department of Art and Architecture, for aesthetic review. Much of the site was intended to have only 20 percent building coverage, with a third of the site left as grassland.[16] The Stanford Industrial Park set a precedent for US universities with large landholdings and little liquidity looking to make money through property speculation as well as forge links with private businesses. It also set an example for the urbanization of the broader Santa Clara Valley (soon to be known as Silicon Valley). By 1977, the San Jose Chamber of Commerce listed fifty-seven industrial parks of various sizes in Silicon Valley.[17]

Once established as an urban form in the United States, the science park was imported wholesale to Britain. It arrived in the early 1970s, in the wake of a decade in which scientific research and development had been at the forefront of British politics.[18] The number of scientists in laboratories and campuses in Britain had been increasing exponentially as a result of military research before and during the Second World War. By the early 1960s, the Labour Party, led by Harold Wilson, looked to scientific expertise as a solution to industrial and imperial decline.[19] Wilson's 1964–70 government oversaw an increase in the size of scientific and technical departments in the country's universities, which were in rapid expansion during this period. And in 1966, following a visit to the United States, Wilson wrote an open to letter to British universities encouraging them to set up science parks in line with the US model.[20] Cambridge University, famous for its fractious 1960s debates between scientist C. P. Snow and literary critic F. R. Leavis over the role of science in society, was particularly affected by the growth of scientific education during this period.[21] In 1967, the university convened a subcommittee under the guidance of Nobel Prize–winning physicist Neville Mott to look at the use

FIGURE 6.1. Horses graze on the grounds of Stanford Industrial Park, 1972.

of scientific research outside the academy, especially its application in the fields of industry, medicine, and agriculture.[22]

When Trinity College Cambridge began to consider locating a science park on the outskirts of the small university town in the late 1960s, it followed Wilson's urging and looked to the United States as a precedent.[23] Like many Oxford and Cambridge colleges as well as Stanford, Trinity owned vast tracts of land. In the early 1970s, Trinity's tenants included an agricultural estate in a small village in Bedfordshire, a boat hire depot on the Grand Union Canal, scattered houses across a large tract of the Romney Marshes in Kent, and even a car tire store in East London.[24] Its status as a registered charity meant that the college benefited from reduced rates of property tax.[25] Trinity College brought to the planning of the Cambridge Science Park its considerable expertise as a landlord. Its finances were already heavily supplemented by rental income. The college's senior bursar, John Bradfield, oversaw this diverse portfolio of landholdings, collecting the rents and approving planning proposals. The site chosen for the park by Bradfield was a flat and featureless patch of ground on the outskirts of the town. Owned by the college since 1443, the site had been a parking spot for US tanks during the Second World War and since then had become an abandoned gravel pit.[26]

Trinity planned the park so that it would resemble a village-like milieu. As in Stanford, Trinity set out to create a "'park' environment of mainly trees and substantial areas of grass."[27] Its public spaces were tended, managed, and policed by Bidwells, a private property developer. The college set about sowing the ground with grass and plants, laying down roads, and turning the gravel pit at the center of the site into an artificial lake. Whimsy was prioritized over function, as the college demolished the original military road on the site, deeming it "too dull and straight."[28] Meanwhile, electricity lines were torn down and hidden underground.[29] A groundskeeper who had worked previously for the new town of Runcorn moved to live full time in the park with his family.[30] The college retained aesthetic control over any proposed developments, and restrictive covenants ensured that only clean, low-rise industries were permitted. Initially, Trinity sought to restrict the number of tenants to sixteen, with a ratio of approximately a square foot of building for every 4.5 square feet of park.[31] The first two tenants were LKB Biochrom, which built a two-story office block and small laboratory on the site, and Laser Scan, which manufactured computer-controlled lasers. By 1989, the park had extended well beyond its initial, modest thirteen-acre site and housed sixty-nine different firms.[32]

The park opted for flexibility and impermanence, anticipating a high turnover of tenants. Companies rented rather than purchased their plot of land, with a twenty-five-year lease that was renewed every five years.[33] Some companies designed and constructed their own buildings, while the park's management designed and constructed others. The latter had malleable internal spaces, which could be reordered to suit the needs of specific tenants without moving expensive equipment.[34] Strips of continuous glass surrounded the buildings, meaning that new entrances and exits could be added quickly, and internal floor space could be subdivided without closing off any exits.[35] Many of the tenants housed laboratories, offices, and small assembly plants, spaces that had to be reconfigured as contracts changed and new technologies emerged.

The park was planned in order to maximize the effectiveness of a new kind of working subject. In 1990, three Open University geographers, Doreen Massey, Paul Quintas, and David Wield, collected data from eighty-eight different businesses located in science parks (with the Cambridge Science Park providing by far the largest number of responders). Their investigation found an elite workforce, separated into small units with a high degree of autonomy and flexibility. There was an almost total absence of trade unions in science parks, with 90 percent of the firms reporting that they employed no unionized workers at all.[36] This lack was several steps ahead of the national trend. Trade union density in the United Kingdom stood at 39.9 percent in 1989, having fallen from 49.9 percent in 1981.[37] When asked by Massey and her team about the low rates of unionization on the site, one manager said that unions were unnecessary as workers felt that they were "well treated" and in a "good environment." As opposed to working in a fixed hierarchy, with clearly assigned tasks, hours, and expectations, most science park workers were expected to be in charge of their own hours, solely motivated by their enthusiasm for the work. Of the managers questioned in Massey, Quintas, and Wield's survey, 67 percent said that their employees were expected to record their own time on projects, and 59 percent said that their staff worked flexible hours. Of these 59 percent, 91 percent said that they had no formal system of timekeeping, and that timekeeping was based on "trust" and "high morale" alone. The same survey found that only 25 percent of science park establishments paid overtime to their workers (compared with 56 percent of nonpark establishments).[38]

Cambridge Science Park was therefore a place where well-being and perceived autonomy were more important than job security and welfare. The park was spatially ordered to suit this new kind of worker, not only through its bucolic, manicured setting, but in its attempts to inculcate a sense of collegiate sociability between different employees as well as collapse the distinction between work and play.[39] Trinity intended for the park to be more than merely an atomized scattering of businesses. The park's newsletter advertised a number of events available to any worker on-site, including games of squash, an annual charity fun run (where different businesses competed against one another), a Christian fellowship that met weekly, and even a weight management course led by a nutrition scientist who worked in the park.[40] In 1983, Trinity opened a social center, which housed a bar furnished by a substantial grant from Barclays bank. The hope was to establish a culture in which businesses would share ideas and resources as well as to provide incentives for flexible workers, who would begin to see their place of employment as a site for leisure and sociability. When opening the social center in the park, the master of Trinity fantasized that the bar would become "a miniature hybrid between Kubla Khan's 'stately pleasure dome' and George IV's Pavilion in Brighton!'"[41] The success of this policy is perhaps best seen in the pages of a spy thriller called *The Cambridge Connection*, written in 2001 by an ex-physicist who used to work in the park. The novel depicts confident and chummy workers who live lives clouded by interbusiness social and sexual intrigue. The novel's protagonist, Harry Bridge, meets the story's love interest for the first time in the social center bar after work.[42]

For these reasons, the worker for whom the park was spatially ordered differed greatly from the worker imagined by the midcentury industrial estate. The shared amenities for the employees in estates like Team Valley, such as the recreation center funded by the government's National Fitness Council, or the regimented canteens with their subsidized and scientifically balanced meals, were intended to maximize the welfare and productivity of a working-class workforce subject to intensive forms of time discipline. There were many ways that the state and private bodies attempted to augment the physical, psychological, and social makeup of the British industrial workforce in the mid-twentieth century. US industrialist Frederick Winslow Taylor's scientific management techniques, increasingly prevalent in large industrial workplaces from the interwar period onward, were one example. The group psychology of the workplace developed at the Tavistock Institute of Human Relations, founded in 1947, was another. These were experiments with subtle and often state-sponsored means of cultivating workplace consensus with the aim of maximizing production.[43] In this vein, Daniel Ussishkin highlighted the efforts of sociologist Talcott Parsons, who was funded by the psychological committee of the Medical Research Council immediately after the Second World War to conduct research into the morale of coal miners. Parsons suggested various fixes that would foster forms of in-group thinking and lead to an "intensification of normative behaviour" among workers. He argued, for instance, that a single color scheme should be chosen for the beams and equipment in a particular colliery to promote feelings of solidarity.[44] In the flexible, supposedly nonhierarchical workplaces of Cambridge Science Park, however, a different idea of worker satisfaction was being cultivated by urban space. Here, morale was seen as an individuated rather than collective affair—something that workers achieved through self-management and interworkplace friendships instead of joint production committees or exercises in collective identification. It was no longer something that could be proscribed from without.

Among the autonomous and flexible workers in science parks, certain hierarchies still endured. Gender profoundly structured their experiences, for instance. The data compiled by Massey's team show that while women were a significant presence in science parks, they tended to be concentrated in low-status work. Of the 138 company founders, only 5 were women, and women made up just 10 percent of the qualified scientists and engineers who worked in the Aston and Cambridge Science Parks. In contrast, women made up 87 percent of the secretarial, administrative, and clerical workforce in these two parks, and across science parks as a whole women made up only 26 percent of all full-time employees.[45] The development of Cambridge Science Park in the 1970s was in line with an explosion of part-time waged work in Britain, with a million part-time jobs created in the 1970s. Ninety percent of all this part-time work in Britain in the 1970s was being performed by women.[46]

The shadow world of mostly female part-time workers was not the ideal subject that the park planners had in mind. This is clear when reading the park's biannual newsletter, a publication in which women are almost totally invisible. In the first eighteen editions, which cover the entire 1980s, just 8.5 percent of all the figures depicted in photographs, cartoons, and sketches were women. Between 1980 and 1995, the newsletter published profiles of prominent members of the science park community. Among the twenty-two of these who appeared during this period, not a single woman was profiled.[47] It is also worth noting that not a single nonwhite person appeared in the magazine at any point in its history. Within elite workforces, then, gender and ethnic divides were marked. One anecdote from Massey and her team's study observes that

> in one company with eight employees it was explained that there were no secretaries, and that all technologists did their own secretarial and administrative tasks. But when we arrived to do our interview we were received by the only woman employee, whose desk was situated, conveniently, nearest the door. It became apparent that not only did this highly qualified engineer act as the firm's receptionist, she also had responsibility for inputting the firm's accounts on a spread-sheet package.[48]

In this sense, Cambridge Science Park bore a deeper structural similarity to the industrial spaces described in the first chapter of this book, with women's labor present yet segregated by perceived levels of skill. The prevalence of women working clerical jobs in Britain (70 percent of all clerical workers were women in the 1970s, when the first science parks appeared) stemmed from the long-standing association of women with rote and deskilled industrial work from the late nineteenth century onward.[49] What's more, as Massey and her team pointed out, the ideal working subject of a British science park worked long and unusual hours and had to be prepared to move long distances at short notice—a combination that was hostile to domestic stability. They quote one park manager as saying that "the ideal [worker] is a bachelor, living at home with a brother and a sister."[50] For this reason, the park's elite workers would have lived lives in which they were serviced by others, whether it was the subordinate, mostly female clerical population of the park or domestic partners at home.[51]

While Cambridge Science Park was organized around a new and self-consciously modern postindustrial worker, it was still developed within the confines of the industrial and regional planning apparatus whose emergence we saw in the first chapter. In 1970, Trinity College's initial application for planning permission was turned down by the Board of Trade on the grounds that science parks were an impractical use of resources for a declining industrial nation. One Board of Trade official, summarizing the attitude within his department, wrote that it was a "slavish and half-baked attempt to follow American fashion," and noted that it was "precisely because [Britain] was so good at pure science and put so much more prestige on Fellows of Trinity winning Nobel Prizes, that our production industries went down the drain."[52]

Following the logic of Britain's postwar regional policy, which used planning permission to channel jobs and capital into depressed regions of the country, it seemed unreasonable for such a large new industrial development to be situated in a remote town with high levels of employment. This advice was at odds with that given by Wilson (by then out of power) to universities encouraging them to create US-style science parks. While an interdepartmental working party had approved the idea of scientific complexes in principle, the Board of Trade cautioned the bursar that it would be difficult to judge whether an applicant for planning permission's desire to be near a university overrode the board's desire to relocate industrial jobs to parts of the country where they would be most needed.[53]

Having been turned down for a site-wide industrial development certificate, which would have allowed the development to proceed, the bursar was forced to make every new tenant on the site apply for their own separate certificate, a process that he likened to collecting stamps.[54] A further hurdle came from the fact that, in 1950, with support from the government, Cambridge County Council had set out to restrict the growth of the town, calling for any large-scale industrial developments in and around the town to be limited.[55] These planning restrictions had to be reluctantly revised in 1971, but tight restrictions on the site were maintained by the council, which demanded that research and development should be prioritized over production.[56]

The park was thus an insurgent exercise—an exceptional development that went against the grain of a regional policy designed to foster an older type of industry. While many involved in the Cambridge Science Park were implicitly critical of Britain's midcentury planning apparatus, the park's planners were not afraid of looking further back into the past, indulging in the patrician rituals associated with a well-endowed Cambridge college. There was something almost *ancien régime* about Trinity College's involvement in the development. Businesses were invited to regular cordial sherry parties on the college's medieval grounds.[57] The social club on-site was named Henry's, after both Henry the VI and Henry the VIII, who were alumni of the college (and whose portraits adorned the pub's interior). One local magazine expressed surprise and amusement about this notoriously backward-looking institution's new high-tech toy: "'Industry' used to be a dirty word in the hallowed cloisters of learning. . . . [Now] I am told, even College masters follow the progress of Acorn shares."[58] Unlike Team Valley or even the later years of Trafford Park, the Cambridge Science Park was not a national, state-directed project. But it was hardly a libertarian start-up either. Scrutinized and restricted by the government and owned by a medieval public institution, the park's humming low-rise buildings still related to the state as a vital presence.

In 1994, Manuel Castells and Peter Hall coauthored a study of planned developments for the promotion of high-tech industry, which they called "technopoles." They established a global typology, exploring the origins of technopoles in Silicon Valley in the 1950s, the massive Soviet research and development plants built in Siberia in the 1960s, and the futuristic compounds built by the Japanese developmental state in the 1980s. Cambridge Science Park was Britain's first iteration of a technopole, a place where scientific knowledge and manufactured products were coproduced in an environment unlike any other in Britain at the time. In this sense, the science park was another instance where Britain's late twentieth-century built environment was aligning itself with the outside world. To quote Castells and Hall, the technopoles on the outskirts of "Cambridge, England, or Cambridge, Massachusetts; Mountain View, California or Munich, Germany" are so similar in appearance that "the hapless traveler, dropped by parachute, would hardly guess the identity of the country, let alone the city."[59] Indeed, just as shopping malls were standardized by input from international bodies of experts, so science parks, by the end of the century, became enmeshed in similar networks. In 1984, the International Association of Science Parks was founded—a body with headquarters split between Spain and China that shared good practices, disseminated through international conferences and events. In the wake of Cambridge, science parks spread quickly through the United Kingdom. In the early 1980s, Britain's first eight science parks created a trade group, the UK Science Parks Association, which in turn became affiliated with the International Association of Science Parks. By 2003, there were fifty-five science parks in the United Kingdom, usually owned by or built near major universities.[60] Even by the mid-1980s, however, these pastoral, suburban, and comprehensively planned developments for postindustrial work were still exceptional. It took a change in planning legislation to usher in an explosion of business parks across Britain.

Stockley Park

In September 1985, the residents of Dawley Road, a suburban backstreet on the distant western fringes of London, were treated to a sickly fragrance—a mixture of pine, vanilla, and decades-old trash. Dawley Road sat on the edge of an enormous new business park called Stockley Park. Building the park required excavating more than 3.5 million cubic meters of industrial and domestic waste, which had been deposited for more than seventy years.[61] To mitigate the dizzying stench unleashed by this process, the developers undertook a sophisticated countersmell operation. Developers built what they claimed (perhaps with some exaggeration) to be the world's largest air freshener, a mobile machine that unleashed alternating bursts of pine and vanilla fragrance. One resident complained after being drenched by concentrated pine-smelling chemicals while cycling past the construction site. The transformation of Stockley Park from a fetid wasteland, known locally as "stinky Stockley," into a giant, mazelike business park, a city within a city, took five years to complete and was a Herculean feat of engineering. It was an undertaking that was perhaps comparable in difficulty to one of the developer's most recent projects before Stockley: a 650-kilometer freeway built in the middle of the Saudi Arabian desert.[62]

As noted, in the early 1980s places like Cambridge Science Park were exceptional—rare oddities that existed tangentially to Britain's postwar planning framework. While science parks were the brainchild of university administrators, business parks like Stockley were a creation of the 1980s' Conservative government. The business parks of the late 1980s and 1990s resembled the science parks that preceded them in their aesthetic and function, although they tended to be larger, less specialist, and subject to fewer planning restrictions. Before the late 1980s, prospective business park builders had faced many of the same planning problems as Trinity College in the early 1970s. British zoning law did not distinguish between high-tech industry, research and development labs, and traditional manufacturing plants, meaning that the owners of a small shed used to manufacture scientific instruments were subject to the same zoning code (or "use class") as a large industrial chemical plant.[63] In 1985, Thatcher's government released a white paper called *Lifting the Burden*, which called for deregulation in a variety of different economic spheres, including the environment, fishing, farming, data protection, and tax rates. The paper also called for a reform of the use class system to take into account this new type of industry.[64] The new B1 use class, approved in 1987 in England and Wales and extended to Scotland and Northern Ireland in 1989, applied equally to offices, research and development centers, and light manufacturing, provided that these were free of "noise, vibration, smell, fumes, smoke, soot, ash, dust or grit."[65]

Until this change, business parks were precocious, marginal curiosities. By the end of the 1980s, however, they were a common feature of the urban landscape. While definitional problems endure, it is clear that the number of developments styled as business parks increased substantially in the late 1980s. One property research company calculated that the square footage of new business park space completed by developers in 1988 was more than five times what it had been just three years earlier. That year, there were four new parks being announced each week.[66] Large private property developers, many of which were insurance companies or pension funds looking for stable

long-term investments, began serially producing business parks.[67] One of the
biggest developers was Arlington Securities, which by the end of the 1980s
owned ten parks across the country and was bought by British Aerospace in
1989 as a means of developing the company's surplus land.[68] Arlington's portfolio included the Aztec West business park on the outskirts of Bristol and
Solent Business Park on the fringes of Southampton, each of which was a large,
comprehensive development that included a luxury hotel and conference facilities. Trafalgar House, a property developer founded in the 1960s, invested
heavily in business parks after the change in planning law. In 1987 the company
was developing four sites, and by 1991 it owned fourteen.[69] The slew of business parks emerging in the late 1980s was concentrated mostly on the outskirts
of major cities or in small towns. Trafalgar's portfolio, for example, was skewed
toward the Home Counties surrounding London, with parks in Weybridge in
Surrey, Basildon in Essex, and Fleet in Hampshire.[70] By 1991, there were six
business parks being built by different developers in Kent, five in Bedfordshire,
and seventeen in Hertfordshire.[71] As with the new shopping malls that were
appearing in cities during the same decade, business parks had wriggled free
from the state-directed developmental aims that guided their predecessors—
industrial estates—and moved to the suburbs, where under the command of
large private developers they were multiplying ferociously.

Of all these new developments, Stockley Park was the most spectacular.
Under discussion since the early 1980s, large areas of Stockley Park were built
before the change in use class, giving it an air of prescience. The park, twenty-
five times larger than the Cambridge Science Park when it opened, was designed to be "analogous to the structure of a town." As well as a large golf
course and nature reserve, the site boasted "a river system in microcosm,"
navigable by boat from the Grand Union Canal and culminating in "a chain
of ponds and rapids, among rocks, leading to a still pool above the weir."[72] By
1989, the park boasted a million square feet of constructed space, most of
which could be found in buildings designed by the park's developer.[73] The
site was overseen by a park manager who had had an extensive prior career in
the armed forces and was patrolled by fourteen full-time private security
guards in yellow jackets, most of whom were also former military personnel
from the local area.[74] CCTV cameras, concealed in miniature wood and glass
pavilions, watched over the park.[75] The park's architects connected buildings
together with spacious underground wiring ducts that remained half empty
in order to accommodate any new technologies that might emerge.[76] While
Stockley Park had enthusiastic support from the London borough of Hillingdon, the development was entirely financed by private funds. It was purchased at an early stage by a property developer named Stuart Lipton, an
entrepreneur made by the 1980s property boom. Lipton was comparable in

success and notoriety to Mountleigh's Clegg, whose company, as we saw in the last chapter, bought and owned the Merry Hill shopping mall. Like Merry Hill, ownership of Stockley Park was passed around between increasingly fragmented property consortia during the 1980s, briefly including Mountleigh itself. A decisive early wave of capital was invested in the project by the Universities Superannuation Scheme, the largest pension program for British university lecturers and administrators.[77]

As a type of urban space, Stockley Park was an import from the US suburbs. Ove Arup and Partners, the architecture firm contracted to plan and design the site, noted that it was struggling to find any precedent in Britain for the type of space that it envisaged. Instead, Arup sent a delegation to visit five different cities in the United States so as to study sites where "the purity of the concept has . . . been realised." These sites included Silicon Valley (where the delegates visited the Stanford Industrial Park) and North Carolina's Research Triangle as well as major science and technology parks in Denver, Atlanta, and New Jersey. Extensive surveys of high-tech firms in the United States were undertaken to profile the kinds of tenants that Stockley was hoping to host. The idea was to attract high-tech firms that combined research and production. In a newsletter produced for local residents, and in words eerily similar to those issuing from Stanford University a generation earlier, the park's management distanced itself from earlier kinds of industry:

> Traditional manufacturing industry is concerned with mass production. . . . The buildings involved are factories, and look like factories—large, dirty and noisy—with mostly manual labour. Modern industries, by comparison, may not even *make* a product at all, in the sense of creating something from raw material. Much of the emerging growth of industry in the UK results from adding value, by adapting a basic product manufactured elsewhere.[78]

While Stockley Park may have been an unfamiliar space to Britons before the change in planning law in the mid-1980s, it would have been a familiar one for many of the US and Japanese technology companies that became its early tenants. The global connections to the United States and Japan were why Stockley Park's proximity to Heathrow Airport was as important to the developers as the Manchester Ship Canal had been to the developers of Trafford Park. Stockley Park was even designed to be aesthetically appealing when viewed from above by planes coming in to land.[79] Among the more permanent tenants were the regional offices of high-tech companies that were headquartered overseas. Apple, the Japanese communications company Fujitsu, and the Taiwanese computer company Acer all had large offices on-site, split between management, production, and customer service facilities. These integrated centers were some of the biggest employers at Stockley, with Fujitsu employing 160 workers.[80]

Stockley provided a veritable onslaught of activities to suit the affluent, flexible workers that it wanted to court. The park's managers hoped that elite employees could be tied together by an infrastructure of health, exercise, and well-being. The park's centerpiece, called the Arena, housed a gym, squash courts, restaurants, a conference center, and a health club. While Team Valley's recreation center, partly funded by the government's National Fitness Council, was free to all workers, the Arena operated along the lines of a private members club. It was marketed as an elite space, adorned with "rich maroon leather" and "sophisticated black marble."[81] Elsewhere, the Arena was touted as being a "country club."[82] This was a space built for elite professionals and managers rather than the lower-paid cleaners, gardeners, or security guards who also worked at the park.

As well as the health club, more intangible forms of well-being were available to some of the workers on the site. A mystical and almost therapeutic quality was attributed to the park's shared amenities. It was described as "a place to work and think in a relaxed and natural environment."[83] Public art was an eye-catching and affordable means of satisfying this ambitious brief. The architects worked with the Public Art Development Trust, a body founded in 1983 to promote works of sculpture in particular.[84] Twenty young artists were recruited at an early stage to work for the development. Perhaps the strangest and most remarked on of their projects were eight bronze women's legs that jutted vertically out of the lake near the Arena. The piece was inscrutable, although heavily sexualized ("If you think you're lucky when you see one pair of nice legs," the park's publicity material leered, "then anyone visiting the Stockley Park Arena will be in for a real treat").Its sculptor, Kevin Atherton, modeled the legs on a fitted cast of Sarah Northey, a British synchronized swimming champion.[85]

While industrial estates were built to reenergize local economies, supplying jobs, training, and often forms of infrastructure such as transportation or electricity, Stockley Park had a different relationship to its surrounding neighborhood. While the park's owners hoped that locals might use the gym (if they were willing to pay the monthly fee) or even get married in the Arena's function rooms, the dominant language was one of charity versus economic development.[86] The park canvassed its tenants for money and recruited volunteers for local charities—in one instance hosting a forty-two-hour sponsored swim in the Arena pool to fund new equipment for the local Hillingdon Hospital.[87] For the most part, however, employees were encouraged to engage in more distant forms of solidarity, with the management hosting blood donations and a sponsored bike ride for a nationwide disability charity.[88] These kinds of

FIGURE 6.2. Kevin Atherton's *Synchronized Sculpture*, Stockley Park. Photograph by Kevin Atherton.

FIGURE 6.3. Stockley Park from the air during its construction. Reproduced with kind permission of Stockley Park Estates Company Limited.

affective communities, bound through voluntarism and ethical imperatives, were distinct from the practices of morale management and conspicuous discipline found on interwar industrial estates. For all this, perhaps the biggest instances of community engagement in Stockley Park were Neighbourhood Watch meetings to discuss questions of security and policing, some of which were attended by several hundred residents and were hosted in the Arena's sports hall.[89]

As at the Cambridge Science Park, then, Stockley called into being a different subject from the workers on mid-twentieth-century industrial estates. On industrial estates, human development was linear. Health, fitness, and diet were calculable, hours were fixed, work was monotonous, and output was easily measured. The distinction between work, leisure, and reproduction was absolute.[90] Stockley, however, was planned around a flexible working subject:

> Traditional businesses are hierarchical which makes for slow progress for the young and eager. The new technology firms are expanding, confident and informed, with no status barriers between grades of staff. . . . A flexible style of working [allows] for rapid career development and for people to match their individual skills to the jobs.[91]

Making this type of worker productive at the level required was a challenge. The site's master plan noted the need to "introduce levels of human activity, interaction and visual perception not usually associated with industrial developments."[92] Successful work frequently hinged on moments of inspiration and chance encounters with other workers that could not be planned precisely, but could be induced through verdant surroundings, displays of public art, lavish meeting rooms, or squash courts where workers could mingle. Like the empty, underground ducts that connected Stockley's buildings—planned to be filled out with communication devices that had yet to be invented—the needs of Stockley's workforce could not yet be precisely anticipated. In other words, like the reformed council estate and shopping mall, business parks operated on the belief that the future needs of their subjects could neither be fully understood nor willfully and permanently remade. It remains to see how the look and feel of business parks along with their guiding assumptions about work and space came to be retrofitted into a much older industrial complex.

Returning to Trafford Park

By 1980, Trafford Park, once one of the most avant-garde industrial developments in the world, resembled a small failed state within the city of Manchester. For most of the 1950s and 1960s, the number of people employed on-site had remained steady at around 50,000. After that it dropped precipitously, reaching 24,500 by 1985. The amount of material transported by the estate's railroad system declined by 90 percent between 1940 and 1971.[93] While Trafford Park suffered from the same problems of offshoring and technological change eroding Britain's urban industrial base in the later postwar period, these issues were compounded by its location. The estate had been well suited for rail and canal access, but was relatively isolated from road networks.[94] Trafford Park felt derelict and eerily deserted by the end of the 1970s. In 1978, a resident of the Village that was built on the estate in the first decade of the century for the workers of Westinghouse's electric company lamented that "there is no sign of people walking around the industrial park at weekends, you could be forgiven for wondering if an Atomic Cloud had passed."[95] Eighty years after the estate opened, one commentator described it as looking like someone "had a big party and forgot to clear up."[96]

Beginning in the 1970s, Trafford Park was subjected to twenty years of failed attempts at regeneration led by local officials concerned about the ruinous appearance of the estate and high levels of unemployment in its surrounding neighborhoods. The estate was made into an enterprise zone by Thatcher's government in 1981. Six years later, and with little sign of any improvement, the government approved the creation of the Trafford Park Development Corporation (TPDC). Urban Development Corporations (UDCs) were modeled on the public development corporations created by postwar governments to plan new towns. These were quasi-state bodies, given powers to buy, sell, and develop land, with boards that were appointed by government ministers. While new town development corporations were tasked with implementing large public building works in relatively depopulated areas, UDCs were mostly concerned with prepping existing urban areas for waves of private property development.[97] Like enterprise zones, they were indicative of a new kind of urbanism that emerged in Britain in the 1980s.[98] They were designed to overrule inner-city local councils and provide incentives for private capital to move into derelict urban areas. By 1990, UDCs were receiving 61 percent of all inner-city expenditures. The first two UDCs were created to redevelop the former docklands of London and Liverpool. The TPDC was one of eight new UDCs created in 1987 and 1988 as part of the Conservative government's revival of interest in urban regeneration. The body comprised eight appointed board members (a mix of local councillors and business leaders) with a full-time staff of fifty-one overseeing an even greater number of outsourced consultants.[99] During the eleven years of its existence, it effected a radical change: transforming Trafford Park into something resembling a giant inner-city business park.

The first order of business was aesthetics. The pastoral capitalism practiced at places like the Stanford Industrial Park, Cambridge Science Park, or

Stockley chimed with a state-sponsored critique of Britain's increasingly ruinous industrial landscape. Britain's industrial growth over two centuries had frequently provoked concern about the aesthetic and environmental degradation left in its wake, and deindustrialization prompted renewed environmental concerns. As the tide of industrial capitalism receded, it left exposed a redundant infrastructure of docks, factories, and warehouses. Many of the urban reforms launched by Thatcher's government in the early 1980s amounted to concerted attacks on Britain's industrial landscape. Derelict land grants, introduced in 1983, were small packets of public money given to private bodies wanting to demolish and redevelop derelict industrial buildings. National garden festivals, held every other year between 1984 and 1992, saw tracts of former industrial land in Liverpool, Glasgow, Stoke-on-Trent, Gateshead, and South Wales demolished and replaced by synthetic, theme-park-esque shows designed to attract tourists from up and down the country as well as across the world.

It is not a surprise, then, that improving the visual appearance of Trafford Park was an urgent priority for the TPDC. The sheer ugliness of the estate was deemed to be a problem as great, if not greater, than the economic issues that it faced. One report claimed that "few would contest that Trafford Park is one of the ugliest working/business environments in the UK and possibly Europe."[100] All the many attempts to regenerate the estate began with a declaration of war on "eyesores." Indeed, in the mid-1970s a number of businesses on the site banded together to launch "Operation Eyesore"—an attempt to improve the estate's outward appearance. This became an official part of the TPDC's mission, with the body accepting that any improvements to Trafford Park would be rendered moot if "prominent eyesores . . . continue to diminish their effect."[101]

The corporation put pressure on individual businesses to improve the outward image of more than two hundred buildings, focusing on the buildings that were most visible to passing cars from the road. Although the large green areas that characterized other business and science parks were impractical in such a dense, inner-city area, the corporation still boasted of planting more than eight hundred thousand trees and shrubs.[102] Trafford Wharf Road, running parallel to the Manchester Ship Canal, was turned into "a continuous strip of trees, shrubs and grass."[103] The canals, once essential shipping lanes, were spruced up and fitted with new bridges to allow leisurely pedestrian walks along their banks. In all, more than forty-two million pounds was spent by the TPDC solely on environmental improvements.[104] Public art was a central part of the corporation's strategy—a means of making people "happier and therefore more productive."[105] The most conspicuous project was the large "skyhook" sculpture that fronted the canal, a representation of a steel anchor connected to a chain vanishing in midair and an unsettling reminder of the Ship Canal's past life.[106]

As in Stockley Park, the relationship between the workplace and wider community was mediated through charity. The TPDC distributed tens of thousands of pounds to local community organizations, sometimes in the form of large, novelty checks.[107] Charity drives raised money to buy computers for local schools, and the development corporation organized campaigns to conserve the local ecology, creating a new environment for the endangered great crested newt.[108] These charitable initiatives came with a renewed emphasis on security and crime control. Businesses were encouraged to cooperate with each other in a complex scheme that pooled information about potential criminals operating in the area.[109] In 1990, the new Trafford Park became one of the earliest commercial adopters of the "Secured by Design" policing strategy described in chapter 4, which sought to remake the built environment in ways that would reduce opportunities and incentives for crime.[110] Once again, Britain's earlier twentieth-century built environment had been found to be unsuitable for the new criminological paradigms arising in the 1980s and 1990s.

Meanwhile, the Trafford Park Village, the small grid of terraced houses commissioned for workers in 1899, continued in place until the early 1980s. For the first four decades of their life, the houses, isolated deep within the park, had all been owned by the estates company and rented out to workers. After the war, the company sold the houses to a private developer, which then offered mortgages to the sitting tenants. By the 1970s, two thousand people lived in the Village's six hundred homes, and the community included two churches, a handful of shops, a swimming pool, four banks, a post office, a library, a pub, and a small mosque.[111] Its gridded streets were still numbered (First Street, Second Street, and so on) from the days when Westinghouse had wanted to cultivate a US feel for the development. Despite a three-year campaign of resistance fought by residents, the council demolished most of the Village in 1981, and all were evicted. The residents who had lived in this unusual neighborhood, surrounded on all sides by factories, had fostered a remarkably close-knit community. The Village's newsletter, the *Park Times*, kept a record of advertisements, poems, letters, and photographs compiled by nostalgic and increasingly desperate local residents over the course of the 1970s. In 1987, six years after the eviction, the land and the physical remains of the small community were bought by the TPDC. In the words of the development corporation's chair, housing was "not a priority" for the new Trafford Park.[112] Instead, the land was turned into an amenities hub for the rest of the estate, similar to Stockley Park's Arena or Cambridge Science Park's social center. One hundred thousand square feet of space was built for small businesses such as shops,

FIGURE 6.4. St. Anthony's communion parade in Trafford Park Village, 1920.
With thanks to Trafford Local Studies.

restaurants, and hotels that would cater to nearby employees.[113] Meanwhile, trendy property developer Urban Splash turned the former Village school into a handful of artistic studios and workshops.[114]

As the landscape of Trafford Park was transformed in the 1980s, the kinds of work available on the estate also underwent a dramatic change. In searching for investors, the TPDC concentrated on attracting high-tech firms from the south of England and the United States.[115] In 1945, 92 percent of Trafford Park's employees worked in manufacturing, with the remaining 8 percent employed in "trades and services."[116] By 1993, the number of manufacturing jobs had fallen to just 42 percent of the total, with the remainder of jobs split evenly among "Real Estate and Business Activities," "Transport Storage and Communication," and "Wholesale and Retail Trade."[117] As in Britain's first science parks, women at the new Trafford Park were concentrated in part-time jobs. While 73 percent of the total workforce was male, women made up 67 percent of all part-time workers on-site.[118] At the same time, the cavernous, teeming factories of the midcentury era had splintered into smaller factories and workshops. Once, 150 firms on the estate had employed more than 50,000 workers, but by 1993 33,000 workers were split between more than 1,200 different companies.[119] In the new Trafford Park, forms of elite service work were incentivized; in the words of the development corporation, it was time to "put the

Porsche before the cart." An area of the park was renamed "downtown," and there banking and finance institutions were prioritized alongside upmarket restaurants and even some private apartment buildings.[120] Although older forms of manufacturing endured in the park, the development company also courted the kinds of high-tech, small-scale manufacturing that wouldn't have been out of place in the Cambridge Science Park, with businesses like the US corporation Photronics, which manufactures semiconductors, opening shop in 1996. That same year, Japanese company Kratos Analytical, which manufactures parts of X-ray machines, set up a facility in the park.

When Trafford Park was first developed at the turn of the twentieth century, it heralded a new kind of industrial space. Despite being the brainchild of a private property speculator, the park became a blueprint for a wave of state-funded industrial estates in areas of high unemployment across the country. Although Trafford Park was larger and more ad hoc than places like the Team Valley or Hillington industrial estates, it was an early sign that "work" in the abstract could be planned for—that grids of infrastructure, laid out in advance near pools of labor, could attract potential factory owners looking to cut down on start-up costs. The estate's warehouses, intricate railroad grid, and imperial supply chains could not survive the gradual erosion of British industry in the last third of the twentieth century. As the development corporation sought to encourage a new kind of work on the estate, it took its cues from science and business parks and the ways in which they cultivated chance connections among elite workers in clean, verdant landscapes lined with works of art. Just as the shopping precincts and housing estates built in the mid-twentieth century came to be reimagined in the 1980s for a new kind of economy as well as a new kind of subject, Trafford Park was transformed from an industrial estate to a business park in the name of urban regeneration.

In the 1920s and 1930s, boosters spoke in raptures about the total nature of the transformation of Trafford Park—describing in vivid detail how it was converted from a lush aristocratic country estate to a thundering industrial machine without a blade of grass in sight.[121] Casting an optimistic eye on one of the earliest attempts to rehabilitate the estate, one observer imagined that the land might return to its wooded, preindustrial state: "Trees and shrubs have been planted along the new roadways which have been constructed. . . . [I]t may soon become green and pleasant as it was over 80 years ago."[122] In the first decades of the twentieth century, the contrast between the ancient de Trafford estate and the industrial complex that replaced it was striking and self-evident. By the 1990s, the difference in appearance between these old patrician landscapes and many modern, high-tech workplaces was harder to identify. Before being evicted en masse in 1981, the residents of Trafford Park Village produced one last commemorative issue of their local newsletter, the

Park Times. On the final page of this edition, a poem, written by an unnamed resident, imagined that the century-long historical arc of this large plot of inner-city land would terminate once again in wilderness, cursed by the ghosts of the aristocrats who once inhabited it:

> With bated breath and gasps of fear
> Flee with flying feet
> You dare not run at night round here
> For fear of what you'll meet!
>
> Menacing mounds of broken brick,
> Block the ill-paved street,
> Witless workmen's wicked trick,
> To break spirit or your feet!
>
> Ghostly ghouls give fearsome fright
> For folks still forced to stay,
> In flickering fear or perilous flight,
> As the village fades away.
>
> Ghosts of Trafford's vanished Hall,
> Banshees, baneful wail,
> Banish buildings, folks and all,
> All "enterprise" to fail.
>
> 'Till once again, the deer can roam,
> And mallards mate with verve!
> "De-Trafford's" Ghost can then come home
> Vast nature to preserve![123]

7

Conclusion

THE BURDEN OF OBSOLESCENCE

I WAS BORN in Britain in 1986 and came of age among many of the urban forms described in this book. Specifically, I grew up in Milton Keynes, a pointillist scattering of business parks, supermarkets, and suburban homes, seventy miles north of London. Milton Keynes was the biggest and perhaps strangest of the more than thirty new towns built by the British state after the war. Despite only recently celebrating its fiftieth birthday, it has become one of the largest conurbations in the South East of England. Milton Keynes has taken on a rich amalgam of cultural meanings for contemporary Britons, associated with middle-class suburban sterility and the termination of ambitious urban plans in neoliberal sprawl.[1] It was not meant to be this way. The original plan called for fifty townships of more than five thousand people threaded together by an elevated municipal monorail, taxpayer funded and free of charge.[2] No resident would live more than a five-minute walk from a monorail stop, and no commute would take more than fifteen minutes. As time passed, this plan was watered down, reconstituted, and eventually shelved completely. During this time, the team working at the Milton Keynes Development Corporation became fascinated by Los Angeles and a different kind of urbanism. The city was caught between contradictory fantasies of the future—developmental modernism and flexible suburban affluence—and between David Lynch's Hollywood and Jean-Luc Godard's *Alphaville*. When Milton Keynes was finally built, it was divided by a grid of major horizontal and vertical roads (named H1, H2, V1, V2, and so on), demarcating more than thirty discrete residential neighborhoods that were intended to mix high- and low-income housing. The shopping precinct, when it was built, was owned and managed by the development corporation, with no doors between its concourses and the streets outside.

By the time we moved to Milton Keynes in 2000, the town had come a long way from both its initial high-modern vision and its consumerist, affluent, and notionally egalitarian realization. The shopping precinct had been expanded and

FIGURE 7.1. View from Enterprise Lane in the Campbell Park housing development, Milton Keynes. Photograph by Pete Williams.

privatized, rebranded as "thecentre:mk" with a nearby theater and restaurant district called "thehub:mk" attached. Even on official maps, these places are marked in all lowercase, all one word. Meanwhile, the discrete neighborhoods, once intended to be socially mixed, had polarized into ghettos and wealthy enclaves. In 2000, children's writer Malcolm Rose published a briefly popular novel about an outbreak of an Ebola-like virus in Milton Keynes. The virus resulted in two neighborhoods, Tinkers Bridge and Passmore, one rich and one poor, being quarantined, forcing them to resolve their deep class differences in order to survive.[3] By the 2000s, the supposedly egalitarian landscape of Milton Keynes was scarred by deep and deepening economic inequality.

My life in Milton Keynes was divided between two urban forms, about half a mile apart. I lived in Campbell Park, a private, high-density housing complex built in 2001 and organized around three courtyards. Our courtyard, my home address for more than five years, was called Enterprise Lane. As a teenager, I went to the meetings of the development's private residents' association and earned pocket money helping organize the association's website. The website featured a forum in which residents discussed the management of the court-yards and parking lots and shared tips about security and the threat of vandalism. The proximity of the development to the city center and nearby "sink estates" meant that intruders were a constant source of anxiety. Since my family moved to a different neighborhood in 2006, these fears appear to have reached something of a crisis point for the residents of Enterprise Lane. I recently returned to the development to find that an extra perimeter fence had been built to shield the approach from the street, undoubtedly intended to instill a greater feeling of defensible space.

Although the shopping precinct was only a ten-minute walk from Enterprise Lane, most people would drive to get there. As a teenager, I was an exception. I walked home from the shopping precinct most days after taking the bus back from school, tacking along a grass verge next to a thundering main road (had I known about the monorail during those years, I would have cursed its absence). The shopping precinct was the focus of my adolescence, where I killed time, met with friends, went on dates, went to the library, and voted in an election for the first time. In my later teenage years, I went there to go to pubs and political protests. The precinct consists of two long parallel atriums, brightly lit and dotted with artificial plants that blast digital birdsongs. There is a clock tower along with a mock indoor "town square" that was used for Christmas pageants, comic book conventions, and home exhibitions. The restaurants and cafés have "outdoor" seating along the internal concourses, which still offer shelter via a roof. The development's attractions range from the spectacular to the mundane, with an indoor ski slope and climbing wall as well as a post office and an unemployment office. For all intents and purposes, the precinct is the civic town center of Milton Keynes. By the time I moved to the city, it had been sold to a property developer and the doors to its concourses were locked after the shops closed in the evening.

For Britons my age, growing up in an urban landscape whose meaning and purpose has been lost or forgotten is a common experience. Journalist Genamour Barrett has written about the experience of growing up in the 1990s and 2000s on a council estate in South East London, remembering a strong sense of community among its residents. As a young girl, she delighted in living high up enough to see fireworks across London and being surrounded by communal spaces in which to play hide-and-seek: "We congregated on balconies, sat for hours in other people's houses, and at any moment you could hear the deafening shrieks of a mother calling her child to come in for dinner." It was a feeling that was lost as social mobility took her family into a suburban housing development, a move toward "a much whiter ideal," and one that left her family exposed to racist harassment.[4] Barrett's childhood community was an insurgent one, formed in spite of Coleman's insistence that communal spaces on council estates bred violence and alienation, or the implicit ideas of midcentury housing officers that stable communities were tied to whiteness.

This book has argued that in the late twentieth century Britain became a postdevelopmental state—a neoliberal political formation characterized by a constant, unresolved negotiation between old and new that played out across its built environment. Many Britons carve lives for themselves out of a disintegrating, repurposed, or hastily repaired developmental infrastructure whose guiding logic no longer animates the politicians, planners, and residents who make and remake towns and cities. While modern societies have always grappled with the burden of obsolescence, the tensions between old and new were felt particularly strongly in the last third of the twentieth century, once Britain's developmental state was in retreat.

In the mid-twentieth century, a variety of new types of urban space were seized on by industrialists, urban planners, politicians, and technocrats to form the foundations of a new economy and a new society. Industrial estates offered the promise that regional imbalances in the economy of Britain and parts of its empire could be solved with dozens of government-financed factory complexes. Shopping precincts, it was hoped, would banish the automobile from town centers and allow the state to plan precisely for consumer demand. Council estates would modernize domestic life and make new communities out of strangers. Each of these imagined that their subjects—industrial workers, shoppers, and council tenants—were malleable and knowable, capable of being remade by the properties of urban space alone. These urban forms had a logic that was unanticipated by some of their early promoters, allowing some to indulge in more radical futures, whether it was the construction of vast district heating schemes tied to industry or the rapid industrial development of parts of Britain's empire.

From the 1970s on, these three urban forms were reimagined and remade. Industrial estates became suburban business parks, central shopping precincts became private shopping malls, and council estates were privatized, hollowed out, and in some cases transformed into securitized compounds like Enterprise Lane. While Britain's developmental spaces were largely the creation of domestic technocrats and planners, these new urban forms were made in the United States and came crashing onto Britain's shores from across the Atlantic Ocean. They were built and owned not by a developmental state but instead by property developers whose portfolios often spanned the world. Their ideal subjects were more elusive—knowledge workers for whom the right kinds of space could enable an intangible feeling of well-being or shoppers capable of almost limitless levels of consumer desire. Those who did not fit this mold were to be policed rather than remade.

I began the research for this book in 2014, when historical time still felt suspended. The project started as a way of accounting for deep structural continuities. The built environment, I argued, was a way of thinking about the different forces, often deemed to be prepolitical, that constrain the machinations of high politics. Since then, history has begun moving extremely quickly. The many ideas and structures that hold neoliberalism together in Britain and elsewhere are starting to dissolve, and the future now feels radically open in ways that were unimaginable just six years earlier. It seems likely that whatever political settlement emerges from our present conjuncture will leave behind a litter of new urban forms. If we are lucky, they will depart in every possible way from those whose history this book charts. We can only hope and agitate for spaces that are owned by neither distant capital nor conservative state technocrats—spaces that are democratic and open to all in ways that can begin to redress the inequalities produced by empire, capital, and patriarchy. In other words, spaces that are shaped by their subjects, rather than the other way around.

NOTES

Introduction

1. The routes taken by planes coming in to land at Heathrow vary depending on weather and which runway the plane is destined for. Planes are held in four stacks on the outskirts of London before being guided onto one of the airport's two runways. Routes from the stack to the runway vary, but the route described in what follows is relatively common.

2. *Thamesmead 1970*, British Film Institute, 1970, accessed March 29, 2019, http://player.bfi .or.uk/film/watch-thamesmead-1970-1970/.

3. Lewis Mumford, *The City in History: Its Origins, Its Transformations, and Its Prospects* (New York: Harvest, 1989), 236. Mumford uses the words "urban form" in two different senses: the first is to describe specific types of urban space, and the second is to depict the city as a totality.

4. For examples of histories of these spaces, see Tom Hulme, "'A Nation Depends on Its Children': School Buildings and Citizenship in England and Wales, 1900–1939," *Journal of British Studies* 54, no. 2 (April 2015): 406–32; Andrew Seaton, "The National Health Service and the Endurances of British Social Democracy, 1948 to the Present" (PhD diss., New York University, in progress); Sabine Clarke, *Science at the End of Empire: Experts and the Development of the British Caribbean, 1940–62* (Oxford: Oxford University Press, 2018); Peter Merriman, *Driving Spaces: A Cultural-Historical Geography of England's M1 Motorway* (Oxford: Blackwell, 2007); David Goldblatt, *The Ball Is Round: A Global History of Soccer* (London: Penguin, 2017); Jordanna Bailkin, *Unsettled: Refugee Camps and the Making of Multicultural Britain* (Oxford: Oxford University Press, 2018).

5. This idea has emerged within geography and critical theory since the 1960s and 1970s. Landmark contributions include Doreen Massey, *For Space* (London: Sage, 2005); Henri Lefebvre, *The Production of Space*, trans. Donald Nicholson Smith (Oxford: Basil Blackwell, 1991); Gaston Bachelard, *The Poetics of Space*, trans. Maria Jolas (Boston: Beacon Press 2004); David Harvey, *The Limits to Capital* (London: Verso, 1999). For an intellectual history of the emergence of this tradition within Marxist and poststructuralist thought, see Ed Soja, *Postmodern Geographies: The Reassertion of Space in Critical Theory* (London: Verso, 2011). For a critique of the utility of the "spatial turn" in critical theory for historians, see Leif Jerram, "Space: A Useless Category for Historical Analysis?," *History and Theory* 52, no. 3 (October 2013): 400–419.

6. For some diverse examples of historical or theoretical work that explicitly deal with questions of how past infrastructure networks or capital outlays shape or constrain politics in the future, see David Edgerton, *The Shock of the Old: Technology and Global History since 1900* (London: Profile, 2008); David Harvey, "Money, Time, Space, and the City," in *The Urban Experience* (Baltimore: Johns Hopkins University Press, 1989); Stephen J. Collier, *Post-Soviet Social: Neoliberalism, Social Modernity, Biopolitics* (Princeton, NJ: Princeton University Press, 2011).

7. John Maynard Keynes, *The Collected Writings of John Maynard Keynes: Volume VII: The General Theory of Employment Interest and Money* (Cambridge: Cambridge University Press, 2013), 383.

8. Important works in this vein include Simon Gunn and Susan C. Townsend, *Automobility and the City in Twentieth-Century Britain and Japan* (London: Bloomsbury Academic, 2019); Otto Saumarez Smith, *Boom Cities: Architect Planners and the Politics of Radical Urban Renewal in 1960s Britain* (Oxford: Oxford University Press, 2019); Charlotte Wildman, *Urban Redevelopment and Modernity in Liverpool and Manchester, 1918–1939* (London: Bloomsbury Academic, 2016); James Greenhalgh, *Reconstructing Modernity: Space, Power, and Governance in Mid-Twentieth-Century British Cities* (Manchester: Manchester University Press, 2018); Elain Harwood, *Space, Hope, and Brutalism: English Architecture, 1945–1975* (New Haven, CT: Yale University Press, 2015); Catherine Flinn, *Rebuilding Britain's Blitzed Cities: Hopeful Dreams, Stark Realities* (London: Bloomsbury Academic, 2018). See also recent and forthcoming work by Alistair Kefford, Aaron Andrews, and Phil Child. A mention must also be made of Erika Hanna, whose work focuses on twentieth-century Ireland, but who has contributed to discussions about British urban history, urban theory, mobility, and photography. The work of Otto Saumarez Smith and Simon Gunn is noteworthy in creating a forum for twentieth-century British urban history, the Society for Promotion of Urban Discussion. All these scholars are consciously following in the footsteps of figures such as Alison Ravetz, Helen Meller, John R. Gold, and Peter Hall, all of whom have been writing canonical, exhaustive histories of twentieth-century housing, architecture, and planning since the 1980s and 1990s. See Alison Ravetz, *The Government of Space: Town Planning in Modern Society* (London: Routledge, 1986); Alison Ravetz, *Council Housing and Culture: The History of a Social Experiment* (London: Routledge, 2001); Helen Meller, *Towns, Plans, and Society in Modern Britain* (Cambridge: Cambridge University Press, 1997); John R. Gold, *The Experience of Modernism: Modern Architects and the Future City, 1928–53* (London: E. and F. N. Spon, 1997); John R. Gold, *The Practice of Modernism: Modern Architects and Urban Transformations* (London: Taylor and Francis, 2007); Peter Hall, *Cities of Tomorrow: An Intellectual History of Urban Planning and Design since 1880*, 4th ed. (London: Wiley Blackwell, 2014).

9. Guy Ortolano has traced the rise and fall of British social democracy through the new town of Milton Keynes. Guy Ortolano, *Thatcher's Progress: From Social Democracy to Market Liberalism through an English New Town* (Cambridge: Cambridge University Press, 2019). Daisy Payling has looked at Sheffield to understand 1980s British political culture. Daisy Payling, "'The Socialist Republic of South Yorkshire': Grassroots Activism and Left-Wing Solidarity in 1980s Sheffield," *Twentieth Century British History* 25, no. 4 (December 2014): 602–27. Tom Hulme has used the histories of Manchester and Chicago to understand interwar citizenship. Tom Hulme, *After the Shock City: Urban Culture and the Making of Modern Citizenship* (Woodbridge, UK: Boydell and Brewer, 2019).

10. For consumerism, see Alistair Kefford, *Planning for Affluence: Cities and the Management of Mass Consumerism in Post-war Britain* (Cambridge: Cambridge University Press, forthcoming); Sarah Mass, "Commercial Heritage as Democratic Action: Historicizing the 'Save the Market' Campaigns in Bradford and Chesterfield, 1969–76," *Twentieth Century British History* 29, no. 3 (September 2018): 459–84; James Greenhalgh, "Consuming Communities: The Neighbourhood Unit and the Role of Retail Spaces on British Housing Estates, 1944–1958," *Urban History* 43, no. 1 (February 2016): 158–74; Erika Rappaport, *Shopping for Pleasure: Women in the*

Making of London's West End (Princeton, NJ: Princeton University Press, 2000). For race and decolonization, see Kennetta Hammond Perry, *London Is the Place for Me: Black Britons, Citizenship, and the Politics of Race* (Oxford: Oxford University Press, 2015); Jordanna Bailkin, *Unsettled*; Kieran Connell, *Black Handsworth: Race in 1980s Britain* (Berkeley: University of California Press, 2019); Marc Matera, *Black London: The Imperial Metropolis and Decolonization in the Twentieth Century* (Berkeley: University of California Press, 2015). See also forthcoming work from Divya Subramanian, Claire Wrigley, Jesse Meredith, and Adam Page. For work on gender and sexuality in twentieth-century British cities, see Judith R. Walkowitz, *Nights Out: Life in Cosmopolitan London* (New Haven, CT: Yale University Press, 2012); Frank Mort, *Capital Affairs: London and the Making of the Permissive Society* (New Haven, CT: Yale University Press, 2010); Matt Houlbrook, *Queer London: Perils and Pleasures in the Sexual Metropolis, 1918–1957* (Chicago: Chicago University Press, 2005); Judy Giles, *The Parlour and the Suburb: Domestic Identities, Class, Femininity, and Modernity* (Oxford: Berg, 2004).

11. For celebrations of Britain's mid-twentieth-century urban landscapes, see Owen Hatherley, *A Guide to the New Ruins of Great Britain* (London: Verso, 2010); Owen Hatherley, *A New Kind of Bleak: Journeys through Urban Britain* (London: Verso, 2013); John Grindrod, *Concretopia: A Journey around the Rebuilding of Postwar Britain* (London: Old Street Publishing, 2014); John Boughton, *Municipal Dreams: The Rise and Fall of Council Housing* (London: Verso, 2018). A dissenting view is taken by Lynsey Hanley, who has been critical of mass housing estates. Lynsey Hanley, *Estates: An Intimate History* (London: Granta, 2012). For critical journalism concerning Britain's contemporary built environment, see Anna Minton, *Big Capital: Who Is London For?* (London: Penguin, 2017); Anna Minton, *Ground Control: Fear and Happiness in the Twenty-First-Century City* (London: Penguin, 2012); James Meek, *Private Island: Why Britain Now Belongs to Someone Else* (London: Verso, 2014). Dawn Foster has written numerous articles in the *Guardian*, *New York Times*, and *Jacobin* about topics such as the Grenfell fire.

12. For a recent work of British urban history that argues that urban change precedes and anticipates political change, see Greenhalgh, *Reconstructing Modernity*. For recent British history monographs from different historiographical contexts that take different types of space as their object, see Aidan Forth, *Barbed Wire Imperialism: Britain's Empire of Camps, 1876–1903* (Berkeley: University of California Press, 2017); Miles Glendinning and Stefan Muthesius, *Tower Block: Modern Public Housing in England, Scotland, Wales, and Northern Ireland* (New Haven, CT: Yale University Press, 1994); Joe Moran, *On Roads: A Hidden History* (London: Profile, 2009). For histories of how specific spaces have outlived or resisted the ideas of those who developed them, see Chandra Mukerji's history of the construction of the Canal du Midi in seventeenth-century France and Yuri Slezkine's history of the House of Government built to house Soviet leaders in the decade after the revolution. Chandra Mukerji, *Impossible Engineering: Technology and Territoriality on the Canal du Midi* (Princeton, NJ: Princeton University Press, 2009); Yuri Slezkine, *The House of Government: A Saga of the Russian Revolution* (Princeton, NJ: Princeton University Press, 2017).

13. For theoretical approaches to how resistance to top-down planning can take the form of everyday acts of reappropriation or subversion, see Margaret Crawford, John Chase, and John Kaliski, eds., *Everyday Urbanism* (New York: Monacelli, 2008); Michel de Certeau, "Walking in the City," in *The Practice of Everyday Life*, trans. Stephen Rendall (Berkeley: University of California Press, 2011). For a more contemporary example of resistance to neoliberal rather than

state-directed urban planning, see Teresa Caldeira, "Imprinting and Moving Around: New Visibilities and Configurations of Public Space in São Paulo," *Public Culture* 24, no. 2 (May 2012): 385–419. For ways that Britain's built environment has been reappropriated by those who use it, see Connell, *Black Handsworth*; Perry, *London Is the Place for Me*; Greenhalgh, *Reconstructing Modernity*.

14. Characterizing mid-twentieth-century Britain's political formation as developmental and technocratic loosely follows David Edgerton, *The Rise and Fall of the British Nation: A Twentieth-Century History* (London: Penguin, 2018); David Edgerton, *The Warfare State: Britain, 1920–1970* (Cambridge: Cambridge University Press, 2006). In telling a story grounded in the history of state-directed development and the implications of its collapse, I am also influenced by Georgi M. Derluguian's history of the Soviet Union and its disintegration. Georgi M. Derluguian, *Bourdieu's Secret Admirer in the Caucuses: A World-System Biography* (Chicago: University of Chicago Press, 2006).

15. For the canonical history of the authoritarian developmental regime imposed by Moses, see Robert A. Caro, *The Power Broker: Robert Moses and the Fall of New York* (New York: Vintage, 1973). For Brasilia, see James Holston, *The Modernist City: An Anthropological Account of Brasilia* (Chicago: University of Chicago Press, 1989). For high-density housing built under Khrushchev in the Soviet Union, see Christine Varga-Harris, *Stories of House and Home: Soviet Apartment Life during the Khrushchev Years* (Ithaca, NY: Cornell University Press, 2015). For a global history of high-density housing programs, see Florian Urban, *Tower and Slab: Histories of Global Mass Housing* (Abingdon, UK: Routledge, 2012).

16. For literature on the slow emergence of top-down urban planning and its prehistory, see Ravetz, *The Government of Space*; Meller, *Towns, Plans, and Society*; Hall, *Cities of Tomorrow*; Daniel T. Rodgers, *Atlantic Crossings: Social Politics in a Progressive Age* (Cambridge, MA: Harvard University Press, 1999).

17. For continuities in the amount of public money spent during the Thatcher administration, see Jim Tomlinson, *Managing the Economy, Managing the People: Narratives of Economic Life in Britain from Beveridge to Brexit* (Oxford: Oxford University Press, 2017), ch. 3. For ways that the Thatcher administration intervened extensively in the British built environment, see Otto Saumarez Smith, "Action for Cities: The Thatcher Government and Inner-City Policy," *Urban History* (2019): 1–18.

18. David Harvey has characterized this shift as marking a transition from the "managerial" to "entrepreneurial" city. David Harvey, "From Managerialism to Entrepreneurialism: The Transformation of Urban Governance in Late Capitalism," *Geografiska Annaler, Series B, Human Geography* 71, no. 1 (1989): 3–17.

19. Otto Saumarez Smith, "The Inner City Crisis and the End of Urban Modernism in 1970s Britain," *Twentieth Century British History* 27, no. 4 (December 2016): 578–98; Aaron Andrews, "Multiple Deprivation, the Inner City, and the Fracturing of the Welfare State: Glasgow, c. 1968–78," *Twentieth Century British History* 29, no. 4 (December 2018): 605–24; Nicholas Deakin and John Edwards, *The Enterprise Culture and the Inner City* (London: Routledge, 1993); Michael Parkinson, "The Thatcher Government's Urban Policy, 1979–1989, a Review," *Town Planning Review* 60, no. 4 (October 1989): 421–40.

20. Amy Edwards, *Financial Times: Investment Culture in Late Twentieth-Century Britain* (Berkeley: University of California Press, forthcoming); Matthew Francis "'A Crusade to Enfranchise the Many': Thatcherism and the Property-Owning Democracy," *Twentieth Century British History* 23. no. 2 (August 2011): 275–97.

21. Brett Christophers, *The New Enclosure: The Appropriation of Public Lands in Neoliberal Britain* (London: Verso, 2018).

22. For classic accounts of neoliberalism as a class project, see David Harvey, *A Brief History of Neoliberalism* (Oxford: Oxford University Press, 2005); Naomi Klein, *The Shock Doctrine: The Rise of Disaster Capitalism* (London: Penguin, 2008).

23. See, for example, Wendy Brown, *Undoing the Demos: Neoliberalism's Stealth Revolution* (New York: Zone Books, 2015); Luc Boltanski and Eve Chiapello, *The New Spirit of Capitalism*, trans. Gregory Elliot (London: Verso, 2018); Pierre Dardot and Christian Laval, *The New Way of the World: On Neo-Liberal Society*, trans. Gregory Elliot (London: Verso, 2014); Bethany Moreton, *To Serve God and Wal-Mart: The Making of Christian Free Enterprise* (Cambridge, MA: Harvard University Press, 2009); Melinda Cooper, *Family Values: Between Neoliberalism and the New Social Conservatism* (Cambridge, MA: MIT Press, 2018). See also Michel Foucault, *The Birth of Biopolitics: Lectures at the Collège de France, 1978–79*, trans. Graham Burchell (Basingstoke, UK: Palgrave Macmillan, 2008).

24. For intellectual histories that trace the emergence of neoliberalism in transatlantic think tanks, see Quinn Slobodian, *The Globalists: The End of Empire and the Birth of Neoliberalism* (Cambridge, MA: Harvard University Press, 2018); Angus Burgin, *The Great Persuasion: Reinventing Free Markets since the Depression* (Cambridge, MA: Harvard University Press, 2012); Daniel Stedman Jones, *Masters of the Universe: Hayek, Friedman, and the Birth of Neoliberal Politics* (Princeton, NJ: Princeton University Press, 2014); Philip Mirowski and Dieter Plehwe, eds., *The Road from Mount Pèlerin: The Making of the Neoliberal Thought Collective* (Cambridge, MA: Harvard University Press, 2009); Ben Jackson, "The Think Tank Archipelago: Thatcherism and Neo-Liberalism," in *Making Thatcher's Britain*, ed. Ben Jackson and Robert Saunders (Cambridge: Cambridge University Press, 2012), 43–61. For the various ways in which these ideas were implemented as policy in different parts of the world, see Marion Fourcade-Gourinchas and Sarah L. Babb, "The Rebirth of the Liberal Creed: Paths to Neoliberalism in Four Countries," *American Journal of Sociology* 108, no. 3 (November 2002): 533–79; Florence Sutcliffe-Braithwaite, "Neo-liberalism and Morality in the Making of Thatcherite Social Policy," *Historical Journal* 55, no. 2 (June 2012): 497–520; Monica Prasad, *The Politics of Free Markets: The Rise of Neoliberal Economic Policies in Britain, France, Germany, and the United States* (Chicago: University of Chicago Press, 2006); Kim Phillips-Fein, *Invisible Hands: The Businessmen's Crusade against the New Deal* (New York: W. W. Norton, 2010).

25. Daniel Rodgers, "The Uses and Abuses of 'Neoliberalism,'" *Dissent* (Winter 2018). For an important critique of the implicit valorization of the white working-class subject in histories of neoliberalism in Britain and the United States, see N.D.B. Connolly, "A White Story," *Dissent* (January 22, 2018), accessed March 30, 2019, https://www.dissentmagazine.org/blog /neoliberalism-forum-ndb-connolly. For an earlier critique, see John Clarke, "Living with/in and without Neo-Liberalism," *Focaal: European Journal of Anthropology* 51 (June 2008): 135–47.

26. Will Davies, *The Limits of Neoliberalism: Authority, Sovereignty, and the Logic of Competition* (London: Sage Publications Ltd., 2014). This particular quote comes from Will Davies, "The Difficulty of 'Neoliberalism,'" Political Economy Research Centre, January 1, 2016, accessed March 29, 2019, http://www.perc.org.uk/project_posts/the-difficulty-of-neoliberalism.

27. For versions of this argument staged in places other than Britain, see Aihwa Ong, *Neoliberalism as Exception: Mutations in Citizenship and Sovereignty* (Durham, NC: Duke University

Press, 2006); Li Zhang, *In Search of Paradise: Middle-Class Living in a Chinese Metropolis* (Ithaca, NY: Cornell University Press, 2010); Collier, *Post-Soviet Social*; Jamie Peck, "Explaining (with) Neoliberalism, *Territory, Politics, Governance* 1, no. 2 (2013): 132–57; James Ferguson, "The Uses of Neoliberalism," *Antipode* 41, no. 1 (January: 2010): 166–84. Meanwhile, Brett Christophers has argued that British neoliberalism is characterized by the privatization of once-public assets. Christophers, *The New Enclosure*.

28. The idea that urban reform could remake individuals and society was present among a diverse number of turn-of-the-twentieth-century philanthropists, town planners, and social reformers. Figures such as Beatrice Webb, Ebenezer Howard, Raymond Unwin, Andrew Mearns, and Charles Booth all in different ways believed that urban space determined the moral as well as social lives of those who lived in or experienced them. Urban reform played a small part in the nineteenth-century emergence of the idea that "the social" was a legible and undifferentiated object of government intervention, distinct from politics and the economy. For histories of the emergence of the social, see James Vernon, "The Ethics of Hunger and the Assembly of Society: The Techno-Politics of the School Meal in Modern Britain," *American Historical Review* 110, no. 3 (June 2005): 693–725; Rodgers, *Atlantic Crossings*; Mary Poovey, *Making a Social Body: Britain, 1830–1864* (Chicago: University of Chicago Press, 1995); Patrick Joyce, ed., *The Social in Question: New Bearings* (London: Routledge, 2002); Nikolas Rose, "The Death of the Social? Refiguring the Territory of Government," *Economy and Society* 25, 3 (August 1996): 327–56. For a case study of the emergence of the social in the British Empire in India, see Mrinalini Sinha, *Specters of Mother India: The Global Restructuring of an Empire* (Durham, NC: Duke University Press, 2006). For other histories of how Britain's social developmental state has sought to shape the lives of its citizens, see James Vernon, *Hunger: A Modern History* (Cambridge, MA: Harvard University Press, 2007); Nikolas Rose, *Governing the Soul: The Shaping of the Private Self* (London: Routledge, 1990); Carolyn Steedman, *Landscape for a Good Woman: A Story of Two Lives* (New Brunswick, NJ: Rutgers University Press, 1987); Daniel Ussishkin, *Morale: A Modern British History* (Oxford: Oxford University Press, 2018); Michal Shapira, *The War Inside: Psychoanalysis, Total War, and the Making of the Democratic Self in Postwar Britain* (Cambridge: Cambridge University Press, 2013).

29. This scholarship tends to emphasize the ways in which disciplinary or coercive power becomes substituted for the cultivation of enterprise—a kind of power that makes only narrow or even nonexistent anthropological claims. Foucault, *The Birth of Biopolitics*; Michael C. Behrent, "Liberalism without Humanism: Michel Foucault and the Free-Market Creed, 1976–1979," *Modern Intellectual History* 6, no. 3 (November 2009): 539–68; Brown, *Undoing the Demos*; Dardot and Laval, *The New Way of the World*; Cooper, *Family Values*. For an alternative account of the production of the neoliberal subject in Britain, see John Clarke, "New Labour's Citizens: Activated, Empowered, Responsibilized, Abandoned?" *Critical Social Policy* 25, no. 4 (November 2005): 447–63. Some historians of Britain are increasingly aware of the ways that the politics of the 1980s were characterized by forms of individualism and autonomy that manifested as a skepticism toward state planning. For the emergence of "popular individualism" in late twentieth-century Britain, see, for example, Emily Robinson, Camilla Schofield, Florence Sutcliffe-Braithwaite, and Natalie Thomlinson, "Telling Stories about Post-War Britain: Popular Individualism and the 'Crisis' of the 1970s," *Twentieth Century British History* 28, no. 2

(June 2017): 268–304. For theories of the individual in 1980s Conservative policy making, see Aled Davies, James Freeman, and Hugh Pemberton, "'Everyman a Capitalist' or 'Free to Choose'?: Exploring the Tensions within Thatcherite Individualism," *Historical Journal* 61, no. 2 (June 2018): 477–501.

30. Certeau, "Walking in the City"; Henri Lefebvre, "Notes on the New Town (April 1960)," in *Introduction to Modernity*, trans. John Moore (London: Verso, 1995); Robert Venturi, Denise Scott Brown, and Steven Izenour, *Learning from Las Vegas* (Cambridge, MA: MIT Press, 1972); Jane Jacobs, *The Death and Life of Great American Cities* (New York: Vintage, 1961).

31. For the ways that Britain's welfare state was organized around the male breadwinning subject, see Susan Pedersen, *Family Dependence and the Origins of the Welfare State: Britain and France, 1914–1945* (Cambridge: Cambridge University Press, 1995). For ways in which black Britons and migrants were excluded from elements of the welfare state, see Perry, *London Is the Place for Me*. For an account of the ways that the welfare state depended on migrant labor while operating through exclusions based on race and gender, see Beverley Bryan, Stella Dadzie, and Susan Scafe, *The Heart of the Race: Black Women's Lives in Britain* (London: Virago, 1985).

32. The authoritarian nature of British neoliberalism along with its mobilization of issues such as race, patriarchy, and authority was noted by both historians and contemporaries. The classic account remains Stuart Hall, "The Great Moving Right Show," *Marxism Today* (January 1979): 14–20. See also Camilla Schofield, *Enoch Powell and the Making of Postcolonial Britain* (Cambridge: Cambridge University Press, 2013); Sutcliffe-Braithwaite, "Neo-liberalism and Morality."

33. Rosemary Wakeman, *Practicing Utopia: An Intellectual History of the New Town Movement* (Chicago: Chicago University Press, 2016); Ortolano, *Thatcher's Progress*, ch. 5.

34. Sam Wetherell, "Freedom Planned: Enterprise Zones and Urban Non-Planning in Post-War Britain," *Twentieth Century British History* 27, no. 2 (March 2016): 266–89.

35. In this sense, the built environment in the postwar period is another area where we can see what James Vernon has called the "worlding" of modern Britain. Tehila Sasson, James Vernon, Miles Ogborn, Priya Satia, and Catherine Hall, "Britain and the World: A New Field?," *Journal of British Studies* 57, no. 4 (October 2018): 677–708.

36. Ruth Craggs and Hannah Neate, "Post-Colonial Careering and Urban Policy Mobility between Britain and Nigeria, 1945–1990," *Transactions of the Institute of British Geographers* 42, no. 1 (September 2016): 44–57; Jesse Meredith, "Decolonising the New Town: Roy Gazzard and the Making of Killingworth Township," *Journal of British Studies* 57, no. 2 (April 2018): 333–62.

37. The earliest and most influential history of US suburbia remains Kenneth Jackson, *Crabgrass Frontier: The Suburbanization of the United States* (Oxford: Oxford University Press, 1987). See also Lizabeth Cohen, *A Consumer's Republic: The Politics of Mass Consumption in Postwar America* (New York: Knopf, 2003); Thomas J. Sugrue, *The Origins of the Urban Crisis: Race and Inequality in Postwar Detroit* (Princeton, NJ: Princeton University Press, 1998); Robert O. Self, *American Babylon: Race and the Struggle for Postwar Oakland* (Princeton NJ: Princeton University Press, 2005); Becky Nicolaides, *My Blue Heaven: Life and Politics in the Working-Class Suburbs of Los Angeles, 1920–1965* (Chicago: University of Chicago Press, 2002). For a summary of this turn, see Kevin Kruse and Thomas J. Sugrue, eds., *The New Suburban History* (Chicago: University of Chicago Press, 2006).

38. One exception is Christopher Klemek, *The Transatlantic Collapse of Urban Renewal: Postwar Urbanism from New York to Berlin* (Chicago: University of Chicago Press, 2011). On transatlantic urban culture, see also Hulme, *After the Shock City*.

39. Jackson, "The Think Tank Archipelago"; Daniel Stedman Jones, *Masters of the Universe: Hayek, Friedman, and the Birth of Neoliberal Politics* (Princeton, NJ: Princeton University Press, 2012).

Chapter 1: The Industrial Estate

1. Andrew Ure, *The Philosophy of Manufactures; Or, an Exposition of the Scientific, Moral, and Commercial Economy of the Factory System of Great Britain* (London: Routledge, 1967), 13–15.

2. For much of the twentieth century, the terms "industrial estate" and "trading estate" were used interchangeably in Britain to describe the same type of space.

3. For the transformation of industrial architecture in the twentieth century, see Joshua B. Freeman, *Behemoth: The Factory and the Making of the Modern World* (New York: W. W. Norton, 2018), chs. 4–6; Gillian Darley, *Factory* (London: Reaktion, 2003); John Winter, *Industrial Architecture: A Survey of Factory Buildings* (London: Studio Vista, 1970). For Britain specifically, see Elain Harwood, *Space, Hope, and Brutalism: English Architecture, 1945–1975* (New Haven, CT: Yale University Press, 2015), ch,. 8; Edgar Jones, *Industrial Architecture in Britain, 1750–1939* (London: Batsford, 1985), ch. 5. For further descriptions of the relative infrastructural autonomy of nineteenth-century textile mills in Britain and elsewhere, see Andreas Malm, *Fossil Capital: The Rise of Steam Power and the Roots of Global Warming* (London: Verso, 2016), esp. ch. 6; Mike Williams, *Cotton Mills in Greater Manchester* (Preston, UK: Carnegie, 1992); Thomas Dublin, *Women at Work: The Transformation of Work and Community in Lowell, Massachusetts, 1826–1860* (New York: Columbia University Press, 1981).

4. US economist William Bredo calculated that there were eighty-one industrial estates in Britain in 1960. William Bredo, *Industrial Estates: Tools for Industrialization* (Glencoe, NJ: Free Press, 1960), 7. According to the Industrial Estates Management Corporation for England, just under a quarter million people were employed in government-owned industrial estates in designed development areas alone on April 1, 1960, when industrial estate management was consolidated into a single national body. This figure does not include industrial estates in new towns. Industrial Estates Management Corporation for England, "Introduction to Industrial Estates and the Part They Play in Location of Industry Policy in Britain," 36, Gateshead Central Library, Local Studies (henceforth GLS), L 338 IND.

5. For the origins of a regionally concentrated industrial policy in Britain, with particular regard to government-financed industrial estates in "special areas" earmarked for development, see Peter Scott, "The Audit of Regional Policy: 1934–1939," *Regional Studies* 34, no. 1 (February 2000): 55–65; Peter Scott, "British Regional Policy, 1945–51: A Lost Opportunity?," *Twentieth Century British History* 8, no. 3 (January 1997): 358–82; Alan Booth, "The Second World War and the Origins of Modern Regional Policy," *Economy and Society* 11, no. 1 (1982): 1–21; Stephen V. Ward, "Interwar Britain: A Study of Government Spending, Planning, and Uneven Economic Development," *Built Environment* 7, no. 2 (1981): 96–108; Stephen V. Ward, *The Geography of Interwar Britain: The State and Uneven Development* (London: Routledge, 1988); Herbert Loebl, *Government Factories and the Origins of British Regional Policy, 1934–1948*

(Aldershot, UK: Avebury, 1988). For Britain's postwar industrial and regional policy with particular regard to government-financed industrial estates, see Peter Scott, "Worst of Both Worlds: British Regional Policy, 1951–64," *Business History* 38, no. 4 (October 1996): 41–64; Martin Chick, *Industrial Policy in Britain, 1945–1951* (Cambridge: Cambridge University Press, 1998); D. W. Parsons, *The Political Economy of British Regional Policy* (Beckenham, UK: Croom Helm, 1986). For postwar industrial planning at the local authority level, see Alistair Kefford, "Disruption, Destruction, and the Creation of 'the Inner Cities': The Impact of Urban Renewal on Industry, 1945–1980," *Urban History* 44, no. 3 (August 2017): 492–515.

6. For accounts of the de Trafford family and the prehistory of Trafford Park, see "Trafford Park under Development," *Sketch*, March 17, 1897; D. A. Farnie, *The Manchester Ship Canal and the Rise of the Port of Manchester, 1894–1975* (Manchester: Manchester University Press, 1980), ch. 6. For two excellent histories of Trafford Park written by local historians, see Karen Cliff and Patricia Southern, *Trafford Park from Old Photographs* (Stroud, UK: Amberley, 2013); Robert Nicholls, *Trafford Park: The First Hundred Years* (Chichester, UK: Philmore and Co., 1996).

7. Ernest Torah Hooley, *The Hooley Book: The Amazing Financier, His Career, and His "Crowd"* (London: John Dicks, 1904), 21–23.

8. P. M. Oppenheimer, "Hooley, Ernest Terah (1859–1947)," *Oxford Dictionary of National Biography* (Oxford: Oxford University Press, 2004).

9. Hooley, *The Hooley Book*, 113–14; Farnie, *The Manchester Ship Canal*, 121.

10. Farnie, *Manchester Ship Canal*, 120.

11. Cliff and Southern, *Trafford Park*, 77. For subsidized electricity, see Farnie, *TheManchester Ship Canal*, 127.

12. Cliff and Southern, *Trafford Park*, 13.

13. For Henry Ford's role in British national development during this period, see Kit Kowol, "An Experiment in Conservative Modernity: Interwar Conservatism and Henry Ford's English Farms," *Journal of British Studies* 55, no. 4 (October 2016): 781–805. For his global scope, see Greg Grandin, *Fordlandia: The Rise and Fall of Henry Ford's Forgotten Jungle City* (London: Icon, 2010).

14. John Dummelow, *A History of the Metropolitan-Vickers Electrical Company Limited* (Manchester: Metropolitan-Vickers Electrical Export Company), 14, 7.

15. Nicholls, *Trafford Park*, 78.

16. Trafford Park Residents' Association, "The Last 'Souvenir' Edition of the Trafford Park Times," 1981, folder 338.09, PAR, 12, Trafford Local Studies (henceforth TLS).

17. Farnie, *TheManchester Ship Canal*, 127.

18. Cliff and Southern, *Trafford Park*, 77–78.

19. Frederick A. Talbot, "Trafford Park: Britain's Workshop and Storehouse," promotional book, 1923, National Archives (henceforth TNA), ZLIB 17/312, 29.

20. Cliff and Southern, *Trafford Park*, 77.

21. Robert L. Wrigley Jr., "Organized Industrial Districts: With Special Reference to the Chicago Area," *Journal of Land and Public Utility Economics* 23, no. 2 (May 1947): 180–98.

22. R. Heiligenthal, "The Planning of Industrial Areas in Germany," *International Housing and Town Planning Bulletin* 32 (August 1933): 14–22.

23. For the emergence of private industrial estates in southern England during the interwar period, see Peter Scott, "Industrial Estates and British Industrial Development, 1897–1939," *Business History* 43, no. 2 (March 2001): 73–98; G. R. Allen, "The Growth of Industry on Trading

Estates, 1920–1939, with Special Reference to Slough Trading Estate," *Oxford Economic Papers* 3, no. 3 (October 1951): 272–300; John Armstrong, "The Development of the Park Royal Industrial Estate in the Interwar Period: A Re-examination of the Aldcroft/Richardson Thesis," *London Journal* 21, no. 1 (1996): 64–79; Michael Cassell, *Long Lease!: The Story of Slough Estates, 1920–1991* (London: Pencorp, 1991).

24. Sidney Pollard, *The Development of the British Economy, 1914–1967* (London: Edward Arnold, 1969), 242–54; Peter Scott, *Triumph of the South: A Regional Economic History of Early Twentieth Century Britain* (Aldershot, UK: Ashgate, 2007), ch. 5. For the effect of this crisis on the northeastern region specifically, see Ward, *The Geography of Interwar Britain*, esp. ch. 1.

25. Miriam Glucksmann, *Women Assemble: Women Workers and the New Industries in Interwar Britain* (London: Routledge, 1990); Denis Linehan, "A New England: Landscape, Exhibition, and Remaking Industrial Space in the 1930s," in *Geographies of British Modernity: Space and Society in the Twentieth Century*, ed. David Glibert, David Matless, and Brian Short (Oxford: Blackwell, 2003); Peter Scott, "Women, Other 'Fresh' Workers, and the New Manufacturing Workforce of Interwar Britain," *International Review of Social History* 45, no. 3 (December 2000): 440–74.

26. Glucksmann, *Women Assemble*.

27. Scott, *Triumph of the South*, ch. 9.

28. Scott, *Triumph of the South*, 77.

29. Frank Trentmann, *Free Trade Nation: Commerce, Consumption, and Civil Society in Modern Britain* (Oxford: Oxford University Press, 2009), part 1; Ross McKibbin, *Parties and People: England, 1914–1951* (Oxford: Oxford University Press, 2010), ch. 2.

30. Stephanie Ward, *Unemployment and the State in Britain: The Means Test and Protest in 1930s South Wales and North-East England* (Manchester: Manchester University Press, 2013); Jim Tomlinson, *Employment Policy: The Crucial Years, 1939–1955* (Oxford: Oxford University Press, 1987), ch. 1; Frederic M. Miller, "The Unemployment Policy of the National Government, 1931–1936," *Historical Journal* 19, no. 2 (July 1976): 453–76; Parsons, *The Political Economy of British Regional Policy*, 5–11.

31. "Places without a Future," *Times*, March 20, 1934.

32. "Places without a Future."

33. The role played by these articles in agitating for the Special Areas Act of 1934 is attested to in Loebl, *Government Factories*; Parsons, *The Political Economy of British Regional Policy*.

34. Beatrix Campbell, "Orwell Revisited," in *Patriotism: The Making and Unmaking of British National Identity*, ed. R. Samuel (London: Routledge, 1989); Dave Russell, *Looking North: Northern England and the National Imagination* (Manchester: Manchester University Press, 2004).

35. James Vernon, *Hunger: A Modern History* (Cambridge, MA: Harvard University Press, 2007), 120–24.

36. Political and Economic Planning, *Report on the Location of Industry: A Survey of Present Trends in Great Britain Affecting Industrial Location and Regional Economic Development, with Proposals for Future Policy* (London: Political and Economic Planning, 1939), 16–17.

37. Quoted in Ward, "Interwar Britain," 103.

38. "Places without a Future III: A Task for One Man," *Times*, March 22, 1934.

39. Loebl, *Government Factories*, 42.

40. Parliamentary Papers, "Reports of Investigations into the Industrial Conditions in Certain Depressed Areas," 1934, Cmd. 4728, 106.

41. Loebl, *Government Factories*, 54; Scott, *Triumph of the South*, 257.

42. The responses to this booklet from its recipients are collected in TNA, LAB 23/153.

43. Scott, "The Audit of Regional Policy," 58.

44. "Trading Companies," Memorandum by the Board of Trade, 2, TNA, BT 64/11.

45. "Memorandum of Understanding of North Eastern Trading Estates Limited," TNA, LAB 18/37.

46. For a full description of Team Valley in its early stages, see Kenelm C. Appleyard, "Government Sponsored Trading Estates," *Journal of the Royal Society of the Arts* 87 (June 30, 1939): 843–63.

47. "Such People Don't Give In," *Daily Mail*, March 29, 1939.

48. "Today's Industrial City of Tomorrow," promotional book, GLS, L 338 NOR.

49. Appleyard, "Government Sponsored Trading Estates," 853.

50. Appleyard, "Government Sponsored Trading Estates," 854; "North-East Workers Praised by Team Valley Estate Chief," undated newspaper clipping, TVTE newspaper cuttings, GLS.

51. Douglass T. Wallis, "The Architect and the Trading Estate," in "Trading Estates: A Review of the Development of Planned Factory Units throughout Great Britain," ed. Douglas G. Wolton, 43, GLS, L 338 WOL.

52. "Today's Industrial City of Tomorrow," promotional book, GLS, L 338 NOR.

53. Appleyard, "Government Sponsored Trading Estates," 856; "Today's Industrial City of Tomorrow."

54. David Matless, *Landscape and Englishness* (London: Reaktion, 1998), 90–95. On interwar eugenics movements in Britain, see Richard Overy, *The Morbid Age: Britain between the Wars* (London: Allen Lane, 2009), ch. 3.

55. Matless, *Landscape and Englishness*, 94.

56. The Central Council of Recreative Physical Training, "Annual Report, 1936–37," 10, TNA, ED 113/61.

57. For a description of the role of the NFC in Team Valley's recreational facilities, see Appleyard, "Government Sponsored Trading Estates," 855. See also "North Eastern Social Trusts Ltd.," grant application, TNA, ED 113/31.

58. Appleyard, "Government Sponsored Trading Estates," 855.

59. Appleyard, "Government Sponsored Trading Estates," 855. See also "North Eastern Trading Estate Ltd., Team Valley Estate Canteens," memo from the factory inspector, TNA, BT 104/29; "Such People Don't Give In."

60. Vernon, *Hunger*, 163–69.

61. "Today's Industrial City of Tomorrow."

62. On the racializing of the poor in the late nineteenth and early twentieth centuries in ways that set working-class people apart as objects for political intervention and reform, see Judith R. Walkowitz, *City of Dreadful Delight: Narratives of Sexual Danger in Late Victorian London* (Chicago: University of Chicago Press, 1992); Gareth Stedman Jones, *Outcast London: A Study in the Relationship between Classes in Victorian Society* (London: Verso, 2013); Seth Koven, *Slumming: Sexual and Social Politics in Victorian London* (Princeton, NJ: Princeton University Press, 2004). On the means by which the interwar unemployed were pathologized, see Ross McKibbin, "The

'Social Psychology' of Unemployment in Inter-War Britain," in *Ideologies of Class: Social Relations in Britain, 1880–1950* (Oxford: Oxford University Press, 1990).

63. Glucksmann, *Women Assemble*; Ruth Cavendish, *Women on the Line* (London: Routledge, 1982); Sue Bruley, "Sorters, Pipers, and Packers: Women in Light Industry in South London, 1920–1960," *Oral History* 25, no. 1 (April 1997): 75–82; Sue Bruley, "'A Very Happy Crowd': Women in Industry in South London in World War Two," *History Workshop Journal* 44 (October 1997): 59–76; Vicky Long, "Industrial Homes and Domestic Factories: The Convergence of Public and Private Space in Interwar Britain," *Journal of British History* 50, no. 2 (April 2011): 434–64; Mike Savage, "Trade Unionism, Sex Segregation, and the State: Women's Employment in 'New Industries' in Inter-War Britain," *Social History* 13, no. 2 (May 1988): 209–30.

64. Savage, "Trade Unionism, Sex Segregation, and the State."

65. "Evidence Submitted by the North East Development Board to the Royal Commission on the Geographical Distribution of the Industrial Population," 13, TNA, HLG 27/41.

66. This figure is from 1948. Cited in Scott, "British Regional Policy," 371.

67. Economic geographer T. W. Freeman's report on North East England noted that of the almost fifty-three thousand employed at Team Valley in 1958, just short of thirty thousand were women. T. W. Freeman, *The Conurbations of Great Britain* (Manchester: Manchester University Press, 1966), 203–4.

68. Scott, "British Regional Policy," 370–72. Scott argues that this is one of the primary reasons for the long-term inability of industrial estates to develop the economies of places like the North East.

69. Glucksmann, *Women Assemble*, 135.

70. For example, workers in the Hoover factory in Perivale in West London worked from 7:30 a.m. to 5:30 p.m., Sunday to Friday. Glucksmann, *Women Assemble*, 137–42.

71. Glucksmann, *Women Assemble*, 136.

72. Herbert Loebl, "Refugees from the Third Reich and Industry in the Depressed Areas of Britain," in *Second Chance: Two Centuries of German-Speaking Jews in the United Kingdom*, ed. Werner E. Mosse (Tübingen: Mohr, 1991), 379, 386–87.

73. "Industries Started by Refugees," *Times*, July 1, 1941.

74. Loebl, "Refugees from the Third Reich," 390, 391.

75. "Refugees in Britain," *Economist*, August 5, 1939.

76. Herbert Loebl, "Entrepreneur, Exporting Expert, and Co-Founder of Joyce, Loebl & Company," *Journal*, May 14, 2012.

77. "Location of Industrial Policy in Britain from 1934–1960 and the British Government's Trading Estates: An Example of Industry in Practice," pamphlets, GLS.

78. "Industrial Estates: 21 Years of Progress," 14, pamphlets, GLS.

79. Hugh Quigley, "The Factory Estate as a Collective Enterprise," in "Trading Estates: A Review of the Development of Planned Factory Units throughout Great Britain," ed. Douglas G. Wolton, 51, GLS, L 338 WOL.

80. Douglas G. Wolton, "The New Industrial Unit," in "Trading Estates: A Review of the Development of Planned Factory Units throughout Great Britain," ed. Douglas G. Wolton, 19, 21, GLS, L 338 WOL.

81. Quoted in Peter Scott, "British Regional Policy," 366.

82. "National Plan for the Location of Industry Urged by Colonel Appleyard," TVTE newspaper cuttings, GLS.

83. Appleyard, "The Future of Trading Estates," 36.

84. "Location of Industry: Trading Estates and Their Assistance to Employers," TVTE newspaper cuttings, GLS; "National Plan for Location of Industry Urged by Colonel Appleyard," TVTE newspaper cuttings, GLS.

85. "Team Valley History: Timeline," GLS, L 338.9, 6; "Oberst Kenelm Appleyard," TVTE newspaper cuttings, GLS.

86. "Team Valley History: Timeline"; "German Firms for Distressed Areas?," *Nottingham Guardian*, newspaper cutting, December 31, 1937, TNA, BT 104/27.

87. Parliamentary Papers, "Royal Commission on the Distribution of the Industrial Population," 1940, Cmd. 6153, part 1.

88. Parliamentary Papers, "Royal Commission," 202–3, 188.

89. Parliamentary Papers, "Employment Policy," 1944, Cmd. 6527, 11–12.

90. Parliamentary Papers, "Royal Commission on the Distribution of the Industrial Population," 136.

91. Scott, "British Regional Policy"; Parsons, *The Political Economy of British Regional Policy*, 82–84.

92. Parliamentary Papers, "Distribution of Industry: A Bill to Provide for the Development of Certain Areas; for Controlling the Provision of Industrial Premises with a View to Securing the Proper Distribution of Industry," 1944–45.

93. "Location of Industrial Policy in Britain from 1934–1960."

94. See, for example, Parliamentary Papers, "Royal Commission on the Distribution of the Industrial Population," ch. 10.

95. Parliamentary Papers, "Final Report of the New Town Committee," 1946, Cmd. 6876, 14–15.

96. Scott, "Worst of Both Worlds."

97. Kefford, "Disruption, Destruction, and the Creation of 'the Inner Cities.'"

98. Bredo, *Industrial Estates*, 7.

99. Industrial Estates Management Corporation for England, "Introduction to Industrial Estates," 36.

100. Scott, "British Regional Policy."

101. "Summary of Comments by Estate Companies," TNA, BT 104/78.

102. Note from Wales and Monmouthshire Industrial Estates to Board of Trade, March 8, 1950, TNA, BT 104/78.

103. "Rules and Constitution of Development Areas Federation of Industrial Estate Associations," TNA, BT 177/243.

104. Swansea Trading Estate Tenants' Association, letter to the Board of Trade, March 7, 1952, TNA, BT 177/243.

105. Letter from F. N. Tribe to W. L. Buxton, August 16, 1935, TNA, BT 64/11.

106. "Committee on Investigator's Reports into Depressed Areas," TNA, CAB 27/577. Cited in Loebl, *Government Factories*, 47.

107. This relationship could be seen as another instance of the framework of governance established between industry, labor, and the state described in Keith Middlemas, *Politics in Industrial Society: The Experience of the British System since 1911* (London: Deutsch, 1979).

108. For East Africa, see Stephen Constantine, *The Making of British Colonial Development Policy, 1914–1940* (London: Cass, 1984). For the Caribbean, see Sabine Clarke, *Science at the End*

of Empire: Experts and the Development of the British Caribbean, 1940–62 (Manchester: Manchester University Press, 2018). For Egypt, see Timothy Mitchell, *Rule of Experts: Egypt, Techno-Politics, Modernity* (Berkeley: University of California Press, 2002). For agricultural development, see Joseph Morgan Hodge, *Triumph of the Expert: Agrarian Doctrines of Development and the Triumph of British Colonialism* (Athens: Ohio University Press, 2007).

109. Hodge, *Triumph of the Expert*, chs. 4–5; James Ferguson, *The Anti-Politics Machine: "Development," Depoliticization, and Bureaucratic Power in Lesotho* (Cambridge: Cambridge University Press, 1990); Joseph M. Hodge, Gerald Hödl, and Martina Kopf, *Developing Africa: Concepts and Practices in Twentieth-Century Colonialism* (Manchester: Manchester University Press, 2014). For state representations of colonial development, see Marc Matera, "An Empire of Development: Africa and the Caribbean in God's Chillun," *Twentieth Century British History* 23, no. 1 (March 2012): 12–37.

110. Clarke, *Science at the End of Empire*.

111. There are two biographies of W. Arthur Lewis: Barbara Ingham and Paul Mosley, *Sir Arthur Lewis: A Biography* (Basingstoke, UK: Palgrave Macmillan, 2013); Robert L. Tignor, *W. Arthur Lewis and the Birth of Development Economics* (Princeton, NJ: Princeton University Press, 2004). For Lewis's later career, see Adom Getachew, *Worldmaking after Empire: The Rise and Fall of Self-Determination* (Princeton, NJ: Princeton University Press, 2019), ch. 5.

112. W. Arthur Lewis, "Economic Development with Unlimited Supplies of Labour," *Manchester School* 22, May 1954.

113. W. Arthur Lewis and F. V. Meyer, "The Analysis of Secondary Industries," Memorandum to Colonial Economic Advisory Committee, Industry Subcommittee, TNA, CO 990/17; W. Arthur Lewis, *The Principles of Economic Planning* (London: Unwin University Books, 1959); W. Arthur Lewis, "An Economic Plan for Jamaica," *Quarterly Journal of Reconstruction* 3 (1944).

114. Lewis, "The Analysis of Secondary Industries," 2; Clarke, *Science at the End of Empire*, 112.

115. Lewis, "The Analysis of Secondary Industries," 2.

116. Lewis, "The Analysis of Secondary Industries," 2.

117. Parliamentary Papers, "East Africa Royal Commission," 1955, Cmd. 9475, 89; L. J. Butler, *Industrialisation and the British Colonial State: West Africa, 1939–1951* (London: Frank Cass, 1997), 102–8.

118. "The African Industrial Estates Development Committee," motion, TNA, CO 822/1399; *Hansard Parliamentary Debates*, Commons, Deb., March 6, 1957, series 5, vol. 566, cc 56–57w.

119. "The African Industrial Estates Development Committee," press handout, TNA, CO 822/1399.

120. "Nigeria: Western Region," TNA, INF 10/241.

121. See, for example, Parliamentary Papers, "The Colombo Plan for Co-Operative Economic Development in South and South-East Asia: Twelfth Annual Report of the Consultative Committee," 1963, Cmd. 2247, 7, 134. See also Economic Commission for Asia and the Far East, "Report of the United Nations Seminar on Industrial Estates in the ECAFE Region to the Committee (Fourteenth Session)," TNA, CO 852/1900.

122. Cassell, *Long Lease!*, ch. 9.

123. Bredo, *Industrial Estates*, xi, 3, 13, 7; A. W. Maldonado, *Teodoro Moscoso and Puerto Rico's Operation Bootstrap* (Gainesville: University Press of Florida, 1997). For Operation Bootstrap's

influence on British development policies on the Caribbean, see Clarke, *Science at the End of Empire*, 97–8, 145–50.

124. Bredo, *Industrial Estates*, 7.

125. Daniel T. Rodgers, *Atlantic Crossings: Social Politics in a Progressive Age* (Cambridge, MA: Harvard University Press, 1998), 7.

Chapter 2: The Shopping Precinct

1. This anecdote is recalled in a series of reflections handwritten later in Gibson's life. Letter B, February 1972, Coventry Archives (henceforth CRO), PA623.

2. Elain Harwood, *Space, Hope, and Brutalism: English Architecture, 1945–1975* (New Haven, CT: Yale University Press), 373.

3. Letter from Gibson to a local newspaper quoted in Nick Tiratsoo, *Reconstruction, Affluence, and Labour Politics: Coventry, 1945–1960* (London: Routledge, 1990), 10.

4. For more technical discussions of typology, see V. J. Bunce, "Revolution on the High Street?: The Emergence of the Enclosed Shopping Centre," *Geography* 68, no. 4 (October 1983): 307–18; Clifford Guy, "Classifications of Retail Stores and Shopping Centres: Some Methodological Issues," *GeoJournal* 45, no. 4 (August 1998): 255–64; Jonathan Reynolds, "The Proliferation of the Planned Shopping Centre," in *Retail Change: Contemporary Issues*, ed. Rosemary D. F. Bromley and Colin J. Thomas (London: UCL Press, 1993).

5. In this sense, the chapter contributes to recent work by British historians who are starting to look at the history of consumerism in the context of the built environment. Some important recent examples include Sarah Mass, "Commercial Heritage as Democratic Action: Historicizing the 'Save the Market' Campaigns in Bradford and Chesterfield, 1969–76," *Twentieth Century British History* 29, no. 3 (September 2018): 459–84; Alistair Kefford, *Planning for Affluence: Cities and the Management of Mass Consumerism in Post-War Britain* (Cambridge: Cambridge University Press, forthcoming); James Greenhalgh, "Consuming Communities: The Neighbourhood Unit and the Role of Retail Spaces on British Housing Estates, 1944–1958," *Urban History* 43, no. 1 (February 2016): 158–74; James Greenhalgh, *Reconstructing Modernity: Space, Power, and Governance in Mid-Twentieth-Century British Cities* (Manchester: Manchester University Press, 2017); Guy Ortolano, "Planning the Urban Future in 1960s Britain," *Historical Journal* 54, no. 2 (June 2011): 477–507; Janina Gosseye, "Milton Keynes' Centre: The Apotheosis of the British Post-War Consensus of the Apostle of Neo-Liberalism?," *History of Retailing and Consumption* 1, no. 3 (September 2015): 209–29; Heinz-Gerhard Haupt, "Small Shops and Department Stores," in *The Oxford Handbook of Consumption*, ed. Frank Trentmann (Oxford: Oxford University Press, 2012); Barbara Usherwood, "Mrs. Housewife and Her Grocer: The Advent of Self-Service Food Shopping in Britain," in *All the World and Her Husband: Women in Twentieth-Century Consumer Culture*, ed. Maggie Andrews and Mary M. Talbot (London: Cassell, 1999).

6. The link between planned shopping centers and economic development in Britain was made in Greenhalgh, *Reconstructing Modernity*. For a similar argument concerning western Europe more broadly, see Janina Gosseye and Tom Avermaete, eds., *Shopping Towns Europe: Commercial Collectivity and the Architecture of the Shopping Centre, 1945–1975* (London: Bloomsbury Academic, 2017).

7. The last twenty years has seen the emergence of a large body of work on the history of the politics, economics, ethics, and social implications of "consumerism" in twentieth-century Britain. Selected works in this vein include Frank Trentmann, *Free Trade Nation: Commerce, Consumption, and Civil Society* (Oxford: Oxford University Press, 2009); Frank Trentmann, *Empire of Things: How We Became a World of Consumers from the Fifteenth Century to the Twenty-First* (London: Allen Lane, 2016); Matthew Hilton, *Consumerism in Twentieth-Century Britain: The Search for a Movement* (Cambridge: Cambridge University Press, 2003); Tehila Sasson, "Milking the Third World?: Humanitarianism, Capitalism, and the Moral Economy of the Nestlé Boycott," *American Historical Review* 121, no. 4 (October 2016): 1196–224; Erika Rappaport, *A Thirst for Empire: How Tea Shaped the Modern World* (Princeton, NJ: Princeton University Press, 2017); John Benson, *The Rise of Consumer Society in Britain, 1880–1980* (London: Longman, 1994).

8. Dave Postles, "The Market as Space in Early Modern England," *Social History* 29, no. 1 (February 2004): 41–58.

9. Robert Tittler, *Architecture and Power: The Town Hall and the English Urban Community, c. 1500–1640* (Oxford: Clarendon, 1991); James Davis, *Medieval Market Morality: Life, Law and Ethics in the English Marketplace 1200–1500* (Cambridge: Cambridge University Press, 2012).

10. Max Weber, *The City* (New York: Free Press, 1966); Karl Polanyi, *The Great Transformation: The Political and Economic Origins of Our Time* (Boston: Beacon, 2001). For an overview of the role of markets in modernization theory, see Jon Stobart and Ilja Van Damme, "Introduction: Markets in Modernization: Transformations in Urban Market Space and Practice, c. 1800–c. 1970," *Urban History* 43, no. 3 (August 2016): 358–71. Mass has shown how battles for the preservation of marketplaces in postwar Britain mobilized a politics of nostalgia. Mass, "Commercial Heritage as Democratic Action."

11. E. P. Thompson, "The Moral Economy of the English Crowd in the Eighteenth Century," *Past and Present* 50 (February 1971): 76–136.

12. For an account of this demographic transition, see James Vernon, *Distant Strangers: How Britain Became Modern* (Berkeley: University of California Press, 2014).

13. James Schmiechen and Kenneth Carls, *The British Market Hall: A Social and Architectural History* (New Haven, CT: Yale University Press, 1999), 26.

14. I am indebted to Schmiechen and Carls for meticulously counting and cataloging these structures using a variety of sources. This figure comes from the appendix to Schmiechen and Carls, *The British Market Hall*.

15. Schmiechen and Carls, *The British Market Hall*.

16. Patrick Joyce, *The Rule of Freedom: Liberalism and the Modern City* (London: Verso, 2003), 86.

17. Katrina Navickas, *Protest and the Politics of Space and Place, 1789–1848* (Manchester: Manchester University Press, 2016).

18. Daniel Defoe, *A Tour through the Whole Island of Great Britain, Vol. 1* (New Haven, CT: Yale University Press, 1991), 148.

19. "Smithfield Cattle Market," *Farmer's Magazine* 19 (1849): 142.

20. The Corporation of the City of London, "A Description of the Metropolitan Meat and Poultry Market, Smithfield," pamphlet, London Metropolitan Archives (henceforth LMA), CLA/017/MP/01/004.

21. Joyce, *The Rule of Freedom*, 83.

22. Victoria Kelley, "The Streets for the People: London's Street Markets, 1850–1939," *Urban History* 43, no. 3 (August 2016): 391–411.

23. Schmiechen and Carls, *The British Market Hall*, 35. Scotland's marketplaces were municipally controlled from a much earlier period.

24. These audit books can be seen at LMA, CLA/017/LC/001.

25. "London Central Meat and Poultry Provision Markets: Annual Report and Accounts," June 17, 1880, 7, LMA, CLA/017/LC/001.

26. Judith R. Walkowitz, *City of Dreadful Delight: Narratives of Sexual Danger in Late Victorian London* (Chicago: University of Chicago Press, 2012); Judith R. Walkowitz, "Going Public: Shopping, Street Harassment, and Streetwalking in Late Victorian London," *Representations* 62 (Spring 1998): 1–30; Erika Rappaport, *Shopping for Pleasure: Women in the Making of London's West End* (Princeton, NJ: Princeton University Press, 2001); Rudi Laermans, "Learning to Consume: Early Department Stores and the Shaping of the Modern Consumer Culture (1860–1914)," *Theory, Culture, and Society* 10, no. 4 (November 1993): 79–102; Geoffrey Crossick and Serge Jaumain, eds., *Cathedrals of Consumption: The European Department Store, 1850–1939* (Aldershot, UK: Ashgate, 1999).

27. Charlotte Wildman, *Urban Redevelopment and Modernity in Liverpool and Manchester, 1918–1939* (London: Bloomsbury Academic, 2016), ch. 3.

28. Erika Rappaport, "Art, Commerce, or Empire?: The Rebuilding of Regent's Street, 1880–1927," *History Workshop Journal* 53, no. 1 (Spring 2002): 94–117.

29. Stobart and Van Damme, "Introduction: Markets in Modernization."

30. As discussed above, see recent and forthcoming work by Alistair Kefford, Sarah Mass, James Greenhalgh, and Guy Ortolano.

31. Ebenezer Howard, *Garden Cities of To-Morrow* (Cambridge, MA: MIT Press, 1965), 54. Urban theorists Peter Hall and Colin Ward have also identified a similarity between Howard's Crystal Palace and modern shopping centers. Peter Hall and Colin Ward, *Sociable Cities: The Legacy of Ebenezer Howard* (Chichester, UK: Wiley, 1998), 21.

32. Howard, *Garden Cities*, 101.

33. For the emergence of town planning as a practice in Britain, see Alison Ravetz, *The Government of Space: Town Planning in Modern Society* (London: Routledge, 2013), esp. chs. 2–3; Helen Meller, *Towns, Plans, and Society in Modern Britain* (Cambridge: Cambridge University Press, 1997), esp. chs. 3–4; Peter Hall, *Cities of Tomorrow: An Intellectual History of Urban Planning and Design in the Twentieth Century* (Chichester, UK: Wiley-Blackwell, 2014), esp. chs. 1 and 4.

34. Meller, *Towns, Plans, and Society*, 41–42; Clara H. Greed, *Women and Planning: Creating Gendered Realities* (London: Routledge, 1994), esp. ch. 7.

35. Daniel T. Rodgers, *Atlantic Crossings: Social Politics in a Progressive Age* (Cambridge, MA: Harvard University Press, 1998).

36. For the development of suburbs in the nineteenth century, see Leonore Davidoff and Catherine Hall, *Family Fortunes: Men and Women of the English Middle Class, 1780–1850* (London: Hutchinson, 1987), ch. 8; Harold James Dyos, *The Victorian Suburb* (Leicester: Leicester University Press, 1961); Todd Kuchta, *Semi-Detached Empire: Suburbia and the Colonization of Britain, 1880 to the Present* (Charlottesville: University of Virginia Press, 2010), ch. 1.

37. Kuchta, *Semi-Detached Empire*, 4.

38. Judy Giles, *The Parlour and the Suburb: Domestic Identities, Class, Femininity, and Modernity* (Oxford: Berg, 2004), ch 1.

39. J. B. Priestley, *English Journey* (Bradford, UK: Great Northern Books, 2009); Patrick Abercrombie, *The Preservation of Rural England* (London: Hodder and Stoughton, 1926); David Matless, *Landscape and Englishness* (London: Reaktion, 1998), part 1.

40. Clough Williams-Ellis, *England and the Octopus* (London: Geoffrey Bles, 1928).

41. Sean O'Connell, *The Car and British Society: Class, Gender, and Motoring, 1896–1939* (Manchester: Manchester University Press, 1998), 19.

42. Alker Tripp, *Town Planning and Road Traffic* (London: Edward Arnold and Co., 1942), 15.

43. O'Connell, *The Car and British Society*, 128.

44. Wilfred Burns, *British Shopping Centres: New Trends in Layout and Distribution* (London: Leonard Hill, 1959), 5.

45. Tripp, *Town Planning and Road Traffic*; Alker Tripp, *Road Traffic and Its Control* (London: Edward Arnold and Co., 1938).

46. Tripp, *Town Planning and Road Traffic*, 62. This was in line with the prevailing public opinion as to the cause of road accidents. O'Connell, *The Car and British Society*, 132.

47. Bill Luckin, "A Never-Ending Passing of the Buck?: The Failure of Drink-Driving Reform in Interwar Britain," *Contemporary British History* 24, no. 3 (September 2010): 363–84.

48. Tripp, *Town Planning and Road Traffic*, 53, 76, 66–67.

49. Gibson's career and work in Coventry have been documented by a number of historians. Junichi Hasegawa, *Replanning the Blitzed City Centre* (Buckingham, UK: Open University Press, 1992); Tiratsoo, *Reconstruction, Affluence, and Labour Politics*; John Grindrod, *Concretopia: A Journey around the Building of Postwar Britain* (Brecon, Wales: Old Street, 2014), ch. 4.

50. Tiratsoo, *Reconstruction, Affluence, and Labour Politics*, 7; Kenneth Richardson and Elizabeth Harris, *Twentieth-Century Coventry* (London: Macmillan, 1972), 277.

51. Tiratsoo, *Reconstruction, Affluence, and Labour Politics*, 7.

52. Donald Gibson, handwritten letters, letter A, February 1972, 3, CRO, PA623.

53. Andrew Saint, "Gibson, Sir Donald Edward Evelyn (1908–1991)," *Oxford Dictionary of National Biography* (Oxford: Oxford University Press, 2004).

54. Donald Gibson, handwritten letters, letter A, February 1972, 1, CRO, PA623.

55. Donald Gibson, "Coventry of Tomorrow: Towards a Beautiful City," pamphlet, 1940, 1, CRO, JN 711.

56. Harwood, *Space, Hope, and Brutalism*, 373.

57. Donald Gibson, "The Rebuilding of Coventry," *Country Life*, December 14, 1940, 525, CRO, JN11B.

58. Tiratsoo, *Reconstruction, Affluence, and Labour Politics*, 10.

59. For a detailed account of the aspirations and limits of postwar urban reconstruction, see Catherine Flinn, *Rebuilding Britain's Blitzed Cities: Hopeful Dreams, Stark Realities* (London: Bloomsbury Academic, 2018). See also Hasegawa, *Replanning the Blitzed City Centre*; Ravetz, *The Government of Space*, ch. 4; Meller, *Towns, Plans, and Society*, ch. 5.

60. Tiratsoo, *Reconstruction, Affluence, and Labour Politics*, 13; Donald Gibson, handwritten notes, letter B, February 1972, 8, CRO, PA623.

61. Richardson and Harris, *Twentieth-Century Coventry*, 294.

62. Donald Gibson, "Coventry Rebuilds," *Architectural Design*, December 1958, 477.

63. D. Rigby Childs, "Coventry: A Survey," *Architects' Journal*, October 8, 1953, CRO, JN11.

64. "New Era for Architecture in Coventry," *Coventry Evening Telegraph*, April 30, 1953.

65. Catherine Flinn, "'The City of Our Dreams'?: The Political and Economic Realities of Rebuilding Britain's Blitzed Cities, 1945–54," *Twentieth Century British History* 23, no. 2 (June 2012): 221–45.

66. For a full list of all sixty-two declaratory orders, see Parliamentary Papers, "Town and Country Planning, 1943–1951: Progress Report by the Minister of Local Government and Planning of the Work of the Ministry of Town and Country Planning," 1951, Cmd. 8204, 181.

67. J. Paton, *A Plan for Plymouth: Report Prepared for the City Council* (Plymouth: Underhill, 1943), 67–70; Jeremy Gould, *Plymouth: Vision of a Modern City* (Swindon: English Heritage, 2010), 33–36.

68. Flinn, *Rebuilding Britain's Blitzed Cities*, esp. chs. 1 and 4.

69. Hasegawa, *Replanning the Blitzed City Centre*, 68, 52.

70. Parliamentary Papers, "Final Report of the New Towns Committee," 1946, Cmd. 6876, 32.

71. Selina Todd has argued that postwar urban reconstruction prioritized new kinds of working-class democratic assembly. Selina Todd, "Phoenix Rising: Working-Class Life and Urban Reconstruction, c. 1945–1967," *Journal of British Studies* 54, no. 3 (July 2015): 679–702.

72. Linely H. Bateman, ed., *History of Harlow* (Harlow: Harlow Development Corporation, 1969), 136; Otto Saumarez Smith, *Boom Cities: Architect Planners and the Politics of Radical Urban Renewal in 1960s Britain* (Oxford: Oxford University Press, 2019), 21.

73. Washington Development Corporation, *Washington New Town Master Plan and Report* (Washington, Tyne and Wear: Washington Development Corporation, 1966), 87–89.

74. Cumbernauld's precinct is eloquently described in Owen Hatherley, *A New Kind of Bleak: Journeys through Urban Britain* (New York: Verso, 2012), 285–311.

75. For urban renewal in 1960s' Britain, see Saumarez Smith, *Boom Cities*; Simon Gunn, "The Rise and Fall of British Urban Modernism: Planning Bradford, 1945–1970," *Journal of British Studies* 49, no. 4 (October 2010): 849–69; Peter Mandler, "New Towns for Old: The Fate of the Old Town Centre," in *Moments of Modernity: Reconstructing Britain, 1945–1964*, ed. Becky Conekin, Frank Mort, and Chris Waters (London: Rivers Oram, 1999); Alistair Kefford, "Disruption, Destruction, and the Creation of 'the Inner Cities': The Impact of Urban Renewal on Industry, 1945–1980," *Urban History* 44, no. 3 (August 2017): 492–515.

76. Mandler, "New Towns for Old," 220.

77. Russell Schiller, "Land Use Controls on U.K. Shopping Centres," in *Shopping Centre Development: Policies and Prospects*, ed. John A. Dawson and J. Dennis Lord (London: Croon Helm, 1985), 44; Peter Shapely, "Governance in the Post-War City: Historical Reflections on the Public-Private Partnerships in the UK," *International Journal of Urban and Regional Research* 37, no. 4 (July 2013): 1288–304.

78. Simon Gunn and Susan Townsend, *Automobility in Twentieth-Century Britain and Japan* (London: Bloomsbury Academic, 2019), esp. part 2.

79. Simon Gunn, "The Buchanan Report, Environment, and the Problem of Traffic in 1960s Britain," *Twentieth Century British History* 22, no. 4 (December 2011): 521–42.

80. Colin Buchanan, *Traffic in Towns* (London: Penguin, 1964), 65–76.

81. Gunn, "The Buchanan Report."

82. For a good summary of these ideas and their effect on new town planning, see Rosemary Wakeman, *Practicing Utopia: An Intellectual History of the New Town Movement* (Chicago: University of Chicago Press, 2016), ch. 4.

83. For the ways that planners tried (and eventually failed) to use shops to create discrete local communities in the decades after the war, see Greenhalgh, "Consuming Communities"; Greenhalgh, *Reconstructing Modernity*, ch. 3.

84. P. Ford and C. J. Thomas, *The Southampton Survey* (Southampton, UK: Southampton County Borough Council, 1953), 7.

85. Parliamentary Papers, "Final Report of the New Towns Committee," 33.

86. Ford and Thomas, *The Southampton Survey*, 7.

87. For self-service shopping in Britain, see Lawrence Black and Thomas Spain, "How Self-Service Happened: The Vision and Reality of Changing Market Practices in Britain," in *Imagining Britain's Economic Future: Trade, Commerce, and Global Markets*, ed. David Thackeray, David Thompson, and Andrew Toye (London: Palgrave, 2018); Gareth Shaw, Louise Curth, and Andrew Alexander, "Selling Self-Service and the Supermarket: The Americanisation of Food Retailing in Britain, 1945–60," *Journal of Business History* 26, no. 4 (October 2004): 568–82; Usherwood, "Mrs. Housewife and Her Grocer."

88. Shaw, Curth, and Alexander, "Selling Self-Service," 574.

89. Harold Hotelling, "Stability in Competition," *Economic Journal* 39, no. 153 (March 1929): 57.

90. William J. Reilly, *The Law of Retail Gravitation* (New York: W. J. Reilly, 1931).

91. Guy Ortolano, *Thatcher's Progress: From Social Democracy to Market Liberalism in a New Town* (Cambridge: Cambridge University Press, 2019), 53.

92. Washington Development Corporation, *Washington New Town Master Plan*, 90–94.

93. Working Party on Shopping Centres, "Technical Appendix," "Sources of Data: The Status of Shopping Centres: Methods of Estimating Demand for Shopping Floor Space," 17, National Archives (henceforth TNA), HLG 136/89.

94. Oliver Marriott, *The Property Boom* (London: H. Hamilton, 1967), 239.

95. "Working Party on Shopping Centres Interim Report," 8, TNA, HLG 136/89. For urban renewal under the Conservative governments of the early 1960s, see Otto Saumarez Smith, "Central Government and Town-Centre Redevelopment in Britain, 1959–1966," *Historical Journal* 58, no. 1 (March 2015): 217–44; Saumarez Smith, *Boom Cities*.

96. Robert Bacon, "The Cowley Shopping Centre: Distributive Trades EDC," 45, TNA, FG 2/319, 2 (emphasis added).

97. Mandler, "New Towns for Old."

98. National Economic Development Office, "Urban Models in Shopping Studies: A Report of the Models Working Party to the Shopping Capacity Sub-Committee of the Economic Development Committee for the Distributive Trade," 5, TNA, FG 4/232.

99. For the role of statistics in economic management in Britain, see Jim Tomlinson, "Managing the Economy, Managing the People: Britain, c. 1931–1970," *Economic History Review* 58, no. 3 (July 2005): 555–85; Jim Tomlinson, *Managing the Economy, Managing the People: Narratives of Economic Life from Beveridge to Brexit* (Oxford: Oxford University Press, 2017). For the early development of the statistics that would underpin projects of national economic development across the world, see Susan Pedersen, *The Guardians: The League of Nations and the Crisis of Empire* (Oxford: Oxford University Press, 2015), ch. 8; Quinn Slobodian, *The Globalists: The*

End of Empire and the Birth of Neoliberalism (Cambridge, MA: Harvard University Press, 2018), ch. 2; Adam Tooze, *Statistics and the German State: The Making of Modern Economic Knowledge* (Cambridge: Cambridge University Press, 2001).

100. For Greenhalgh, rising affluence along with more demanding and sophisticated consumers thwarted attempts by planners to use clusters of shops to forge neighborhood communities. Greenhalgh, "Consuming Communities."

101. Jonathan Raban, *Soft City* (London: Picador, 2008), 97.

102. The architect changed his name from Gruenbaum to Gruen shortly after moving to the United States. There are two biographies of Gruen: M. Jeffrey Hardwick, *Mall Maker: Victor Gruen, Architect of an American Dream* (Philadelphia: University of Pennsylvania Press, 2003); Alex Wall, *Victor Gruen: From Urban Shop to New City* (Barcelona: Actar, 2005). Gruen himself published a number of books including a posthumous autobiography: Victor Gruen, *Shopping Town: Designing the City in Suburban America*, trans. Anette Baldauf (Minneapolis: University of Minnesota Press, 2017).

103. Gruen, *Shopping Town*, ch. 2.

104. Hardwick, *Mall Maker*, 8–13, 20.

105. For the early twentieth-century emergence of these spaces in the United States, see William Leach, *Land of Desire: Merchants, Power, and the Rise of a New American Culture* (New York: Pantheon, 1993); Alan Trachtenberg, *The Incorporation of America: Culture and Society in the Gilded Age* (New York: Hill and Wang, 2007), 130–36. For their lavish interior designs, see Trentmann, *Empire of Things*, ch. 4.

106. Trachtenberg, *The Incorporation of America*, 131.

107. Hardwick, *Mall Maker*, 31.

108. Victor Gruenbaum and Elsie Krummeck, "Shopping Center," *Architectural Forum*, May 1943, 101.

109. Hardwick, *Mall Maker*, 72–78.

110. Victor Gruen, "The Future of Planned Shopping Centers," speech to Harvard University Graduate School of Business, April 17, 1957, Library of Congress, Victor Gruen Collection (henceforth LoCVGC), box 82.

111. Victor Gruen, "Renewing Cities for the Automobile Age," speech to the National Housing Center in Washington, DC, January 3, 1957, LoCVGC, box 82.

112. Clarence Stein and Catherine Bauer, *Store Buildings and Neighborhood Shopping Centers* (New York: Record and Guide, 1934).

113. On the designation of Radburn as a garden city for the motor age, see Clarence Stein, "Toward New Towns for America," *Town Planning Review* 20, no. 3 (October 1949): 203–82.

114. Lizabeth Cohen, "From Town Center to Shopping Center: The Reconfiguration of Community Marketplaces in Postwar America," *American Historical Review* 101, no 4 (October 1996), 1050–81.

115. Victor Gruen, "What Is a Shopping Center?," press release from Victor Gruen Associates advertising the Shopping Centers of Tomorrow exhibition of 1954, LoCVGC, OV 2.

116. Victor Gruen Associates, "Shopping Centers of Tomorrow: An Architectural Exhibit Circulated by the American Federation of Arts," promotional material, ca. 1954, LoCVGC, OV 1.

117. Victor Gruen, *Shopping Towns USA* (New York: Reinhold, 1960), 11, 140.

118. Victor Gruen, "What Is a Shopping Center?"

119. "Gruen's Shopping Centers of Tomorrow," *Southwest Builder and Contractor*, n.d., LoCVGC, OV 1.

120. See, for example, Walkowitz, *City of Dreadful Delight*, 46–52. Cohen has also shown how shopping malls contributed to the spatial segregation of female employment. Cohen, "From Town Center to Shopping Center."

121. Hardwick, *Mall Maker*, 129.

122. James J. Farrell, *One Nation under Goods: Malls and the Seduction of American Shopping* (Washington, DC: Smithsonian, 2003), 9.

123. Barry Maitland, *Shopping Malls: Planning and Design* (London: Construction Press, 1985), 13; "Third Annual Southdale Circus Presents Performances," *Hopkins Minnesota Suburban Press*, August 17, 1961, LoCVGC, OV 6.

124. Thomas W. Hanchett, "US Tax Policy and the Shopping Center Boom of the 1950s and 1960s," *American Historical Review* 101, no. 4 (October 1996): 1082–110.

125. See, for example, Thomas J. Sugrue, *The Origins of the Urban Crisis: Race and Inequality in Postwar Detroit* (Princeton, NJ: Princeton University Press, 1998); Kenneth T. Jackson, *Crabgrasss Frontier: The Suburbanization of the United States* (Oxford: Oxford University Press, 1987); Lizabeth Cohen, *A Consumers' Republic: The Politics of Mass Consumption in America* (New York: Knopf, 2003).

126. Gruen, *Shopping Town*, 214.

127. Quoted in Hardwick, *Mall Maker*, 216.

128. Marriott, *The Property Boom*, 232.

129. Matthew Hilton, *Prosperity for All: Consumer Activism in an Era of Globalisation* (Ithaca, NY: Cornell University Press); Matthew Hilton, *Consumerism in Twentieth-Century Britain*; John Benson, *The Rise of Consumer Society in Britain*; Jan L. Logeman, *Trams or Tail Fins?: Public and Private Prosperity in Postwar West Germany and the United States* (Chicago: University of Chicago Press, 2012); Frank Trentmann, *Empire of Things*; Lizabeth Cohen, *A Consumers' Republic*.

130. Hilton, *Prosperity for All*, 51–75.

Chapter 3: The Council Estate

1. For the global spread of high-density public housing schemes, see Florian Urban, *Tower and Slab: Histories of Global Mass Housing* (New York: Routledge, 2012); Anne Power, *Hovels to High Rise: State Housing in Europe since 1850* (New York: Routledge, 1993).

2. Miles Glendinning and Stefan Muthesius, *Tower Block: Modern Public Housing in England, Scotland, Wales, and Northern Ireland* (New Haven, CT: Yale University Press, 1994), ch. 31; E. W. Cooney, "High Flats in Local Authority Housing in England and Wales since 1945," in *Multi-Storey Living: The British Working-Class Experience*, ed. Anthony Sutcliffe (London: Croom Helm, 1974).

3. Ray Forrest, Alan Murie, and Peter Williams, *Home Ownership: Differentiation and Fragmentation* (London: Unwin Hyman, 1990), 22.

4. This figure of 1.6 million was an estimate prepared by the Department of Housing and Local Government: J. S. Gill to Mr. Instone, "Right to Buy: Sales of Flats," memo, April 25, 1988, National Archives (henceforth TNA), AT 131/19. The delegation of house building to hundreds

of local authorities, along with definitional problems, has meant that it is difficult to get an exact figure for the number of flats on comprehensively planned housing estates. For the information on the ratio of flats to houses within 1980 council housing stock, see Ray Forrest and Alan Murie, *Selling the Welfare State: The Privatisation of Public Housing* (London: Routledge, 1991), 121–22.

5. For council estates and working-class community formation, see Ben Jones, *The Working Class in Mid-Twentieth-Century England: Community, Identity, and Social Memory* (Manchester: Manchester University Press, 2012); James Greenhalgh, *Reconstructing Modernity: Space, Power, and Governance in Mid-Twentieth-Century British Cities* (Manchester: Manchester University Press, 2017). For council estates and the politics of housing policy, see Power, *Hovels to High Rise*; Alison Ravetz, *Council Housing and Culture: The History of a Social Experiment* (London: Routledge, 2001); John Burnett, *A Social History of Housing: 1815–1985* (London: Methuen, 1986). For council housing and gender, see Claire Langhamer, "The Meanings of Home in Post-war Britain," *Journal of Contemporary History* 40, no. 2 (April 2005): 341–62; Kevin Guyan, "Masculinities, Planning Knowledge, and Domestic Space in Britain, c. 1941–1961" (PhD diss., University College London, 2016). For council housing and consumerism, see Alistair Kefford, "Housing the Citizen-Consumer in Post-War Britain: The Parker Morris Report, Affluence, and the Even Briefer Life of Social Democracy," *Twentieth Century British History* 29, no. 2 (June 2018): 255–58; Matthew Hollow, "The Age of Affluence Revisited: Council Estates and Consumer Society in Britain, 1950–1970," *Journal of Consumer Culture* 16, no. 1 (2016): 279–96. For the architecture of council estates, see Elain Harwood, *Space, Hope, and Brutalism: English Architecture, 1945–1975* (New Haven, CT: Yale University Press, 2015), ch 2; Glendinning and Muthesius, *Tower Block*. For works on council housing written outside the academy, see Lynsey Hanley, *Estates: An Intimate History* (London: Granta, 2007); Owen Hatherley, *A Guide to the New Ruins of Great Britain* (London: Verso, 2011); Anna Minton, *Big Capital: Who Is London For?* (London: Penguin, 2017), esp. chs. 4–5; John Boughton: *Municipal Dreams: The Rise and Fall of Council Housing* (London: Verso, 2018); John Grindrod, *Concretopia: A Journey around the Rebuilding of Postwar Britain* (Brecon, Wales: Old Street, 2014).

6. Friedrich Engels, *Conditions of the Working Class in England* (Oxford: Oxford University Press, 2009), 61–63.

7. Engels, *Conditions of the Working Class*, 77, 85.

8. For selected readings on the origins of Britain's state housing project, see Ravetz, *Council Housing and Culture*; Power, *Hovels to High Rise*; Mark Swenarton, *Homes Fit for Heroes: The Politics and Architecture of Early State Housing in Britain* (London: Routledge, 2018); Burnett, *A Social History of Housing*; Peter Malpass, *Housing and the Welfare State: The Development of Housing Policy in Britain* (Basingstoke, UK: Palgrave Macmillan, 2005); Anne Power, *Property before People: The Management of Council Housing* (London: Allen and Unwin, 1987), part 1. For selected readings on liberal reform and the nineteenth-century city, see Helen Meller, *Towns, Plans, and Society in Modern Britain* (Cambridge: Cambridge University Press, 1997), chs. 2–3; Chris Otter, *Victorian Eye: A Political History of Light and Vision in Britain* (Chicago: University of Chicago Press, 2008); Patrick Joyce, *The Rule of Freedom: Liberalism and the Modern City* (London: Verso, 2003).

9. James B. Russell, "Life in One Room: Some Serious Considerations for the Citizens of Glasgow," lecture, 1888, 3, Glasgow City Archives, D/HE/1/5/4/14; Helen Clark and Elizabeth

Carnegie, *She Was Aye Workin': Memories of Tenement Women* (Glasgow: City of Glasgow Press, 2003), 18.

10. Russell, "Life in One Room," 13, 6, 9 (emphasis added).

11. For the politics of these philanthropic interventions, see Seth Koven, *Slumming: Sexual and Social Politics in Late Victorian London* (Princeton, NJ: Princeton University Press, 2004). For the housing conditions of the London poor in the late nineteenth century, see Gareth Stedman Jones, *Outcast London: A Study in the Relationship between Classes in Victorian London* (London: Verso, 2013).

12. J. E. Connor and B. J. Critchley, *The Red Cliffs of Stepney: The Buildings of the East End Dwellings Co., the 4% Industrial Dwellings Co., and Associated Groups* (Colchester, UK: Connor and Butler, 1987), 23.

13. Minutes of the East End Dwelling Company, May 26, 1884, 13, Tower Hamlets Local History Library and Archive, B/CAP/A/1/1.

14. Quoted in Beatrice Potter Webb, *My Apprenticeship* (London: Longmans, 1929), 261–62.

15. Webb, *My Apprenticeship*, 262–63.

16. These details come from Jerry White, *Rothschild Buildings: Life in an East End Tenement Block* (London: Pimlico, 2003), 34–56.

17. Ravetz, *Council Housing and Culture*, 37–39. For the politics of the early LCC, see John Davis, "London Government, 1850–1920: The Metropolitan Board of Works and the London County Council," *London Journal* 26, no 1 (May 2001): 47–56.

18. One exception was artist and socialist William Morris, who in 1884 called for London to be filled with tall flats resembling "vertical streets" with communal living spaces. E. P. Thompson, *William Morris: From Romantic to Revolutionary* (New York: Pantheon Books, 1977), 685.

19. Swenarton, *Homes Fit for Heroes*; Andrew Saint, "Spread the People: The LCC's Dispersal Policy, 1889–1956," in *The Politics and the People of London: 1889–1965*, ed. Andrew Saint (London: Hambledon Press, 1989); David Rooney, "Visualization, Decentralization, and Metropolitan Improvements: 'Light-and-Air' and London County Council Photographs," *Urban History* 40, no. 3 (August 2013): 462–82.

20. Ebenezer Howard, *Garden Cities of To-Morrow* (Cambridge, MA: MIT Press, 1965).

21. Raymond Unwin, "Cottage Plans and Common Sense," *Fabian Society*, tract 109, 1902; Barry Parker and Raymond Unwin, *The Art of Building a Home: Collection of Lectures and Illustrations* (London: Longmans and Co., 1901). For the housing of early garden cities, see Mervyn Miller, *Letchworth: The First Garden City* (Chichester, UK: Phillimore, 1989); Tony Rook, *Welwyn Garden City through Time* (Stroud, UK: Amberley, 2013).

22. David Butler and Gareth Butler, *British Political Facts* (Basingstoke, UK: Palgrave Macmillan, 2011), 377.

23. Alison Ravetz, "From Working-Class Tenement to Modern Flat: Local Authorities and Multi-Storey Housing between the Wars," in *Multi-Storey Living: The British Working-Class Experience*, ed. Anthony Sutcliffe (London: Croom Helm, 1974), 122.

24. Judy Giles, *The Parlour and the Suburb: Domestic Identities, Class, Femininity, and Modernity* (Oxford: Berg, 2004); Deborah Sugg Ryan, *Ideal Homes, 1918–1939: Domestic Design and Suburban Modernism* (Manchester: Manchester University Press, 2018); David Jeremiah, *Architecture and Design for the Family in Britain, 1900–70* (Manchester: Manchester University Press, 2000), chs. 1–3.

25. Local Government Board, Committee Report, *Provision of Dwellings for the Working Classes in England and Wales and Scotland (Tudor Walters Report)* (London: HMSO, 1918); Jeremiah, *Architecture and Design for the Family*, 41–45.

26. Sheffield Housing Deputation, *Multi-Storey Housing in Some European Countries: Report of the City of Sheffield Housing Deputation* (Sheffield: Housing Deputation, 1955), 36.

27. Robert J. Gordon, *The Rise and Fall of American Growth: The U.S. Standard of Living since the Civil War* (Princeton, NJ: Princeton University Press, 2016).

28. Ravetz, "From Working-Class Tenement to Modern Flat," 132–33; Hanley, *Estates*, 85. For the emergence of an international network of expertise concerning urban development, see Daniel T. Rodgers, *Atlantic Crossings: Social Politics in a Progressive Age* (Cambridge, MA: Harvard University Press, 1998); Christopher Klemek, *The Transatlantic Collapse of Urban Renewal: Postwar Urbanism from New York to Berlin* (Chicago: University of Chicago Press, 2011).

29. Ravetz, *Council Housing and Culture*, esp. ch. 7; Meller, *Towns, Plans, and Society*, ch. 5; Hanley, *Estates*, chs 2–3; Boughton, *Municipal Dreams*, chs 4–5; Glendinning and Muthesius, *Tower Block*.

30. For construction methods, see Glendinning and Muthesius, *Tower Block*, chs. 7–8 and 10. For critiques of these building methods, see Peter Scott, "Friends in High Places: Government-Industry Relations in Public Sector House-Building during Britain's Tower Block Era," *Business History* (April 2018): 1–21; Patrick Dunleavy, *The Politics of Mass Housing in Britain, 1945–75: A Study of Corporate Power and Professional Influence in the Welfare State* (Oxford: Clarendon, 1981).

31. Hatherley, *The New Ruins of Great Britain*; John R. Gold, *The Practice of Modernism: Modern Architects and Urban Transformations, 1954–1972* (London: Taylor and Francis, 2007).

32. Andrew Saint, *Park Hill: What's Next?* (London: Architectural Association, 1996), 9.

33. Matthew Hollow, "Governmentality on the Park Hill Estate: The Rationality of Public Housing," *Urban History* 37, no. 1 (May 2010): 117–35.

34. City of Sheffield Housing Committee, "Park Hill Redevelopment," February 1961, Sheffield Local Studies Library (henceforth SLS), 331–833 SF.

35. Central Housing Advisory Committee, *Design of Dwellings: Report of the Design of Dwellings Sub-Committee* (London: HMSO, 1944), 21.

36. "Park-Hill Sheffield," SLS, MP1738 S; Hollow, "Governmentality on the Park Hill Estate," 128.

37. Just 5 percent of households had central heating during this period. James Obelkevich, "Consumption," in *Understanding Post-War British Society*, ed. Peter Catterall and James Obelkevich (London: Routledge, 1994), 145.

38. Department of Scientific and Industrial Research, Heating and Ventilation (Reconstruction) Committee, District Heating Subcommittee, draft report, 129, TNA, DSIR 4/1916.

39. Sheffield Housing Deputation, "Multi-Storey Housing," 36.

40. Christine L. Corton, *London Fog: The Biography* (Cambridge, MA: Harvard University Press, 2015), esp. ch. 8 and conclusion.

41. Obelkevich, "Consumption," 145.

42. Glendinning and Muthesius, *Tower Block*, 18–19. For the potential for new domestic technologies to transform women's labor, see Suzette Worden, "Powerful Women: Electricity in the Home, 1919–1940," in *A View from the Interior: Feminism, Women, and Design*, ed. Judy Attfield and Pat Kirkham (London: Women's Press, 1989); Sugg Ryan, *Ideal Homes*; Giles, *The*

Parlour and the Suburb; Kefford, "Housing the Citizen Consumer in Post-War Britain"; Matthew Hollow, "The Age of Affluence Revisited: Council Estates and Consumer Society in Britain, 1950–1970," *Journal of Consumer Culture* 16, no. 1 (March 2016): 279–96.

43. Glendinning and Muthesius, *Tower Block*, 16.

44. Kefford, "Housing the Citizen Consumer in Post-War Britain," 235–36.

45. The Solid Fuel Advisory Council, T. R. Fawkes, sales district manager, sample letter, TNA, COAL 78/2661; Women's Solid Fuel Council, "1983/4 Annual Report," 11, TNA, COAL 78/2661.

46. Stephen Kotkin, *Magnetic Mountain: Stalinism as a Civilization* (Berkeley: University of California Press, 1995); Stephen J. Collier, *Post-Soviet Social: Neoliberalism, Social Modernity, Biopolitics* (Princeton, NJ: Princeton University Press, 2011).

47. National District Heating Association, *District Heating in the Union of Soviet Socialist Republics with Briefs on Other European Countries* (Pittsburgh: National District Heating Association, 1967).

48. Charlotte Johnson, "District Heating as Heterotopia: Tracing the Social Contract through Energy Infrastructure in Pimlico, London," *Economic Anthropology* 3, no. 1 (January 2016): 94–105.

49. The results can be found in TNA, DSIR 4/1914.

50. Building Research Station, "Introductory Note on Translations: District Heating in Russia," library communication no. 150/1, July 1943, TNA, DSIR 4/1914.

51. District Heating Subcommittee, "Draft Report," 14–15.

52. Parliamentary Papers, "Final Report of the New Towns Committee," July 1946, Cmd. 6876, 24.

53. G. Gourdeau, *The Problem of District Heating* (London: n.p., 1949).

54. *District Heating for the New Britain* (National Coal Board, 1970), 27, 26.

55. Gourdeau, *The Problem of District Heating*.

56. Gourdeau, *The Problem of District Heating*.

57. "Children's Library at Pimlico," *Architecture and Building News*, October 12, 1960, City of Westminster Archive Centre (henceforth CWA), WCC C137, Churchill Gardens.

58. F. Turpin, *District Heating: A Brief Introduction to Planning Requirements* (London: Haywood Books, 1966), 145.

59. "Shivering Tenants Are Told 'The Heating Season Is Over,'" *West London Press*, June 3, 1960, CWA, WCC C138, Churchill Gardens.

60. Department of the Environment, "Right to Buy: District Heating," memo, April 23, 1982, TNA, AT 88/165.

61. These details come from Valerie G. Wigfall, *Thamesmead* (Stroud, UK: History Press, 2008), ch. 6; "Thamesmead Gets the GLC's First Community Officer," press release, June 21, 1968, London Metropolitan Archives (henceforth LMA), GLC/DG/PRB/35/004/364.

62. Quoted in Wigfall, *Thamesmead*, 72, 67.

63. "Thamesmead, 1973–74," annual report, Greenwich Heritage Centre (henceforth GHC), Thamesmead Annual Reports.

64. Steve St. Clare and Angela Dines, "Thamesmead Social Survey," Greater London Council Research memorandum, 1975, LMA, GLC/DG/PUB/01/083/0730.

65. Wigfall, *Thamesmead*, 68–69.

66. Pearson Phillips, "Living in Debt in Dreamland," *Observer*, November 9, 1975, GHC, Thamesmead Town Planning.

67. Nikolas Rose, *The Powers of Freedom: Reframing Political Thought* (Cambridge: Cambridge University Press, 1999), 168.

68. Radhika Natarajan, "Organizing Community: Commonwealth Citizens and Social Activism in Britain, 1948–1982" (PhD diss., University of California at Berkeley, 2013); Sam Wetherell, "Painting the Crisis: Community Arts and the Search for the 'Ordinary' in 1970s and '80s London," *History Workshop Journal 76*, no. 1 (October 2013): 235–49.

69. This is to take just a fraction of what is a vast historical literature. For examples of work on these three themes, see Karuna Mantena, *Alibis of Empire: Henry Maine and the Ends of Liberal Imperialism* (Princeton, NJ: Princeton University Press, 2010); Lise Butler, "Michael Young, the Institute of Community Studies, and the Politics of Kinship," *Twentieth Century British History 26*, no. 2 (February 2015): 203–24; Daniel Immerwahr, *Thinking Small: The United States and the Lure of Community Development* (Cambridge, MA: Harvard University Press, 2015).

70. For a spatial history of community formation in Britain, see Guy Ortolano, *Thatcher's Progress: From Social Democracy to Market Liberalism through an English New Town* (Cambridge: Cambridge University Press, 2019), ch. 4; Greenhalgh, *Reconstructing Modernity*, esp. chs. 3–4; Jones, *The Working Class in Mid-Twentieth-Century England*, esp. chs. 3–4. For an overview of the ways that community as been conceived of and politicized, see Jon Lawrence, *Me, Me, Me: Individualism and the Search for Community in Postwar Britain* (Oxford: Oxford University Press, 2019).

71. Howard, *Garden Cities of To-Morrow*.

72. Unwin, "Cottages and Common Sense," 15.

73. Clarence Perry, *The Neighborhood Unit* (London: Routledge, 2001).

74. For the global spread of the neighborhood unit, see Rosemary Wakeman, *Practicing Utopia: An Intellectual History of the New Town Movement* (Chicago: University of Chicago Press, 2016), chs. 1–2. For its application in Britain, see Greenhalgh, *Reconstructing Modernity*, ch. 3; Ortolano, *Thatcher's Progress*, 148–50. For the way that community formation in new towns was influenced by comparable experiments in Britain's empire, see Jesse Meredith, "Decolonising the New Town: Roy Gazzard and the Making of Killingworth Township," *Journal of British Studies 57*, no. 2 (April 2018): 333–62.

75. For a contemporary overview of the role of voluntary organizations in community formation on interwar estates, see Elizabeth Macadam, *The New Philanthropy: A Study of Relations between the Statutory and Voluntary Social Services* (London: Allen and Unwin, 1934), 158–61.

76. New Estates Community Committee, *New Housing Estates and Their Social Problems* (National Council of Social Service, 1935), 3.

77. Ravetz, *Council Housing and Culture*, 137.

78. Ministry of Education, *Community Centres* (London: HMSO, 1944), 5.

79. Parliamentary Papers, "Capital Investment in 1948," December 1947, Cmd. 7268, 15.

80. This was the argument, for example, of Michael Young and Peter Wilmott's best-selling sociological study of Bethnal Green published in 1957. Michael Young and Peter Willmott, *Family and Kinship in East London* (London: Penguin Modern Classics, 2007). For waning faith in the neighborhood unit in Britain, particularly in the context of new town planning, see Ortolano, *Thatcher's Progress* 150–53.

81. For example, Kenny Cupers has shown how urban planners in Britain, the United States, and France continued to be influenced by the idea of habitat in the 1950s and 1960s. "Habitat" was a notion drawn from ecology referring to the idea that "reshaping dwelling space would also reshape the very people in it." Kenny Cupers, "Human Territoriality and the Downfall of Public Housing," *Public Culture* 29, no. 1 (January 2017): 165–80.

82. Gold, *The Practice of Modernism*, 204–7; Glendinning and Muthesius, *Tower Block*, part B.

83. Quoted in Glendenning and Methusius, *Tower Block*, 121.

84. Central Housing Advisory Committee, *The Needs of New Communities: A Report on Social Provision in New and Expanding Communities* (London: Central Housing Advisory Committee, 1967), 3.

85. National Council of Social Service, *Creative Living: The Work and Purposes of a Community Association* (London: National Council of Social Service, 1964), 9, 30.

86. National Association of Women's Clubs and the National Council of Social Service, *Planning a Women's Club—or Section—Programme* (London: National Council of Social Service, 1954), 3–6.

87. Selected works on exclusive practices along the lines of race within Britain's welfare state include Kennetta Hammond Perry, *London Is the Place for Me: Black Britons, Citizenship, and the Politics of Race* (Oxford: Oxford University Press, 2015); Beverley Bryan, Stella Dadzie, and Sanne Scafe, *The Heart of the Race: Black Women's Lives in Britain* (London: Virago, 1985); Jordanna Bailkin, *Afterlife of Empire* (Berkeley: University of California Press, 2012); Rob Waters, *Thinking Black: Britain, 1964–1985* (Berkeley: University of California Press, 2018); Kathleen Paul, *Whitewashing Britain: Race and Citizenship in the Postwar Era* (Ithaca, NY: Cornell University Press, 1997). For ways that black Britons experienced urban space, see Kieran Connell, *Black Handsworth: Race in 1980s Britain* (Berkeley: University of California Press, 2019); Marc Matera, *Black London: The Imperial Metropolis and Decolonization in the Twentieth Century* (Berkeley: University of California Press, 2015); Paul Gilroy, "Police and Thieves," in *The Empire Strikes Back: Race and Racism in 70s Britain*, ed. Centre for Contemporary Cultural Studies (London: Routledge, 1992).

88. Elizabeth Mary Burney, *Housing on Trial: A Study of Immigrants and Local Government* (Oxford: Oxford University Press, 1967), 3; John Davis, "Rents and Race in 1960s London: New Light on Rachmanism," *Twentieth Century British History* 12, no. 1 (January 2001): 69–92.

89. Perry, *London Is the Place for Me*, ch. 3; Camilla Schofield and Ben Jones, "'Whatever Community Is, This Is Not It': Notting Hill and the Reconstruction of 'Race' in Britain after 1958," *Journal of British Studies* 58, no. 1 (January 2019): 142–73. One exception is the new town of Killingworth, whose architect and planner, Roy Gazzard, drew on his expertise as an urban planner in colonial Uganda to, in his words, "socially engineer" a mixed community. Cited in Meredith, "Decolonizing the New Town."

90. Ruth Glass, *Newcomers: The West Indians in London* (London: Centre for Urban Studies, 1960).

91. Schofield and Jones, "Whatever Community Is, This Is Not It," 143.

92. Burney, *Housing on Trial*, 74.

93. Burney, *Housing on Trial*, 3.

94. Perry, *London Is the Place for Me*, 83–86.

95. Burney, *Housing on Trial*, 58–59. For further evidence of housing discrimination on the grounds of race in London's local government in the 1960s and 1970s, see London Housing

Research Group, Working Party on Race and Housing, *Race and Local Authority Housing: A Report of the London Housing Research Group* (London: Community Relations Commission, 1977); Commission for Racial Equality, *Race and Council Housing in Hackney: Report of a Formal Investigation* (London: Commission for Racial Equality, 1984). For discrimination in Birmingham, see John Rex and Robert Moore, *Race, Community, and Conflict: A Study of Sparkbrook* (Oxford: Oxford University Press, 1967). For Nottingham, see Alan Simpson, *Stacking the Decks: A Study of Race, Inequality, and Council Housing in Nottingham* (Nottingham: Nottingham and District Community Relations Council, 1981). For discrimination across Britain, see Nicholas Deakin, "Housing and Ethnic Minorities—an Overview," *Journal of Ethnic and Migration Studies* 6, no. 1–2 (December 1977): 4–7.

96. Burney, *Housing on Trial*, 73.

97. Commission for Racial Equality, *Race and Council Housing in Hackney*, 36.

98. Commission for Racial Equality, *Living in Terror: A Report on Racial Violence and Harassment in Housing* (London: Commission for Racial Equality, 1987), 9, 21. See also Bethnal Green and Stepney Trades Council, *Blood on the Streets: A Report by Bethnal Green and Stepney Trades Council on Racial Attacks in East London* (London: Bethnal Green and Stepney Trades Council, 1978).

99. Power, *Property before People*, ch. 5

100. In 1985, sociologist Sidney Jacobs referred to council housing as the "British road to apartheid." Sidney Jacobs, "Race, Empire, and the Welfare State: Council Housing and Racism," *Critical Social Policy* 5, no. 13 (June 1985): 6–28.

101. London Housing Research Group, *Race and Local Authority Housing*; J. J. Gribbin, "The Implications of the 1976 Race Relations Act for Housing," *Journal of Ethnic and Migration Studies* 6, no. 1–2 (June 1977): 99–104.

102. *Thamesmead, 1970* (British Film Institute, 1970), 25 min., accessed April 4, 2019, http://player.bfi.or.uk/film/watch-thamesmead-1970-1970/; *Living at Thamesmead* (British Film Institute, 1974), 25 min., accessed April 4, 2019, http://www.bfi.org.uk/films-tv-people/4ce2b6d2d506c. For an excellent analysis of this short film, see Owen Hatherley, *Militant Modernism* (Winchester, UK: O Books, 2008), 38–39.

103. Phillips, "Living in Debt in Dreamland."

104. "Thamesmead: A Riverside Development," 1967, 6, GHC, Thamesmead Town Planning, 6.

105. "Thamesmead, 1973–74," annual report; *Living at Thamesmead*.

106. Wigfall, *Thamesmead*, 73, 75.

107. Photographs, "Thamesmead Community Centre: Clubroom Activities," LMA, SC/PHL/02/0179–124.

108. Peggy Grey, *Radio Thamesmead: Survey of a Community Radio Station* (London: Volunteer Centre, 1988), 4.

109. Report, "Thamesmead: Housing a Balanced Community," 1974, LMA, GLC/DG/PUB/01/070/0616.

110. A 1970 survey of Thamesmead's first 440 residents showed that more than a quarter (125) came from Southwark, while significant numbers came from Newham (88), Tower Hamlets (30), and Lambeth (25). GLC Strategy Branch, "Survey of Ingoing Tenants: Preliminary Tabulations," January 1970, LMA, GLC/DG/PUB/01/209/U0567.

111. Quoted in Wigfall, *Thamesmead*, 61.

112. Information Sheet, "Some Facts about Thamesmead," GHC, Thamesmead Town Planning.

113. Leslie Donnelly, "Thamesmead Community Profile," 1986, 27, 34, 40, GHC, Thamesmead Town Planning.

114. Peter Chadwick and Ben Weaver, *The Town of Tomorrow: 50 Years of Thamesmead* (London: Here Press, 2019), 162.

115. The need to stimulate public participation in urban planning was the headline recommendation of a high-profile 1969 report authored by the Labour member of Parliament Arthur Skeffington. Committee on Public Participation in Planning, *People and Planning (the Skeffington Report)* (London: HMSO, 1969).

116. Schofield and Jones, "Whatever Community Is, This Is Not It."

117. For the ways that race challenged the limits of the universalist claims of welfare, see Natarajan, "Organizing Community"; Schofield and Jones, "Whatever Community Is, This Is Not It." For "community" as a spontaneous and pluralist site that was mobilized against the grain of state power, see Wetherell, "Painting the Crisis"; David Ellis, "Pavement Politics: Community Action in Leeds, c. 1960–1990" (PhD diss., University of York, 2015). For noncommunitarian challenges to claims about the homogeneity of the social body, see Emily Robinson, Camilla Schofield, Florence Sutcliffe-Braithwaite, and Natalie Thomlinson, "Telling Stories about Post-War Britain: Popular Individualism and the 'Crisis' of the 1970s," *Twentieth Century British History* 28, no. 2 (June 2017): 268–304.

118. Wigfall, *Thamesmead*, 59.

119. Tony Aldous, "London's New Town," GHC, Thamesmead Town Planning. 30, 31.

120. Melvin Webber, "Order in Diversity: Community without Propinquity," in *Cities and Space: The Future Use of Urban Land*, ed. Lowdon Wingo (Baltimore: Johns Hopkins University Press, 1963).

Chapter 4: The Private Housing Estate

1. David Butler and Gareth Butler, *British Political Facts*, 10th ed. (Basingstoke, UK: Palgrave Macmillan, 2011), 377.

2. Ray Forrest, Alan Murie, and Peter Williams, *Home Ownership: Differentiation and Fragmentation* (London: Unwin Hyman, 1990), 22.

3. Department for Communities and Local Government, *English Housing Survey: Social Rented Sector, 2016–17* (London: Department for Communities and Local Government, 2018), 3.

4. Ray Forrest and Alan Murie, *Selling the Welfare State: The Privatisation of Public Housing* (London: Routledge, 1988), 110.

5. Miles Glendinning and Stefan Muthesius, *Tower Block: Modern Public Housing in England, Scotland, Wales, and Northern Ireland* (New Haven, CT: Yale University Press, 1994), 313.

6. This figure was an estimate prepared by the Department of Housing and Local Government. J. S. Gill to Mr. Instone, "Right to Buy: Sales of Flats," memo, April 25, 1988, National Archives (henceforth TNA), AT 131/19. The delegation of house building to hundreds of local authorities, along with definitional problems, has meant it is difficult to get an exact figure for the number of flats on comprehensively planned housing estates.

7. Aled Davies, "'Right to Buy': The Development of a Conservative Housing Policy, 1945–1980," *Contemporary British History* 27, no. 4 (December 2013): 421–44; Matthew Francis, "'A Crusade to Enfranchise the Many': Thatcherism and the 'Property-Owning Democracy,'" *Twentieth Century British History* 23, no. 2 (June 2012): 275–97.

8. Jim Tomlinson, *Managing the Economy, Managing the People: Narratives of Economic Life in Britain from Beveridge to Brexit* (Oxford: Oxford University Press), 76.

9. *Hansard Parliamentary Debates*, Commons, Deb., May 24, 1979, series 5, vol. 967, c1223.

10. For Wandsworth's right-wing local government during this period, see Simon James, "The Cradle of Privatisation: Wandsworth Borough Council, 198–87," *Britain and the World* 4, no. 2 (2011): 294–302.

11. Cited in Adam Smith Institute, ed., *Altered Estates* (London: Adam Smith Institute, 1988), 26.

12. Miss J. Crowley to Wandsworth House Sales Coordinator, "Re: 5000th Sale in Wandsworth," memo, May 4, 1984, TNA, AT 88/184.

13. Councilor P. Bingle to Mr. W. Spendlove, memo, November 25, 1983, TNA, HLG 118/4253.

14. Miss J. Crowley to Wandsworth House Sales Coordinator, "Re: 5000th Sale in Wandsworth." For the total number of dwellings on the Ethelburga Estate, see Patrick Baty, "Ethelburga Estate, Battersea," accessed March 29, 2019, http://patrickbaty.co.uk/2013/09/19/ethelburga-estate/

15. "Right to Buy: District Heating," memo, April 23, 1982, TNA, AT 88/165.

16. "Right to Buy: District Heating: Favourable to Disconnection," memo, April 8, 1982, TNA, AT 88/165.

17. "Agreement Made between London Borough of Wandsworth and the Consumer," sample lease agreement, TNA, AT 88/165.

18. Charlotte Johnson, "District Heating as Heterotopia: Tracing the Social Contract through Energy Infrastructure in Pimlico, London," *Economic Anthropology* 3, no. 1 (January 2016): 94–105.

19. "Service Charges," draft speech, May 1980, TNA, HLG 118/3542.

20. Willis Goodhart and Andrew Walker, "Joint Opinion," April 27, 1981, TNA, HLG 118/3542.

21. John O'Brien, "How to Calculate Service Charges," extract from report of a Housing Centre seminar, May 21, 1981, TNA, AT 131/19.

22. Beresford, cited in Adam Smith Institute, *Altered Estates*, 26.

23. Mrs. A. E. Nott to Mr. Lewis, letter, July 16, 1986, TNA, AT 131/19.

24. "Local Authority Tenants (Heating Charges)," April 20, 1982, TNA, AT 88/165.

25. Hugh Corner to Mr. Armstrong, "Housing Act 1980: Sale of Flats," letter, January 6, 1982, TNA, HLG 118/3705.

26. Lesley Creedon to Hugh Corner, "RTB: Building Society Mortgages," memo, June 9, 1982, TNA, HLG 118/3705.

27. J. N. Raynor to J. S. Gill, "Housing Act 1980: Right to Buy," letter, January 26, 1987, TNA, AT 88/165.

28. "Report on Flats as Mortgage Securities," draft report, January 1987, 1, 5, TNA, AT 131/19. Ortolano has uncovered a similar reluctance among mortgage lenders to give loans to those living in modernist houses in the new town of Milton Keynes. Guy Ortolano, *Thatcher's*

Progress: From Social Democracy to Market Liberalism through an English New Town (Cambridge: Cambridge University Press, 2019), 132–40.

29. Figure quoted in Richard Vinen, *Thatcher's Britain: The Politics and Social Upheaval of the Thatcher Era* (London: Simon and Schuster, 2009), 205.

30. S. Mullin to Mr. Gill, "Mortgages on High Rise Flats," memo, July 22, 1992, TNA, AT 131/18.

31. "Mortgage Lenders Black High Rise Flats," Thames Television report transcript, April 22, 1992, TNA, AT 131/18.

32. Mira Bar-Hillel, "How 'Right to Buy' Has Turned Sour," *Evening Standard*, December 2, 1992, TNA, AT 131/18.

33. Diane Boliver, "The Tower Block Tenants Who Are Forced to Live in Misery," *Guardian*, June 6, 1992, TNA, AT 131/18.

34. Mr. Gill to Mr. Instone, "Right to Buy: Sales of Flats."

35. "Right to Buy: Measures to Increase Sales of Flats," note of a meeting with Birmingham City Council, June 13, 1985, TNA, HLG 118/4408.

36. Alison Ravetz, *Council Housing and Culture: The History of a Social Experiment* (London: Routledge, 2001), 203.

37. James Meek, *Private Island: Why Britain Now Belongs to Someone Else* (London: Verso, 2014), 214–15. For more on housing associations, see Anna Minton, *Big Capital: Who Is London For?* (London: Penguin, 2017), ch. 4; John Boughton, *Municipal Dreams: The Rise and Fall of Council Housing* (London: Verso, 2018), chs. 7–8.

38. Jon Lawrence and Florence Sutcliffe-Braithwaite, "Margaret Thatcher and the Decline of Class Politics," in *Making Thatcher's Britain*, ed. Ben Jackson and Robert Saunders (Cambridge: Cambridge University Press, 2012), 143–47; Francis, "A Crusade to Enfranchise the Many"; Davies, "Right to Buy."

39. J. J. Gribbin, "The Implications of the 1976 Race Relations Act for Housing," *Journal of Ethnic and Migration Studies* 6, no. 1–2 (June 1977): 99–104.

40. For "residualization," see Ian Cole and Robert Furbey, *The Eclipse of Council Housing* (London: Routledge, 1994), 82–88; Anne Power, *Property before People: The Management of Twentieth Century Council Housing* (London: Allen and Unwin, 1987), ch. 5; Peter Malpass, *Reshaping Housing Policy: Subsidies, Rents, and Residualisation* (London: Routledge, 1990).

41. This has contributed to a racialization of the "inner city" in Britain in the late twentieth century, a process identified by contemporary sociologists. See, for example, Gareth Millington, *"Race," Culture, and the Right to the City: Centres, Peripheries, Margins* (Basingstoke, UK: Palgrave Macmillan, 2011); Gareth Millington, "The Outer-Inner City: Urbanization, Migration, and 'Race' in London and New York," *Urban Research and Practice* 5, no. 1 (March 2012): 6–25; Michael Keith, *After the Cosmopolitan?: Multicultural Cities and the Future of Racism* (London: Routledge, 2005).

42. Geoff Dench, Kate Gavron, and Michael Young, *The New East End: Kinship, Race, and Conflict* (London: Profile, 2006), 299 and esp. conclusion.

43. See, for example, Robert Moore, "'Careless Talk': A Critique of Dench, Gavron, and Young's *The New East End*," *Critical Social Policy* 28, no. 3 (August 2008): 349–60. See also Madeline Bunting, "Kin Outrage," *Guardian*, April 25, 2007.

44. Patrick Dunleavy, *The Politics of Mass Housing in Britain: A Study of Corporate Power and Professional Influence in the Welfare State* (Oxford: Clarendon, 1981). These critiques were also

being made by the architects of council estates, some of whom, such as Sydney Cook, turned toward building low-rise modernist estates in the 1970s. See Mark Swenarton, *Cook's Camden: The Making of Modern Housing* (London: Lund Humphries, 2017).

45. Sheffield Housing Department, "Park Hill Survey," 1962, 8, Sheffield Local Studies Library (henceforth SLS), 331.833 SQ; Margaret Willis, *Living in High Flats: An Investigation* (London: London County Council Architecture Department, 1955), 2.

46. A later survey of Park Hill residents found that 39 percent of housewives with children under the age of five were dissatisfied with living above the ground floor. Department of the Environment, *The Estate outside the Dwelling: Reactions of Residents to Aspects of Housing Layout* (London: HMSO, 1972).

47. Oscar Newman, *Defensible Space: People and Design in the Violent City* (London: Architectural Press, 1972), 1.

48. Jane Jacobs, *The Death and Life of Great American Cities* (New York: Vintage, 1961), ch. 2.

49. Michael Young and Peter Willmott, *Family and Kinship in East London* (London: Penguin Modern Classics, 2007).

50. Newman, *Defensible Space*, 2–3.

51. Newman, *Defensible Space*, 51.

52. Kenny Cupers, "Human Territoriality and the Downfall of Public Housing," *Public Culture* 29, vol. 1 (January 2017): 165–80.

53. David Garland sees the emergence of situational crime prevention as part of a broader authoritarian restructuring of police and penological practices in Britain and the United States in the 1970s and 1980s. Garland contends that these changes, which included things like tougher sentences, more intrusive methods of surveillance, and an intensification of political rhetoric around crime control, bought to an end a modernist and welfarist view of crime control that operated with a perfectable subject in mind. David Garland, *The Culture of Control: Crime and Social Order in Contemporary Society* (Chicago: University of Chicago Press, 2001), ch. 3. For a more detailed account of the institutional emergence of situational crime prevention and its adoption as police practice, see Ben Taylor, "Science and the British Police: Surveillance, Intelligence, and the Rise of the Professional Police Officer, 1930–2000" (PhD diss., King's College London, 2015), ch. 5.

54. See, for example, Home Office Research Unit, *Designing Out Crime* (London: HMSO, 1980).

55. C. Ray Jeffery, *Crime Prevention through Environmental Design* (Beverly Hills: Sage, 1971); Derek B. Cornish and Ron Clarke, eds., *The Reasoning Criminal: Rational Choice Perspectives on Offending* (New Brunswick, NJ: Transaction Publishers, 2014).

56. Gary S. Becker, "Crime and Punishment: An Economic Approach," *Journal of Political Economy* 76, no. 2 (March 1968): 169–217.

57. Michel Foucault, *The Birth of Biopolitics: Lectures at the Collège de France, 1978–79*, trans. Graham Burchell (Basingstoke, UK: Palgrave Macmillan, 2008), 199.

58. The classic account of the way that urban crime became racialized in Britain in the 1970s remains Stuart Hall, Chas Critcher, Tony Jefferson, John Clarke, and Brian Roberts, *Policing the Crisis: Mugging, the State, and Law and Order* (Basingstoke, UK: Palgrave Macmillan, 2013).

59. This is not to say that Newman wasn't influential in Britain before the mid-1980s. Anarchist urban planner Colin Ward had been an advocate for Newman's ideas through the 1970s. Researchers in the Home Office such as Sheena Wilson and Tony Marshall had also called for

architectural reform explicitly on the terms established by Newman in the late 1970s. Cupers, "Human Territoriality and the Downfall of Public Housing," 180–81.

60. Alice Coleman, *Utopia on Trial: Vision and Reality in Planned Housing*, 2nd ed. (London: Hilary Shipman, 1990), 6.

61. Coleman, *Utopia on Trial*, 17–18.

62. Coleman, *Utopia on Trial*, 157.

63. Coleman, *Utopia on Trial*, 168–69.

64. P. A. Bearpark to Alan Ring, memo, January 19, 1988, TNA, PREM 19/2240; P.J.C. Mawer to P. A. Bearpark, memo, January 28, 1988, TNA, PREM 19/2240.

65. King's College Design Improvement Team, "Ledbury Estate: Design Disadvantagement Report," 2–4, 7, 1989, n.p. Seen with the permission of Alice Coleman, October 2014.

66. King's College Design Improvement Team, "Ledbury Estate," 11.

67. Quoted in Adam Smith Institute, *Altered Estates*, 1.

68. "Ledbury Estate: Design Disadvantagement Report," 14, 17.

69. For a summary of the projects undertaken by DICE, see Department of the Environment, *The Design Improvement Controlled Experiment (DICE): An Evaluation of the Impact, Costs, and Benefits of Estate Re-Modeling* (London: Department of the Environment, 1997).

70. Sheffield Department of Design and Building Services, "Hyde Park Technical Appraisal," 25, 1987, Sheffield Archives and Local Studies (henceforth SLA), ACC 2010/36, box 1.

71. "Hyde Park: 1991 Student Games Village and Future Housing Scheme," SLA, ACC 2010/36, box 1.

72. Quoted in Andrew Saint, ed., *Park Hill: What Next?* (London: Architectural Association, 1996), 63.

73. Department of the Environment, *The Design Improvement Controlled Experiment*, 2.

74. Anna Minton, *Ground Control: Fear and Happiness in the Twenty-First-Century City* (London: Penguin, 2012), ch. 4.

75. Secured by Design, "New Homes 2014," accessed April 2, 2019, https://www.securedbydesign.com/images/downloads/New_Homes_2014.pdf.

76. Katrina Moss and Ken Pease, "Crime and Disorder Act 1998: Section 17. A Wolf in Sheep's Clothing?," *Crime Prevention and Community Safety: An International Journal* 1, no. 4 (October 1999): 14–19.

77. "MP Lays Foundation Stone for Cascades," newspaper cutting, May 21, 1987, Tower Hamlets Local History Library and Archives (henceforth THA), 331.1, folder 8.

78. Annabel Walker, "High Rise to Luxury," *Sunday Times*, November 2, 1986, THA, 331.1, folder 8.

79. Peter Malpass and Alan Murie, *Housing Policy and Practice* (Basingstoke, UK: Palgrave Macmillan, 1999), 98.

80. See, for example, Teresa Caldeira, *City of Walls: Crime Segregation and Citizenship in São Paulo* (Berkeley: University of California Press, 2001); Edward J. Blakely and Mary Gail Snyder, *Fortress America: Gated Communities in the United States* (Washington, DC: Brookings Institution Press, 1997); Mike Davis, *City of Quartz: Excavating the Future in Los Angeles* (London: Verso, 2006).

81. Dulwich Society, "Baroness Margaret Thatcher, 1926–2013," June 25, 2013, accessed April 2, 2019, http://www.dulwichsociety.com/2013-summer/861-baroness-margaret-thatche.

82. Rowland Atkinson, John Flint, and Diane Lister, *Gated Communities in England* (London: Office of the Deputy Prime Minister, 2003).

83. "London Docklands: New Homes Exhibition," promotional book, Museum of London Docklands Archive (henceforth MLDA), Docklands Forum, 44, set 2, box 5.

84. "A Total Concept," advertising brochure, THA, 331.1, LC 7838, box 2.

85. "London Docklands," 29.

86. Walker, "High Rise to Luxury"; Michael Baumgarten, "Docklands Development at New Concordia Wharf," *Architects' Journal*, July 4, 1984, 57.

87. "London Docklands," 8.

88. For detailed descriptions of heating systems, see "St Hilda's Wharf," advertising brochure, THA, 331.4, LP. 7819; "Eaton Terrace," advertising brochure, THA, 331.9, folder 9; "Gun Wharf," advertising brochure, THA, 331.1, folder 9.

89. Chris Ward, "2.5 Million!," *South London Press*, March 6, 1987, Southwark Local History Library and Archive (henceforth SLH), PC 711.312 BER.

90. Tim Dwelly, "A Fifty-Fifty Future," *ROOF*, May–June 1990, THA, 331.1, folder 8.

91. "Free Trade Wharf," advertising brochure, THA, 331.1, LP 8619. See also the detailed security arrangements described for Prospect Wharf. "Prospect Wharf," advertising brochure, MLDA, Docklands Forum, set 2, box 5.

92. See, for example, "London Borough of Wandsworth Housing Committee Minutes," November 16, 1978, 6.

93. "Hyde Park Village," 21, SLS, local pamphlets, 728.314 SSTQ.

94. Clive Norris and Gary Armstrong, *The Maximum Surveillance Society: The Rise of CCTV* (Oxford: Berg: 1999), ch. 2; Taylor, "Science and the British Police," ch. 5. The use of CCTV to monitor residualized council estates can be contrasted to the spread of neighborhood watch schemes during the same period. The ideal participant of these more activist schemes, as Chris Moores has shown, tended to be middle class. Chris Moores, "Thatcher's Troops?: Neighborhood Watch Schemes and the Search for 'Ordinary' Thatcherism in 1980s Britain," *Contemporary British History* 31, no. 2 (April 2017): 230–55.

95. Norris and Armstrong, *The Maximum Surveillance Society*, 43.

96. Advertising brochure, Horseshoe Court and Russia Court, MLDA, Docklands Forum, set 2, box 5.

97. Advertising brochure, "Prospect Wharf," MLDA, Docklands Forum, set 2, box 5.

98. Matthew Antrobus, "Homes of Their Own," *Architects' Journal*, October 18, 1989, THA, 331.1, folder 11.

99. Nigel Cox, *Running a Flat Management Company* (Bristol: Jordans, 1993), 1.

100. For a specimen of a constitution designed for residents, see Federation of Private Residents' Associations, "The Federation of Private Residents' Associations Information Pack" (London: Federation of Private Residents' Associations, 1993).

101. Federation of Private Residents' Association, *Newsletter*, Spring 1980.

102. Federation of Private Residents' Association, *Newsletter*, Spring 1991.

103. Federation of Private Residents' Association, *Newsletter*, Summer 1987.

104. Federation of Private Residents' Association, *Newsletter*, Autumn 1993.

105. For reasons of anonymity, the name of the housing complex has been changed, as have any individuals referred to in the printed materials. The materials were viewed with the permission of the association's chair in October 2014.

106. Parker Grange Residents' Association, "Minutes," February 12, 1985.

107. Parker Grange Residents' Association, "Minutes," December 9, 1983.

108. Parker Grange Residents' Association, "Minutes," April 25, 1987.

109. Parker Grange Resident's Association, "Memorandum: Maintenance Charges 1984."

110. Mr. Fairclough to Mr. Jones, Parker Grange Residents' Association file of correspondence, January 14, 1985.

111. Parker Grange Residents' Association, "Minutes," December 1, 1985.

112. Parker Grange Residents' Association, "Minutes," December 1, 1985.

113. Parker Grange Residents' Association, "Minutes," April 25, 1987.

114. These issues arise, respectively, in Parker Grange Residents' Association, "Minutes," April 30, 1988; Parker Grange Residents' Association, "Minutes," April 24, 1991; Parker Grange Residents' Association, "Minutes," April 30, 1988.

115. Parker Grange Residents' Association, "Minutes," April 18, 1990.

116. Details taken from the development's website, accessed April 2, 2019, http://www.embassygardens.com/. For a further description of Embassy Gardens, see Minton, *Big Capital*, 23–24.

117. Rob Davies, "Complex Chain of Companies That Worked on Grenfell Tower Raises Oversight Concerns," *Guardian*, June 16, 2017; Pete Apps, "Grenfell: The Paper Trail," *Inside Housing*, accessed April 2, 2019, https://social.shorthand.com/insidehousing/32LVIu5Itu/grenfell-the-paper-trail.

118. Robert Booth and Celia Wahlquist, "Grenfell Tower Residents 'Brushed Away' Fire Safety Concerns," *Guardian*, June 14, 2017.

119. Channel 4 News, "Musician Akala: People Died in London Fire Because They Were Poor," interview by Jon Snow, June 15, 2017, accessed April 2, 2019, https://www.channel4.com/news/akala-people-died-in-london-fire-because-they-were-poor.

120. Nadine El-Enany, "The Colonial Logic of Grenfell," *Verso* (blog), July 3, 2017, accessed April 2, 2019, https://www.versobooks.com/blogs/3306-the-colonial-logic-of-grenfell.

Chapter 5: The Shopping Mall

1. "Seismologists Called in to Advise on Merry Hill Tower at Dudley, West Midlands," *Construction News*, April 13, 1990.

2. "Romantic Paris Weekend Awaits Miss Merry Hill," *Merry Hill Express*, promotional newspaper, April 1987, Dudley Archives and Local History Service (henceforth DLA), R 83580.

3. "Security First at Merry Hill," *Merry Hill Magazine*, promotional newspaper, Spring 1997, DLA, R 87000.

4. "The World's Tallest Tower for Britain," *Times*, November 8, 1989.

5. See, for example, Margaret Crawford, "The World in a Shopping Mall," in *Variations on a Theme Park: The New American City and the End of Public Space*, ed. Michael Sorkin (New York: Hill and Wang, 1992); John Goss, "'The Magic of the Mall': An Analysis of Form Function and Meaning in the Contemporary Retail Built Environment," *Annals of American Geographers* 83, no. 1 (March 1993): 18–47; Michael Sorkin, "See You in Disneyland!," in *Variations on a Theme Park: The New American City and the End of Public Space*, ed. Michael Sorkin (New York: Hill and Wang, 1992). Shopping malls also feature in Robert Putnam's famous account of the decline

of US public life. Robert Putnam, *Bowling Alone: The Collapse and Revival of American Community* (New York: Simon and Schuster, 2000), 211. Meanwhile, Zygmunt Bauman describes the condition of postmodernity as being like "a life long confinement to a shopping mall." Zygmunt Bauman, *Intimations of Postmodernity* (London: Routledge, 1992), vii.

6. Crawford, "The World in a Shopping Mall," 4.

7. In 1996, the *American Historical Review* published a roundtable exchange about the history of US shopping malls. See Lizabeth Cohen, "From Town Center to Shopping Center: The Reconfiguration of Community Marketplaces in Postwar America," *American Historical Review* 101, no. 4 (October 1996): 1050–81; Kenneth Jackson, "All the World's a Mall: Reflections on the Social and Economic Consequences of the American Shopping Center," *American Historical Review* 101, no. 4 (October 1996): 1111–21; Thomas W. Hanchett, "US Tax Policy and the Shopping Center Boom of the 1950s and 1960s," *American Historical Review* 101, no. 4 (October 1996): 1082–110. See also Lizabeth Cohen, *A Consumers' Republic: The Politics of Mass Consumption in Postwar America* (New York: Knopf, 2003); Kenneth Jackson, *Crabgrass Frontier: The Suburbanization of the United States* (Oxford: Oxford University Press, 1987); Joel Garreau, *Edge City: Life on the New Frontier* (New York: Doubleday, 1991).

8. Cohen, "From Town Center to Shopping Center," 1079.

9. Arlene M. Dávila, *El Mall: The Spatial and Class Politics of Shopping Malls in Latin America* (Berkeley: University of California Press, 2016); Joel Stillerman and Rodrigo Salcedo, "Transposing the Urban to the Mall: Routes, Relationships, and Resistance in Two Santiago, Chile, Shopping Centers," *Journal of Contemporary Ethnography* 41, no. 3 (March 2012): 309–36; Nicholas Jewell, *Shopping Malls and Public Space in Modern China* (London: Routledge, 2016); Stefan Al, *Mall City: Hong Kong's Dreamworlds of Consumption* (Honolulu: Hawaii University Press, 2016).

10. Dávila, *El Mall*, 4–5.

11. Victoria de Grazia, *Irresistible Empire: America's Advance through Twentieth-Century Europe* (London: Belknap, 2005).

12. For an early version of this argument relating to the financialization of landownership, see Doreen Massey and Alejandrina Catalano, *Capital and Land: Landownership by Capital in Great Britain* (London: Edward Arnold, 1978).

13. Jackson, *Crabgrass Frontier*; Kevin M. Kruse and Thomas Sugrue, eds., *The New Suburban History* (Chicago: University of Chicago Press, 2006).

14. Jackson, *Crabgrass Frontier*, 23.

15. William Severini Kowinski, *The Malling of America: Travels in the United States of Shopping* (New York: W. Morrow, 1985) 20–21. For the spread of malls in the United States, see also Cohen, "From Town Center to Shopping Center"; James J. Farrell, *One Nation under Goods: Malls and the Seduction of American Shopping* (Washington, DC: Smithsonian, 2003).

16. For the importation of self-service shopping from the United States to Britain, see Barbara Usherwood, "Mrs. Housewife and Her Grocer: The Advent of Self-Service Food Shopping in Britain," in *All the World and Her Husband: Women in Twentieth-Century Consumer Culture*, ed. Maggie Andrews and Mary M. Talbot (London: Cassell, 1999); Gareth Shaw, Louise Curth, and Andrew Alexander, "Selling Self-Service and the Supermarket: The Americanisation of Food Retailing in Britain, 1945–60," *Journal of Business History* 26, no. 4 (October 2004): 568–82. For Europe, see de Grazia, *Irresistible Empire*, ch. 8.

17. Massey and Catalano, *Capital and Land*, ch. 6; Peter Scott, *The Property Masters: A History of the British Commercial Property Sector* (London: E. and F. N. Spon, 1996), ch. 6. For a contemporary account by a property journalist, see Oliver Marriott, *The Property Boom* (London: Hamish Hamilton, 1967).

18. Massey and Catalano, *Capital and Land*, ch. 6; Scott, *The Property Masters*, ch. 1. For a longer history of the emergence of a market in property in Britain, see Desmond Fitz-Gibbon, *Marketable Values: Inventing the Property Market in Modern Britain* (Chicago: University of Chicago Press, 2018).

19. Scott, *The Property Masters*, 46.

20. "L.C.C.'s Big Reconstruction Scheme: Redevelopment of Elephant and Castle Area," *Municipal Journal and Local Government Administrator*, October 25, 1946, Southwark Local History Library and Archive (henceforth SLH), Elephant and Castle Shopping Centre, press cuttings, 658.87.

21. Patrick Abercrombie, *County of London Plan, 1943* (London: Macmillian, 1943), 10–11.

22. Marriott, *The Property Boom*, 214.

23. Minutes of the London County Council, Town Planning Committee Report (No. 2), July 11, 1960.

24. "Elephant and Castle Shopping Centre: Terms and Conditions of Lease for Standard Shop Tenant," contract, SLH, Elephant and Castle Shopping Centre, press cuttings, 648.87.

25. "The Largest Shopping Centre in London," promotional book, 18, 14, 15, SLH, Elephant and Castle Shopping Centre, press cuttings, 648.87.

26. Commercial editor, "New Pattern for Shopping: In or Out of Town?," *Financial Times*, August 22, 1962.

27. "Elephant and Castle Progress Report," *Borough: The Quarterly Journal of the Southwark Chamber of Commerce* 9, no. 1 (1966), 11, SLH, Elephant and Castle Shopping Centre, press cuttings, 648.87; "Elephant and Castle Shopping Centre," *Post-War Buildings*, 2012, 2, SLH, Elephant and Castle Shopping Centre, press cuttings, 648.87.

28. Marriott, *The Property Boom*, 220–21.

29. Richard Allen, "Shopkeepers Defy Charges," *South London Press*, July 30, 1991, SLH, Elephant and Castle Shopping Centre, press cuttings, 648.87.

30. Marriott, *The Property Boom*, 231.

31. The planned shopping precinct can be seen as a public counterpart to the modernization of domestic labor described in Judy Giles, *The Parlour and the Suburb: Domestic Identities, Class, Femininity, and Modernity* (London: Bloomsbury Academic, 2004); Deborah Sugg Ryan, *Ideal Homes, 1918–1939: Domestic Design and Suburban Modernism* (Manchester: Manchester University Press, 2018). For the status of women as consumers in the immediate postwar period, see Maggie Andrews and Mary M. Talbot, eds., *All the World and Her Husband: Women in Twentieth-Century Consumer Culture* (London: Cassell, 1999); Matthew Hilton, "The Female Consumer and the Politics of Consumption in Twentieth-Century Britain," *Historical Journal* 45, no. 1 (April 2002): 103–28.

32. Elephant and Castle Second Anniversary Pamphlet, SLH, Elephant and Castle Shopping Centre, press cuttings, 648.87; "Elephant and Castle Progress Report," 11.

33. Elephant and Castle Second Anniversary Pamphlet.

34. "Elephant and Castle Progress Report," 11.

35. Elephant and Castle Second Anniversary Pamphlet.

36. For an overview of these developments, see V. J. Bunce, "Revolution on the High Street?: The Emergence of the Enclosed Shopping Centre," *Geography* 68, no. 4 (October 1983): 307–18; Jonathan Reynolds, "The Proliferation of the Planned Shopping Centre," in *Retail Change: Contemporary Issues*, ed. Rosemary D. F. Bromley and Colin J. Thomas (London: UCL Press, 1993).

37. Russell Schiller, "Land Use Controls on U.K. Shopping Centres," in *Shopping Centre Development: Policies and Prospects*, ed. J. D. Dawson and J. Dennis Lord (London: Croon Helm, 1985).

38. "Application by Brent Cross (Hendon) Joint Development Company Ltd.," Planning Application, 1968, National Archives (henceforth TNA), MT 106/25.

39. "Brent Cross: Current Issues Fact File," 1999, Barnet Local Studies and Archives (henceforth BLA), L711.552.GRE.

40. "Brent Cross, Current Issues Fact File."

41. I. Shepherd and P. Newby, "The Brent Cross Regional Shopping Centre—Characteristics and Early Effects," survey of shoppers, 1978, 11, BLA, L381.45.

42. H. R. Mann, "The Brent Cross Shopping Centre Impact Study: The First Home Interview Survey," 1977, 33, BLA, 711.552.GRE.

43. In 1975, there were fifteen million licensed automobiles for a population of fifty-five million. David Butler and Gareth Butler, *British Political Facts*, 10th ed. (Basingstoke, UK: Palgrave Macmillan, 2011), 399–400.

44. Mann, "The Brent Cross Shopping Centre Impact Study," 68.

45. Michael Freedland, "Shades of Disneyland," *Evening Standard*, October 9, 1976, BLA, L381.45.

46. Leana Pooley, "Will You Go Shopping in the North End?," *Evening Standard*, March 1, 1976, BLA, L381.45.

47. Tom Dyckhoff, "The Sprawl of the Mall," *Times*, March 8, 2006, BLA, L381.45.

48. Shepherd and Newby, "The Brent Cross Regional Shopping Centre," 11; Freedland, "Shades of Disneyland."

49. Ortolano has shown how British urban planners in the 1960s and 1970s were coming to realize that the pleasurable aspects of consumption could be an antidote to suburban anomie. Guy Ortolano, "Planning the Urban Future in 1960s Britain," *Historical Journal* 54, no. 2 (June 2011): 477–507.

50. In a widely circulated report, the investment bank Credit Suisse calculated that there were 1,211 shopping malls in the United States in 2017, and many were facing closure in the coming years. See, for example, Chris Isadore, "Malls Are Doomed: 25% Will Be Gone in 5 Years," CNN, June 2, 2017, accessed April 5, 2019, https://money.cnn.com/2017/06/02/news/economy/doomed.

51. For Brazil, see Aliansce Shopping Centers, "Brazilian Shopping Mall Market," accessed April 8, 2019, http://ir.aliansce.com.br/enu/brazilian-shopping-mall-market. For India, see Anaj Puri, "The Rise and Growth of Indian Malls," *Deccan Herald*, June 24, 2018, accessed April 5, 2019, https://www.deccanherald.com/business/economy-business/rise-and-growth-indian-malls-676834.html.

52. Fung Business Intelligence Group, "Shopping Malls," October 2018, 4, accessed April 5, 2019, https://www.fbicgroup.com/sites/default/files/SCR2018_4_Shopping_malls.pdf.

53. In 2016, the British Council of Shopping Centres changed its name to Revo.

54. Dávila, *El Mall*, esp. ch. 4; Stillerman and Salcedo, "Transposing the Urban to the Mall."

55. This is not a comprehensive list.

56. This built on attempts to understand the psychology of shoppers conducted earlier in the twentieth century. For high streets, see Rachel Bowlby, *Carried Away: The Invention of Modern Shopping* (London: Faber, 2000). For supermarkets, see Usherwood, "Mrs. Housewife and Her Grocer"; Vance Packard, *The Hidden Persuaders* (New York: David McCay, 1957).

57. Bowlby, *Carried Away*, ch. 4.

58. Louis G. Redstone, *New Dimensions in Shopping Centers and Stores* (New York: McGraw Hill, 1973), 73, 80.

59. Maitland, *Shopping Malls*, 13.

60. Nadine Beddington, *Design for Shopping Centres* (London: Butterworth Scientific, 1982), 1.

61. Maitland, *Shopping Malls*, 112. See also Clive Darlow, *Enclosed Shopping Centres* (London: Architectural Press, 1972), ch. 3.

62. Tia DeNora, *Music in Everyday Life* (Cambridge: Cambridge University Press, 2000), 132.

63. Jonathan Sterne, "'Sounds Like the Mall of America': Programmed Music and the Architectonics of Commercial Space," *Ethnomusicology* 41, no. 1 (Winter 1997): 22–50.

64. Redstone, *New Dimensions*, 80, 90.

65. Peter G. Martin, *Shopping Centre Management* (London: E. and F. N. Spon, 1982), 191.

66. "Pig Patrol," *Shopping Center World*, April 1972.

67. "Protecting Shoppers Means Protecting Profits," *Shopping Center World*, September 1984.

68. Collie Knox, *Steel at Brierley Hill, 1857–1957* (Manchester: Newman Neame Northern Ltd., 1957), 12–13.

69. This was the policy of the 1968 Urban Programme and 1978 Inner Urban Areas Act.

70. Department of the Environment, *Policy for the Inner Cities* (London: HMSO, 1977); Otto Saumarez Smith, "The Inner City Crisis and the End of Urban Modernism in 1970s Britain," *Twentieth Century British History* 27, no. 4 (December 2016): 578–98; Otto Saumarez Smith, "Action for Cities: The Thatcher Government and Inner-City Policy," *Urban History* (forthcoming); Aaron Andrews, "Multiple Deprivation, the Inner City, and the Fracturing of the Welfare State: Glasgow, c. 1968–78," *Twentieth Century British History* 29, no. 4 (December 2018): 605–24.

71. For a fuller history of this policy, see Sam Wetherell, "Freedom Planned: Enterprise Zones and Urban Non-Planning in Post-War Britain," *Twentieth Century British History* 27, no. 2 (March 2016): 266–89.

72. Reyner Banham, Paul Barker, Peter Hall, and Cedric Price, "Non-Plan: An Experiment in Freedom," *New Society*, March 20, 1969.

73. Peter Hall, "Green Fields and Grey Areas," speech delivered to the Royal Town Planning Institute annual conference, Chester, June 15, 1977. Reprinted in Peter Hall, "The Enterprise Zone: British Origins, American Adaptations," working paper no. 350, Institute of Urban and Regional Development, Berkeley, 1981.

74. "Ministerial Committee on Economic Strategy: Enterprise Zone Report," September 21, 1979, 8, TNA, CAB 134/4336. Reference to removal of discrimination based on race and sex

found in "Official Group on the Impact of Government on Industry Sub Group on Enterprise Zones/Pilot Areas," July 30, 1979, TNA, 277/3500.

75. Alastair Ross Goobey, *Bricks and Mortals: Dream of the 80s and the Nightmare of the 90s— Inside Story of the Property World* (London: Century Business, 1992), 184–88.

76. Architect planner Colin Buchanan had also proposed monorails as a solution to traffic congestion. For unrealized monorail plans in the 1960s, see Guy Ortolano, *Thatcher's Progress: From Social Democracy to Market Liberalism through an English New Town* (Cambridge: Cambridge University Press, 2019), 47–50; Simon Gunn, "The Buchanan Report, Environment, and the Problem of Traffic in 1960s Britain," *Twentieth Century British History* 22, no. 4 (December 2011): 521–42.

77. "Memories Are Made of This," *Dudley News*, August 26, 1988, DLA, NPC/220.

78. "Carole Ann Rice Takes a Lighthearted Look at the Joys of Shopping," *Merry Hill Magazine*, Winter 1993, DLA, R87000.

79. "Monorails of Australia: Oasis-Jupiter Broadbeach," accessed April 5, 2019, http://www.monorails.org/tMspages/Broadb.html.

80. "Illusions of Grandeur," *Interior Design*, January 1990, DLA, MP59(S).

81. Amy Edwards, "Manufacturing Capitalists: The Wider Share Ownership Council and the Problem of 'Popular Capitalism,' 1958–1992," *Twentieth Century British History* 27, no. 1 (March 2016): 100–123.

82. "Illusions of Grandeur."

83. Goobey, *Bricks and Mortals*, ch. 6.

84. Angela MacKay, "70m Deal as Clegg Leaves Mountleigh," *Times*, November 9, 1989.

85. Goobey, *Bricks and Mortals*, 194. See also the career of Iranian speculator Vincent Tchenguiz and his role in developing securitized rents in the 1990s, described in Andrew Leyshon and Nigel Thrift, "The Capitalization of Almost Everything: The Future of Finance and Capitalism," *Theory, Culture, and Society* 24, no. 7–8 (December 2007): 97–115.

86. "Giant Store Moves in to Shop City," *Dudley Express and Star*, November 13, 1986, DLA, NPC/200.

87. Goobey, *Bricks and Mortals*, 116.

88. "Giant Store Moves in to Shop City"; Angela Mackay, "Partners with the Gift of Timing," *Times*, November 9, 1989.

89. "Giant Store Moves in to Shop City."

90. The figure was obtained by tallying the total number of listings on the British Council of Shopping Centres' online directory. Regionally, the figures break down as follows: Scotland, 74; North, 179; Midlands, 125; eastern region, 28; London and South East, 219; south and west region, 85; and Northern Ireland, 39. These figure were calculated in 2013. Since that date, the British Council of Shopping Centres (now called Revo) no longer makes its listings public.

91. Geographers and journalists have recently drawn attention to the difficulty of distinguishing between public and private space in British cities. See Anna Minton, *Ground Control: Fear and Happiness in the Twenty-First-Century City* (London: Penguin, 2009); Andy Pratt, "The Rise of Quasi-Public Space and Its Consequences for Cities and Culture," *Palgrave Communications* 3, no. 1 (2017): 1–4; Daithi Mac Sithigh, "Virtual Walls?: The Law of Pseudo-Public Spaces," *International Journal of Law in Context* 8, no. 3 (September 2012): 394–412.

92. "Dossers' Haven May Soon Be Closed at Night," *Oxford Mail*, October 14, 1983; "Consuming Westgate," *Oxford Mail*, May 13, 1983; "Tramps Force Shops Switch," *Oxford Mail*, April 14, 1983; "Showpiece of Squalor," *Oxford Mail*, April 1, 1982.

93. "Showpiece of Squalor."

94. "A Jab Jibe at Shops Centre," *Oxford Mail*, May 5, 1983.

95. "Spare a Thought for Our Drunks and Punks!," *Oxford Mail*, March 12, 1982.

96. "Council Wants Partner for Oxford Centre," *Estates Gazette*, October 27, 1984, Sainsbury's Archive (henceforth TSA), BRA 2/2/2.

97. "Westgate Shopping Centre: Closure of Malls, Security, and Other Improvements," report to the Oxford City Council Estates Committee, November 15, 1983, 7, TSA, BRA 2/2/2.

98. Kevin Gray and Susan Francis Gray, *Elements of Land Law*, 5th ed. (Oxford: Oxford University Press, 2009), 1344–57.

99. "Possible Night-Time Closure of Westgate Centre, Oxford," report to the Oxford City Council Estates Committee, March 17, 1983, 3, TSA, BRA 2/2/2.

100. Ibid, 4.

101. "Possible Night-Time Closure of Westgate Centre, Oxford," report to the Oxford City Council Estates Committee, March 17, 1983, 3, 4, TSA, BRA 2/2/2. Criminologist Alison Wakefield identified a similar blurring between pastoral and policing practices among private security guards in British shopping malls elsewhere. Alison Wakefield, "Situational Crime Prevention in Mass Private Property," in *Ethical and Social Perspectives on Situational Crime Prevention*, ed. Andrew von Hirsch, David Garland, and Alison Wakefield (Oxford: Hart, 2000).

102. Kevin Gray and Susan Francis Gray, "Civil Rights, Civil Wrongs, and Quasi-Public Space," *European Human Rights Law Review* 4 (1999): 46–102.

103. For the precedent used to uphold the arbitrary rights of landowners or property owners to exclude individuals, see Gray and Gray, *Elements of Land Law*, 1330–43; Kevin Gray and Susan Francis Gray, "Private Property and Public Property," in *Property and the Constitution*, ed. Janet McClean (Oxford: Hart, 1999).

104. Amalgamated Food Employees Union Local 590 v. Logan Valley Plaza Inc., 391 U.S. 308. (1968). See also Cohen, *A Consumers' Republic*, 274–91.

105. PruneYard Shopping Center v. Robbins, 447 U.S. 74 (1980).

106. Cohen, *A Consumers' Republic*, 275.

107. Harrison v. Carswell (1976), 2 SCR 200. For the Australian context, see Leonie Sandercock, "From Main Street to Fortress: The Future of Malls as Public Spaces, or 'Shut Up and Shop,'" *Just Policy* 9 (March 1997): 27–34; Malcolm Voyce, "Shopping Malls in Australia: The End of Public Space and the Rise of 'Consumerist Citizenship'?," *Journal of Sociology* 42, no. 3 (September 2006): 269–86.

108. Anthony Alexander, *Britain's New Towns: Garden Cities to Sustainable Communities* (London: Routledge, 2009), ch. 10.

109. For a description of the design and construction of the Milton Keynes Shopping Centre, see Janina Gosseye, "Milton Keynes' Centre: The Apotheosis of the British Post-War Consensus or the Apostle of Neo-Liberalism?," *History of Retailing and Consumption* 1, no 3 (September 2015): 209–29.

110. Appleby and Others v. the United Kingdom, 44306/98, European Court of Human Rights, 2003, VI.

111. Andy Pratt, "The Rise of Quasi-Public Space"; Katherine Astill, "The Right to Protest in a Quasi-Public Space," *Guardian*, October 28, 2010. For ownership patterns of Britain's land as a whole, see Brett Christophers, *The New Enclosure: The Appropriation of Public Land in Neoliberal Britain* (London: Verso, 2018).

112. See, for example, Mike Devereux and David Littlefield, "A Literature Review on the Privatisation of Public Space," accessed April 5, 2019, http://eprints.uwe.ac.uk/31529.

113. Isadore, "Malls Are Doomed."

114. For images of the mall, see http://matthewniederhauser.com/research/2011/02/23/south-china-mall-the-empty-temple-of-consumerism, accessed April 5, 2019.

115. Emma Featherstone, "UK High Street Sees Sharp Decline in Shoppers in September," *Independent*, October 16, 2017; Sarah Butler, "Apocalypse Now for Britain's Retailers as Low Wages and the Web Cause Ruin," *Guardian*, February 17, 2018.

Chapter 6: The Business Park

1. "Either a Borrower or a Lender Be," *Cambridge Science Park Newsletter*, Spring 1983, Cambridgeshire Archives and Local Studies, Cambridgeshire Collection (henceforth TCC), ZK.9.b.878.

2. This is based on a calculation of the number of developments calling themselves "business parks" made by a property research firm. Andy King, *U.K. 2000: An Overview of Business Parks* (London: Applied Property Research Ltd., 1988), 1.

3. For an extensive list of subcategories, see E.D.B. Waldy, *Business Parks* (London: Fletcher King, 1986), 7–8.

4. This was the headline finding of three Cambridge University economists commissioned by the Department of the Environment in 1985 to chart the geography of deindustrialization. Stephen Fothergill, Michael Kitson, and Sarah Monk, *Urban Industrial Change: The Causes of the Urban-Rural Contrast in Manufacturing Employment Change* (London: HMSO, 1985), 2, 5.

5. For deindustrialization and structural changes in the labor market, see Jim Tomlinson, "De-industrialization Not Decline: A New Meta-Narrative for Post-War British History," *Twentieth Century British History* 27, no. 1 (March 2016): 76–99; Andrew Newell, "Structural Change," in *Work and Pay in Twentieth Century Britain*, ed. Nicholas Crafts, Ian Gazeley, and Andrew Newell (Oxford: Oxford University Press 2007); Arthur McIvor, *Working Lives: Work in Britain since 1945* (Basingstoke, UK: Palgrave Macmillan, 2013); Guy Standing, "Globalization, Labour Flexibility, and Insecurity: The Era of Market Regulation," *European Journal of Industrial Relations* 3, no. 1 (March 1997): 7–37. For women and waged work in postwar Britain, see Sara Connolly and Mary Gregory, "Women and Work since 1970," in *Work and Pay in Twentieth Century Britain*, ed. Nicholas Crafts, Ian Gazeley, and Andrew Newell (Oxford: Oxford University Press 2007); Helen McCarthy, "Social Science and Married Women's Employment in Post-War Britain," *Past and Present* 233, no. 1 (November 2016): 269–305; Helen McCarthy, "Women Marriage and Work in Post-War Britain," *Women's History Review* 26, no. 1 (February 2016): 46–61; Marie Hicks, *Programmed Inequality: How Britain Discarded Women Technologists and Lost Its Edge in Computing* (Cambridge, MA: MIT Press, 2017); Dolly Smith Wilson, "A New Look at the Affluent Worker: The Good Working Mother in Post-War Britain," *Twentieth Century British History* 27, no. 2 (January 2006): 206–29; Sarah Stoller, "Inventing the Working Parent: Work,

Gender, and Feminism in Neoliberal Britain" (PhD diss., University of California at Berkeley, forthcoming). On casualization and the rise of part-time work, see Veronica Beechey and Tessa Perkins, *A Matter of Hours: Women, Part-Time Work, and the Labour Market* (Cambridge, UK: Polity, 1987); Miriam Glucksmann, *Cottons and Casuals: The Gendered Organization of Time and Space* (Abingdon, UK: Routledge, 2012); Christoph Hermann, *Capitalism and the Political Economy of Work Time* (London: Routledge, 2015). For other reflections on late twentieth-century knowledge work, see Luc Boltanski and Eve Chiapello, *The New Spirit of Capitalism*, trans. Gregory Eliot (London: Verso, 2005), esp. chs. 1–2; Fred Turner, *From Counterculture to Cyberculture: Stewart Brand, the Whole Earth Network, and the Rise of Digital Utopianism* (Chicago: University of Chicago Press, 2006), esp. chs. 1 and 6.

6. For an experiential history of office work in postwar Britain, see Joe Moran, *Reading the Everyday* (London: Routledge, 2005), ch. 2. For a history of suburban office complexes in the United States, see Louise Mozingo, *Pastoral Capitalism: A History of Suburban Corporate Landscapes* (Cambridge, MA: MIT Press, 2014). For France, see Rosemary Wakeman, "Dreaming the Atlantis: Science and the Planning of Technopolis, 1955–1985," *Osiris* 18, no. 1, (January 2003): 255–70. For a global history of high-tech working landscapes, see Manuel Castells and Peter Hall, *Technopoles of the World: The Making of Twenty-First-Century Industrial Complexes* (London: Routledge, 1994).

7. Speech to donors by unnamed administrator, 1960, Stanford University Archive (henceforth SUA), Public Affairs Office Records, 1960–1980, SC0105, box 1, folder 7.

8. In the 1970s, the park changed its name from the Stanford Industrial Park to the Stanford Research Park.

9. John M. Findlay, *Magic Lands: Western Cityscapes and American Culture after 1940* (Berkeley: University of California Press, 1992), ch. 3.

10. Findlay, *Magic Lands*, 118–19.

11. "US Industrial Park in Brussels Display," *New York Times*, May 9, 1958; Findlay, *Magic Lands*, 117.

12. Mozingo, *Pastoral Capitalism*.

13. AnnaLee Saxenian, *Regional Advantage: Culture and Competition in Silicon Valley and Route 128* (Cambridge, MA: Harvard University Press, 1996), ch. 1. See also Langdon Winner, "Silicon Valley Mystery House," in *Variations on a Theme Park: The New American City and the End of Public Space*, ed. Michael Sorkin (New York: Hill and Wang, 1992).

14. Castells and Hall, *Technopoles of the World*, 15–16; Saxenian, *Regional Advantage*, 20–27.

15. "Ampex Corperation Lease," SUA, Public Affairs Office Records, 1960–1980, SC677, box 2.

16. Speech to donors by unnamed administrator, SUA, SC0105, box 1, folder 7.

17. Findlay, *Magic Lands*, 152.

18. For accounts of the emergence of British science parks, see Helen Lawton Smith, *Universities, Innovation, and the Economy* (London: Routledge, 2006); Tony Taylor, "High Technology Industry and the Development of Science Parks," *Built Environment* 9, no. 1 (1983): 72–78.

19. David Edgerton, *Warfare State: Britain, 1920–1970* (Cambridge: Cambridge University Press, 2005), ch. 4.

20. Lawton Smith, *Universities, Innovation, and the Economy*, 12.

21. Guy Ortolano, *The Two Cultures Controversy: Science, Literature, and Cultural Politics in Postwar Britain* (Cambridge: Cambridge University Press, 2011), ch. 3.

22. "Relationship between the University and Science-Based Industry: Notice by the Council of the Senate," *Cambridge University Reporter*, October 22, 1969.

23. "A University Promotes Commercial Enterprise," May 23, 1973, National Archives (henceforth TNA), BT 177/2765; "IDC Position," May 23, 1973, TNA), BT 177/2765.

24. Trinity College Reports, *Senior Bursar's Report*, June 5, 1970 and October 2, 1970, Trinity College Archives (henceforth TCA).

25. Norma Carter and Chris Watts, *The Cambridge Science Park* (London: Surveyors, 1984).

26. "A Cambridge Science Park: A Proposal by Trinity College for the Early Provision of Suitable Accommodation for Science-Based Industry in Cambridge," TNA, BT 177/2765.

27. Carter and Watt, *Cambridge Science Park*, 28.

28. Trinity College Reports, *Senior Bursar's Report*, February 16, 1973, TCA.

29. "A Cambridge Science Park: A Proposal by Trinity College."

30. "Cambridge Science Park News Bulletin 4," *Cambridge Science Park Newsletter*, October 1980, TCC, ZK.9.b.878.

31. "A Cambridge Science Park: A Proposal by Trinity College."

32. "Cambridge Science Park Directory," January 1989, TCC, D.09.1503. The directory lists sixty-nine occupants.

33. "Cambridge Science Park: A Trinity College Scheme," Report, TNA, BT 177/2765.

34. "Cambridge Science Park," TCC, D04.1401.

35. Carter and Watt, *Cambridge Science Park*, 33.

36. Doreen Massey, Paul Quintas, and David Wield, *High-Tech Fantasies: Science Parks in Society, Science, and Space* (London: Routledge, 1991), 104.

37. OECD and J. Visser, "Institutional Characteristics of Trade Unions, Wage Setting, State Intervention, and Social Pacts," ICTWSS database, accessed June 8, 2019, http://www.uva-aias.net/en/ictwss/.

38. Massey, Quintas, and Wield, *High-Tech Fantasies*, 104, 93, 102.

39. Luc Boltanski and Eve Chiapello have argued that the late twentieth century saw the blurring of the distinction between work and home (or production and reproduction) that Max Weber identified as a constitutive part of the emergence of capitalism. Boltanski and Chiapello, *The New Spirit of Capitalism*, 154–56.

40. "Science Park Christian Fellowship," *Cambridge Science Park Newsletter*, Autumn 1985, TCC, ZK.9.b.878.

41. "Fostering the Wall Plaque Industry," *Cambridge Science Park Newsletter*, Autumn 1984, TCC, ZK.9.b.878; "Pastime and Good Company at the Trinity Centre," *Cambridge Science Park Newsletter*, Autumn 1984, TCC, ZK.9.b.878.

42. Raymond Harrowell, *The Cambridge Connection* (Cambridge, UK: Vanguard, 2001).

43. Daniel Ussishkin, *Morale: A Modern British History* (Oxford: Oxford University Press, 2017), ch. 5; Nikolas Rose, *Governing the Soul: The Shaping of the Private Self* (London: Routledge 1990), part 2.

44. Daniel Ussishkin, "Morale and the Postwar Politics of Consensus," *Journal of British Studies* 52, no. 3 (July 2013): 722–43.

45. Massey, Quintas, and Wield, *High-Tech Fantasies*, 110–12.

46. Beechey and Perkins, *A Matter of Hours*, 1, 2. See also Smith Wilson, "A New Look at the Affluent Worker."

47. From my own analysis of the Cambridge Science Park newsletter, TCC ZK.9.b.878.

48. Massey, Quintas, and Wield, *High-Tech Fantasies*, 110–12.

49. Hicks, *Programmed Inequality*, 9.

50. Massey, Quintas, and Wield, *High-Tech Fantasies*, 109.

51. The construction of the park preceded the increasing politicization of the "working parent." Stoller, "Inventing the Working Parent," esp. ch. 4. For the compatibility of neoliberal politics and postindustrial work with patriarchal ideas and practices grounded in the family, see Melinda Cooper, *Family Values: Between Neoliberalism and the New Social Conservatism* (Cambridge, MA: MIT Press, 2018).

52. "Science Parks: Regional Implications," TNA, BT 177/2765.

53. Memo from M. W. Hunt, May 5, 1970, TNA, BT 177/2765.

54. Trinity College Reports, *Senior Bursar's Report*, February 16, 1973, TCA.

55. For these proposals, see William Holford and Henry Myles Wright, *A Report to the Town and Country Planning Committee of the Cambridgeshire County Council* (Cambridge: Cambridge University Press, 1950).

56. Trinity College Reports, *Senior Bursar's Report*, October 15, 1971, TCA. The birth of the park coincided with a massive increase in high-tech work in Cambridge and nearby—a development that became known as the "Cambridge Phenomenon." The number of high-tech firms in Cambridgeshire increased from 30 in 1959 to 322 in 1984. See Castells and Hall, *Technopoles of the World*, 93–100.

57. Trinity College Reports, *Senior Bursar's Report*, October 15, 1971, TCA.

58. "Cambridge Science Parks: A Breakthrough," *Cambridgeshire Life*, May 1984.

59. Castells and Hall, *Technopoles of the World*, 1.

60. UK Science Park Association, *Evaluation of the Past and Future Economic Contribution of the UK Science Park Movement* (Cambridge: United Kingdom Science Park Association, 2003), 1.

61. "Stockley Park: Heathrow, Summer 1989," promotional booklet, Hillingdon Local Studies and Archives (henceforth HLS), ADB 15/15, box 1.

62. "Stockley Park: Heathrow," promotional monthly newsletter, September 1985, HLS, ADB 15/15, box 1.

63. King, *U.K. 2000*, 3.

64. Parliamentary Papers, *Lifting the Burden: Presented to the Minister without Portfolio*, 1985, Cmd. 7571.

65. Town and Country Planning (Use Classes) Order, 1987, ca. 764.

66. King, *U.K. 2000*, 5, 1.

67. For the ways that pension funds restructured the ownership of British capital in the postwar period, see Aled Davies, "Pension Funds and the Politics of Ownership in Britain, c. 1970–1986," *Twentieth Century British History* 30, no. 1 (March 2019), 81–107.

68. Angela Jameson, "Arlington Securities Ready for Market Return," *Times*, July 14, 2003.

69. Christopher Warman, "A Valuable Pitch in the Business Park," *Times*, December 11, 1987; Christopher Warman, "Parks That Really Do 'the Business,'" *Times*, October 23, 1991.

70. Warman, "A Valuable Pitch in the Business Park."

71. Rodney Hobson, "Parks Mean Business," *Times*, February 8, 1991; "Why the Parks Prove So Popular," *Times*, May 29, 1990; Chris Harris, "A New Spirit of Enterprise," *Times*, May 1, 1991.

72. "Stockley Park: A Development Proposal," May 1983, 14, HLS, ADB 15/15, box 2.

73. "Stockley Park: Heathrow," promotional booklet, HLS, ADB 15/15, box 1.

74. "Stockley Park: Heathrow," promotional monthly newsletter, December 1988, HLS, ADB 15/15, box 1.

75. "Stockley Park: Heathrow," promotional monthly newsletter, April 1989, HLS, ADB 15/15, box 1.

76. "Stockley Park: Heathrow," promotional monthly newsletter, August 1986, HLS, ADB 15/15, box 1.

77. Alastair Ross Goobey, *Bricks and Mortals: The Dream of the 80s and the Nightmare of the 90s—the Inside Story of the Property World* (London: Century Business, 1992), ch. 4.

78. "Stockley Park: Strategy for Development and General Specification," development proposal by Arup Associates, 3, 13–14, HLS, ADB 15/15, box 1.

79. "Stockley Park: Strategy for Development and General Specification," 24.

80. "Stockley Park: Heathrow," promotional monthly newsletter, September 1986 and June 1987, HLS, ADB 15/15, box 1.

81. "Stockley Park: Heathrow," promotional monthly newsletter, October 1988, HLS, ADB 15/15, box 1.

82. "Stockley Park: Heathrow," promotional monthly newsletter, January 1988, HLS, ADB 15/15, box 1.

83. "Stockley Park: Heathrow," promotional booklet, HLS, ADB 15/15, box 1.

84. "Stockley Park: Heathrow," promotional monthly newsletter, October 1987, HLS, ADB 15/15, box 1.

85. "Stockley Park: Heathrow," promotional monthly newsletter, July 1988, HLS, ADB 15/15, box 1.

86. "Stockley Park: Heathrow," promotional monthly newsletter, July 1988, HLS, ADB 15/15, box 1. For the rise of charities and NGOs in postwar Britain, see Matthew Hilton, *The Politics of Expertise: How NGOs Shaped Modern Britain* (Oxford: Oxford University Press, 2013).

87. "Stockley Park: Heathrow," promotional monthly newsletter, August 1990, HLS, ADB 15/15, box 1.

88. "Stockley Park: Heathrow," promotional monthly newsletter, March 1991, HLS, ADB 15/15, box 1.

89. "Stockley Park: Heathrow," promotional monthly newsletter, November 1988, HLS, ADB 15/15, box 1.

90. The significance of this shift from "work" as it was theorized in the abstract in terms of labor time by Ricardian, Marxist, and classical economics, to "work" as a set of choices and decisions made by rational opportunistic subjects was identified as a constitutive element of neoliberal thought early as 1979 by Michel Foucault. Michel Foucault, *The Birth of Biopolitics: Lectures at the Collège de France, 1978–79,* trans. Graham Burchell (Basingstoke, UK: Palgrave Macmillan, 2008), ch. 9.

91. "Stockley Park: Heathrow," promotional monthly newsletter, February 1986, HLS, ADB 15/15, box 1.

92. "Stockley Park: A Development Proposal," May 1983, 14, HLS, ADB 15/15, box 2.

93. Robert Nicholls, *Trafford Park: The First Hundred Years* (Chichester, UK: Philmore and Co., 1996), 117, 128, 127.

94. "Trafford Park Industrial Estate," Board of Trade Research Subcommittee report, 6, TNA, HLG 79/428.

95. Trafford Park Residents' Association, "The Last 'Souvenir' Edition of the Trafford Park Times," 1981, folder 338.09, PAR, 12, Trafford Local Studies (henceforth TLS).

96. "Regeneration Statement," Trafford Park Development Corporation, 12, TLS, TRA 1706 2/2.

97. For more accounts of the history of the TPDC and UDCs more broadly, see Nicholas Deakin and John Edwards, *The Enterprise Culture and the Inner City* (London: Routledge, 1993); Peter Hall, *Cities of Tomorrow: An Intellectual History of Urban Planning and Design since 1880*, 4th ed. (London: Wiley-Blackwell, 2014), ch. 11; Michael Parkinson, "The Thatcher Government's Urban Policy, 1979–1989, a Review," *Town Planning Review* 60, no. 4 (October 1989): 421–40.

98. UDCs are further evidence that Thatcherite urbanism, rather than marking a retreat of the role of the state, was characterized by expensive instances of legislative activism. Otto Saumarez Smith, "Action for Cities: The Thatcher Government and Inner-City Policy," *Urban History* (forthcoming); Sam Wetherell, "Freedom Planned: Enterprise Zones and Urban Non-Planning in Post-War Britain," *Twentieth Century British History* 27, no. 2 (March 2016): 266–89.

99. Deakin, *Enterprise Culture and the City*, 10, 77.

100. "Trafford Park: A Dynamic Future Built on a Proud Past," Trafford Park Development Corporation, TLS, TRA 1706 1/2.

101. "1992 Annual Report," Trafford Park Development Corporation, TLS, TRA 1706 1/2.

102. "Regeneration Statement," Trafford Park Development Corporation, 12, 18, TLS, TRA 1706 2/2.

103. "1992 Annual Report."

104. "Regeneration Statement," 12, 54.

105. "Art in the Park," *Trafford Park Profile Magazine*, 1992, 12, Greater Manchester County Record Office (henceforth MCRO), box 2, A/TPDC.

106. "Regeneration Statement," 61, photographic insert.

107. Press Release, "Trafford Park Development Corporation Demonstrates Commitment to the Local Community," December 13, 1990, MCRO, A/TPDC, box 1, folder 4/1.

108. "Largest Computer Provision for Schools Launched by a Development Corporation," press release, September 6, 1990, MCRO, A/TPDC, box 1 4/1; "New Home for Great Crested Newts at Trafford Park Ecology Park," April 20, 1990, MCRO, A/TPDC, box 1 4/1.

109. "Trafford Park Business Watch Success," press release, June 18, 1990, MCRO A/TPDC, box 1, folder 4/1.

110. "Trafford Park Plays Key Role at National Launch of Secured by Design: Commercial," press release, May 26, 1992, MCRO, A/TPDC, box 1, folder 4/1.

111. Brian Hope, "The Trafford Park Story: Village Life," *Manchester Evening News*, February 26, 1978, TLS, TLA 338.09.

112. "Trafford Park: Manchester UDC: In Profile," interview with Peter Hadfield, TPDC chair, TLS, TRA 942.731.

113. Nicholls, *Trafford Park*, 151.

114. "1995 Annual Report," Trafford Park Development Corporation, TLS, TRA 1706 1/2.

115. Deakin, *Enterprise Culture and the City*, 79.

116. These figures are my own calculations based on data from Board of Trade Regional Office Note on Trafford Park, 1946, Table 1: Stretford Exchange: Insured Population in Main Industries, TNA, HLG 79/428.

117. "Trafford Park Company Census," Trafford Park Development Corporation, TLS, TRA 1706 1/2. This was still above the national average for manufacturing employment.

118. "Trafford Park Company Census."

119. "1993 Annual Report," Trafford Park Development Corporation, TLS, TRA 1706 1/2.

120. "Trafford Park: A Dynamic Future Built on a Proud Past," Trafford Park Development Corporation, TLS, TRA 1706 1/2.

121. See, for example, A. Southern, *Trafford Park: Britain's Workshop and Storehouse* (Trafford Park Estates, 1923).

122. McBride, "Trafford Park: A Thesis," 17.

123. "The Last 'Souvenir' Edition of Trafford Park Times," 4.

Chapter 7: Conclusion

1. Lauren Pikó, *Milton Keynes in British Culture: Imagining England* (London: Routledge, 2019).

2. Guy Ortolano, "Planning the Urban Future in 1960s Britain," *Historical Journal* 54, no. 2 (June 2011): 477–507; Guy Ortolano, *Thatcher's Progress: From Social Democracy to Market Liberalism through an English New Town* (Cambridge: Cambridge University Press, 2019), ch. 1.

3. Malcolm Rose, *Plague* (London: Scholastic, 2000).

4. Gena-mour Barrett, "Living on an Estate Gave Me a Community I Never Knew I Needed," in *Know Your Place: Essays on the Working Class by the Working Class*, ed. Nathan Connolly (St Ives, UK: Dead Ink Books, 2017), 159.

INDEX

A NOTE ON THE TYPE

This book has been composed in Arno, an Old-style serif typeface in the
classic Venetian tradition, designed by Robert Slimbach at Adobe.

CPSIA information can be obtained
at www.ICGtesting.com
Printed in the USA
JSHW042331111222
34693JS00004BA/5